Wearing Ideology

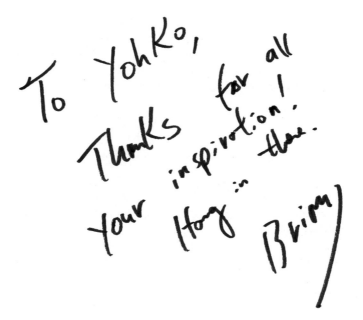

To Yohko,
Thanks for all
your inspiration!
Hang in there.
Brian

Dress, Body, Culture

Series Editor **Joanne B. Eicher**, *Regents' Professor, University of Minnesota*

Books in this provocative series seek to articulate the connections between culture and dress which is defined here in its broadest possible sense as any modification or supplement to the body. Interdisciplinary in approach, the series highlights the dialogue between identity and dress, cosmetics, coiffure, and body alterations as manifested in practices as varied as plastic surgery, tattooing, and ritual scarification. The series aims, in particular, to analyze the meaning of dress in relation to popular culture and gender issues and will include works grounded in anthropology, sociology, history, art history, literature, and folklore.

ISSN: 1360-466X

Previously published titles in the Series

Helen Bradley Foster, *"New Raiments of Self": African American Clothing in the Antebellum South*

Claudine Griggs, *S/he: Changing Sex and Changing Clothes*

Michaele Thurgood Haynes, *Dressing Up Debutantes: Pageantry and Glitz in Texas*

Anne Brydon and Sandra Niesson, *Consuming Fashion: Adorning the Transnational Body*

Dani Cavallaro and Alexandra Warwick, *Fashioning the Frame: Boundaries, Dress and the Body*

Judith Perani and Norma H. Wolff, *Cloth, Dress and Art Patronage in Africa*

Linda B. Arthur, *Religion, Dress and the Body*

Paul Jobling, *Fashion Spreads: Word and Image in Fashion Photography*

Fadwa El-Guindi, *Veil: Modesty, Privacy and Resistance*

Thomas S. Abler, *Hinterland Warriors and Military Dress: European Empires and Exotic Uniforms*

Linda Welters, *Folk Dress in Europe and Anatolia: Beliefs about Protection and Fertility*

Kim K.P. Johnson and Sharron J. Lennon, *Appearance and Power*

Barbara Burman, *The Culture of Sewing*

Annette Lynch, *Dress, Gender and Cultural Change*

Antonia Young, *Women Who Become Men*

David Muggleton, *Inside Subculture: The Postmodern Meaning of Style*

DRESS, BODY, CULTURE

Wearing Ideology
State, Schooling and Self-Presentation in Japan

Brian J. McVeigh

Oxford • New York

First published in 2000 by
Berg
Editorial offices:
150 Cowley Road, Oxford, OX4 1JJ, UK
838 Broadway, Third Floor, New York, NY 10003-4812, USA

Berg is an imprint of Oxford International Publishers Ltd.

Library of Congress Cataloging-in-Publication Data
A catalogue record for this book is available from the Library of Congress.

British Library Cataloguing-in-Publication Data
A catalogue record for this book is available from the British Library.

ISBN   1 85973 485 5 (Cloth)
       1 85973 490 1 (Paper)

Typeset by JS Typesetting, Wellingborough, Northants.
Printed in the United Kingdom by Biddles Ltd, Guildford and King's Lynn.

Contents

Preface

Two things impressed me after I first arrived in Japan in the summer of 1987. The first was the number of people in uniform. From service personnel to "office ladies", "elevator girls," and dark-suited office workers, everybody, it seemed, was uniformed. But it was especially the students who caught my attention. There seemed to be a youthful army, attired in blue or black and armed with heavy school and gym bags, that patrolled the streets, scouted the alleys, guarded the corners and made sorties on trains, subways and buses. Uniforms, of course, are not unique to Japan, but, except for some societies perhaps (such as China, where the blue "Mao suit" was the *de rigueur* daily outfit for several decades), their ubiquity in Japan is striking. The second impression was what the Japanese call *kawaisa* or "cuteness", a daily aesthetic that seemed to paint a vast collection of objects with sweetness, color and juvenility. An innumerable range of things were coated with images of cuteness: pens, pencils, school bags, shirts, slippers, coats, condoms, store fronts, signs, advertisements, public notices, billboards, bank books, food packaging. Other objects were manufactured cuteness itself: assorted knick-knacks of puppies, kittens, bears, mice, pigs, frogs and other animals, as well as teddy bears, mascots and picture books entirely dedicated to "cute" themes, such as little animals. Like uniforms, cuteness is certainly not unique to Japan (however, I would wager that, based on my travels, the pervasiveness of this daily aesthetic is more salient in Japan than in other societies).

I never thought that ten years after arriving in Japan I would discern a connection between uniforms (things serious *(majime)*, formal, regulated and standardized) and cuteness (things cheerful *(akarui)*, friendly, playful and spontaneous). Even further from my mind ten years ago was that I would argue that an examination of something as mundane as uniforms and as seemingly inconsequential as cuteness reveals connections that are indeed meaningful and consequential. These connections, as I argue in this book, link socialization, self-presentation, political economy and material culture, as well as schooling, gender and national identity.

Acknowledgments

I owe Professor Joanne B. Eicher, the General Editor of the Dress, Body, Culture Series, and Kathryn Earle, Editorial Director at Berg Publishers, an immense debt of gratitude for encouraging me to write this book after spotting my article on uniforms in Japan (McVeigh 1997a). They gave me a very rare and invaluable opportunity to link my various interests in the effects of political economy on psyche and self-presentation as mediated via objects and the body. I am also grateful for the helpful suggestions of the anonymous reviewers.

My debt of gratitude begins with Woo Chan Lee and Anna Puga who worked with me on a research project that led to the discussion of "cuteness" in this book while at the Inter-University Center for Japanese in Yokohama (1987–8). Special thanks also to all my students in Japan who graciously subjected themselves to my questioning. This book would not have been possible without the invaluable support of my research assistants: Toyama Haruko, who searched for materials both in the United States and Japan and offered me ideas; Joshua Howard, who tracked down sources in the United States; and Nishimura Itsue, who provided sources from Japan. Also, Beth Coleman provided rich insights and useful materials. I am also grateful to Ken Henshall, Paul Noguchi, Takie Sugiyama Lebra, Valerie Steele, Daniel Miller, Konno Hisako, Laura Miller, Donna Storey, Meg Miller, Sakaedani Akiko, Valerie Wilson Trower, Inamura Katsuko, Don Trower, Katalin Ferber, Kathe Geist, Penny Herbert, Perri Strawn, Jilly Traganou and Sharon Kinsella, all of whom helped make this book what it is. The editorial skills of M. Geneviere Malcolm also improved this book. My wife Lana deserves immeasurable gratitude for sharing with me all those experiences and years in Japan.

Finally, I would like to thank Berg publishers for granting me permission to use previously published material from "Wearing Ideology: How Uniforms Discipline Bodies and Minds in Japan" (*Fashion Theory: The Journal of Dress, Body & Culture* 1(2): 189–214, 1997) and the *Journal of Material Culture* for allowing me to reproduce "Commodifying Affection, Authority and Gender in the Everyday Objects of Japan" (1(3): 291–312, 1996). I would also like to thank the following individuals for permitting me to reproduce their research results: Funada Sakiko (*"Gakkô fuku ni taisuru chakuyôsha no ishiki ni tsuite,"* Nihon ifuku gakkai shi, 35(2): 13–59, 1992); Nomura Mariko (*"Shiritsu joshi chûgaku – kôtô gakkô no seifuku ni tsuite: sonoseiritsu to gaiteiki o mukaeta genjô,"* Nihon shigaku kyôiku kenkyûjo kiyô, 28(1): 199–223, 1993 and *"Seifuku ni kansuru seito no ishiki ni tsuite: ankêto chôsa yori,"* Nihon shigaku kyôiku kenkyûjo kiyô, 29(1): 229–57, 1994); Uchino Michiko (*"Fusorio koso ga utsukushî: seifuku no danjobetsu kyôsei wa seisabetsu,"* Kikan joshi kyôiku mondai, 63: 54–60 (April 1995); Uno Kôji and Nogami Akiko (*"Ginkô no joshi jûgyô-in no seifuku,"* Ôsaka shôin joshi daigaku ronshû, 27(17): 93–101, 1990; *"Sen-i kanren kaisha no joshi jûgyô-in no seifuku,"* Ôsaka shôin joshi daigaku ronshû, 29(10): 133–45, 1992; *"Shôjikai no joshi jûgyô-in no seifuku,"* Ôsaka shôin joshi daigaku ronshû, 30(5): 95–105, 1993; and *"Basugaido no seifuku,"* Ôsaka shôin joshi daigaku ronshû, 31(3): 115–23, 1994); and Uno Kôji, Nogami Akiko and Sakurai Mutsuko (*"Tetsudôgyô no danshi jûgyô-in no seifuku,"* Ôsaka shôin joshi daigaku ronshû, 28(13): 149–56, 1991).

Note to Reader

Japanese names follow the Japanese convention of family names written first and followed by given names. The abbreviations JT, DY and AEN stand for *Japan Times, Daily Yomiuri* and *Asahi Evening News,* respectively. Officially, the yen is pegged at ¥360 to one US $1.00. During the time I spent in Japan, however, it fluctuated from 79 to 141 yen to one US dollar.

1

Introduction: Approaches and Definitions

Japan is a uniformed society. There are the *sararîman* ("salary man", i.e. white-collar workers) in their dark-blue suits, white shirts and conservative ties; young men, concerned with presenting the appropriate and "uniform" self, carrying briefcases (sometimes with nothing inside); the OLs ("office ladies", i.e. secretaries) in their prim company uniforms; sharply dressed and hatted "elevator girls" whose robotic but delicate gestures and soft voices guide customers on and off department store elevators; housewives in their aprons and large slippers; the cab drivers, bus drivers and train station personnel in their white gloves; the elderly guards and tour guides, dressed in pseudo-military style uniforms, who politely usher people in and out, to and fro;[1] the identically clad school toddlers with their yellow caps and oversized backpacks; and the older male students in their military-inspired navy blue uniforms and the female students in their "sailor uniforms". Indeed, it sometimes seems as if everyone in Japan is in uniform. Even the gangsters have a type of regulated dress comprised of flashy suits, loud neckties, expensive jewelry, sunglasses and closely cropped hair (cf. Raz 1992: 20). Many societies, of course, have uniforms, but it is hard to find a place where people so enthusiastically and systematically outfit themselves in uniforms as in modern Japan. But why do dress uniformity and uniforms play such a salient role among the Japanese?

If Japan is often perceived as a uniformed society, there is another image that may come as somewhat as a surprise. For many Westerners, Japan possesses a unique and refined culture, steeped in a centuries-old tradition of graceful taste and cultivated sensibility. This elegant aesthetic finds expression in the bright colors of the woodblock print, exquisite pottery, the delicate beauty of a scroll painting, or the powerful simplicity of calligraphy. Japanese artistic creations are admired for their suggestiveness, sublimity and a certain coolness of sentiment.[2] But scenes of colorful kimono-wrapped women demurely serving tea (or doll-like, admiring cherry blossoms), austere Zen rock gardens, or solemn temples nestled among pine trees, are as much a product of tourist brochures and official state ideology as they are a part of Japanese tradition. The real Japan – at least the Japan of the ordinary worker, housewife and student – presents a remarkably different view. In contrast to the accepted stereotypical images in the West, the average Japanese lives in a more mundane, commercialized and somewhat garish world. It is in this world – in crowded local shops, department stores, train stations, subways, buses and on noisy streets and narrow alleys – where, if anything catches the observer's eye, it is the number of "cute" (*kawai*) things. One does not have to stay long in Japan to notice that images of cuteness are more evident than the idealized and prepackaged "traditional" images consumed in the West. Indeed, it seems as if, next to images of dress uniformity, a "cult of cuteness" thrives.

How do these two very different styles – one concerned with uniformity, order and regulation and the other with cuteness, spontaneity and quirkiness – relate? I attempt to answer this question in this book, but first a few words about uniforms are in order.

In the most basic terms, my contentions are about ideology and clothing. In more particular terms, my goal is to examine the interrelated dynamics of state, capital, material culture, body, socialization, subjectivity and self-presentation. These facets of sociopolitical and economic life – implicated in the *habiti* of production and consumption – form numerous connections, but my concern is to study how they all converge in the nexus of dress uniformity. More specifically, I examine uniforms, but in particular, student uniforms. Besides exploring the linkages between state, capital, socialization, subjectivity, self-presentation as expressed via material culture, I will also examine how they relate to schooling (where much of socialization occurs); consumerism (the complement to capitalist production); and gender differences and construction (a theme that cannot be ignored since gender is the most important distinction societies make). At first glance, the various topics I address may appear unrelated, even incongruous. But my basic contention is that dress uniformity and uniforms – especially student uniforms – are a disciplinary link between the individual and the political structures and their allied economic interests, and the practice of donning standardized clothing every day reinforces a host of associated values that maintain both the rationalizing projects of the state and economic interests. This is not to say that those who wear uniforms readily and completely agree with these rationalizing projects, but wearing a uniform is a sign that one at least is playing their role in these projects to a significant degree. The linkages between state and dress is complex, multiform, and multilayered. Even though such a connection is not simply deterministic or causal, this does not mean that there is no relationship. The primary purpose of this book is to delineate this relationship by examining how schools, as aspects and agents of the state, influence what students don. One can certainly argue to what degree the state is behind the uniformization of students, but it is difficult to deny that from their point of view, schools are linked to an officialdom of statist and nationalist implications.

This book, then, is not about fashion per se, i.e. it is not about the chic, the singular, or what is in vogue. Rather it is about *le quotidien* – what is frequent, familiar and common. The 'everydayness' of putting on, wearing and caring for uniforms and daily accouterments, while not as fashionable and spectacular as the latest style, haute couture and the newest trend, is more important because of its repetitive, multitudinous and ubiquitous nature. Such extensiveness of action stretched over a lifetime shapes attitudes far more powerfully than what is episodic or currently in fashion. Uniforms, defined as tangible symbols of the ability of the enormous and extensive politico-economic structures to shape bodily practices, and by implication, subjectivity and behavior, are notable because, as examples of material culture, they are utilized on a massive scale on a daily basis.

I do not focus on the uniforms of military, police and other security personnel because their highly regulated and standardized dress and accouterments are expressions of uniformity (though important for their own reasons) that are at once obvious and common to many other societies (to a lesser degree, the same could be said of athletes). I also pay little attention to a huge range of casualness and clothing styles that are usually regarded as non-uniformed, though in Japan, the dressing patterns and practices of white-collar workers (*sararîman*) and even housewives can be characterized as relatively uniformed (especially the former). Also, because my interest is in how the grand projects of modernity are articulated through the everyday and for the sake of keeping my arguments focused, I do not examine the history of uniformed dress in Japan.[3] Also, I do not investigate "traditional" clothing and related items (on which there is an abundant amount of material in Japanese) by which many non-Japanese commentators seemed so fascinated and charmed, and to which not a few Japanese point to as examples of "traditional" culture. The most famous example of "traditional" attire is the kimono, an open-front, ankle-length, wide-sleeved, one-piece dress that has no buttons and is worn with a broad belt (see Chapter 4). Other examples of "traditional" clothing include the *hakama* (a long divided skirt), *haori* (a loose short coat), *hanten* (traditionally a short workman's livery coat though now commonly worn as a quilted jacket), *happi* (another short workman's livery coat though now worn for various festive occasions), *tanzen* (a large padded kimono for winter),[4] *yukata* (a light cotton kimono worn in summer), *haramaki* (stomach wrap), *geta* (clogs), *zôri* (flat, thonged sandals) and a whole range of attire used for the martial arts.[5] Of course, it needs to be said that designating certain objects of material culture as "traditional" is a very modern project in itself whose effect is to establish national identity-building binaries: *our* cultural heritage/*your* practical things; past/present; we/them; self/other; Japan/the West; and the Japanese/the rest.

The remainder of this chapter is devoted to laying the theoretical ground-work, working definitions and outline of subsequent chapters.

Theoretical Framework: The State's Construction of Subjectivity and Self-Presentation

This work is not a conventional ethnography that focuses on a well-defined community or group of people. However, this work is certainly ethnographic in spirit, being based on daily observations and interviews while I have lived in Japan since 1987 (as a graduate student, researcher, and professor).

In the most broad sense, I adopt a "cultural psychological" approach (whose particular application to my purposes is found in Chapter 2), which briefly defined is the study of "the way cultural traditions and social practices regulate, express, transform and permutate the human psyche, resulting less in psychic unity for humankind than in ethnic divergences in mind, self, and emotion" (Shweder 1990: 1). My intention is to demonstrate how culture constructs mind and how cognition is a form of social action (e.g. values about being a good worker and forms of self-presentation). My working premise is that, in a certain sense, mind and society are ultimately indissociable and that psychological processes *are* social practices. Shweder explicates the meaning of cultural psychology by explaining *what it is not*:

(1) It is not general psychology, whose primary aim is to describe a presupposed "central (abstract and transcendent = deep or interior or hidden) processing mechanism inherent (fixed and universal) in human beings" (Shweder 1990: 4). Many researchers are not concerned with "all the concrete, apparent, variable, and particular stuff, substance, or content that is operated upon by the processor or may interfere with its operations" (Shweder 1990: 4). But in this book, I am very much concerned with the "concrete, apparent, variable, and particular stuff and content" – e.g. statist and capitalist projects of massive collectivities, school regulations and environment, notions of gender and especially the objects and sensory experiences of material culture— that shape the subjectivities of students/workers.

(2) It is not cross-cultural psychology, which is "a subdiscipline of general psychology that shares with general psychology the Platonic aim of character-izing the inherent central processing mechanism of the mental life" (Shweder

1990: 9). Rather, my concern in this book is with the particular context and concrete specifics, which are just important as acultural universals, that go into constituting minds. Thus, I intend to describe how socializing experiences (school rules, activities and ceremonials), material culture (clothing, uniforms and accessories), bodily management (cleaning, covering and restraining), and culturally specific norms (diligent students, persistent workers and other roles) produce distinctive subjectivities.

(3) It is not psychological anthropology, which attempts to "make use of the stuff of culture to characterize or discover a central processing device" (Shweder 1990: 14). Psychological anthropology is ultimately reductionistic since it assumes that the sociocultural environment is relatively pliant, "operated upon by, or expressive of, deep and invariant psychological laws or processes or motivation, affect and intellect" (Shweder 1990: 15). Unlike some psychological anthropologists, I do not believe that society can be reduced to or explained by the workings of mental central processing devices. Instead, I am more interested in describing how sociocultural environments – in this case, Japan's politico-economic force field and at the more local level, schools – constructs the attitudes, sentiments and thinking of individuals.

(4) It is not ethnopsychology, which investigates mind in the same way it approaches folk beliefs about botany or kinship, i.e. it is not person-centered enough (Shweder 1990: 16). I am not interested in describing abstract taxonomies which are divorced from the intentions of individual social actors and have little relation to motivated, volitional, goal-aspiring subjects and agents.

More specifically, in order to apprehend the concrete, variable, particular stuff, i.e. contextual politico-economic forces that produce subjectivities via material culture, I adopt a symbolic interactionist approach. This approach is useful because it is basically concerned with the *le quotidien*, the routinized, the face-to-face, and gives attention to the terms that the social actors under examination actually employ to negotiate their own social reality. The symbolic interactionist approach also allows us to appreciate the observation that social organization is "an ongoing interactional process rather than a fixed interactional product" (Brissett and Edgley 1990a: 283). Though much could be said about the import of symbolic interactionism, four premises will suffice for my present purposes: first, personhood is constructed through social interaction; second, human beings act towards others and things on the basis of the meanings that persons and things have for them; third, meanings emerge from the processes of social interaction; and finally, individuals, through symbolic interaction, actively modify meanings through interpretation.[6]

Some sociologists have criticized symbolic interactionism for its "astructural bias" and for being "apolitical". Some contend that it has been unable to deal with macro-structural issues and "avoids historical, economic, institutional, and political issues" (Denzin 1992: 56) (for recent critiques, see Prendergast and Knotternus 1990 and Reynolds 1990). However, Denzin counters these criticisms and points out that many symbolic interactionists have directly addressed issues of social organization and structure (1992: 59–60) (e.g. Hall 1987). In any case, there is no reason why symbolic interactionism cannot be methodologically employed to analyze institutional, political and economic aspects of social existence.

Dramaturgical Analysis

Even more specifically, I will adopt what is called the "dramaturgical variety" of symbolic interactionism (cf. Brisset and Edgley eds. 1990b, Goffman 1959, Perinbanayagam 1982, 1985). There are four reasons why I do so.

(1) *To Offer a More Sophisticated Analysis of Self-Presentation*. In this work, in order to be faithful to the cultural psychological premise that individual and institution, intention and ideology and self and society are all indissoluble, I want to frame my dramaturgical analysis within the context of political economic forces. Such theoretical framing allows me to push the implications of a social constructivist view of the self, thereby offering what I hope is a more sophisticated analysis of the dynamics of one of the major themes of this work: self-presentation. I also aim to illustrate "the importance of appearance for any general theory of self" (Stone 1990). All too often, terms such as self, presentation and performance are unfortunately and unhelpfully employed in a vague and misleading manner. Part of my agenda is to offer a more useful analysis which recognizes that social life and our minds consist of "various levels of understanding and awareness, not of layers covering a fundamental core which could be duly revealed by proper scientific work" (Brissett and Edgley 1990b: 37).

(2) *Social Actors Are Agents and Subjects Who Make Meaning*. Dramaturgy "asserts the power of human beings as subjects of their destiny" (Brissett and Edgley 1990b: 3), i.e. as subjects, individuals are not merely "role-taking" but also "role-making" (Turner 1990: 86). Therefore, I adopt a dramaturgical approach because it allows an escape from the "billiard ball" view of human action in which people are pushed along by larger forces; individuals do not merely "react", they "act". People act not because of "needs" or "forces", but "simply in order to make their conduct meaningful to those around them as well as to themselves, and they typically do so retrospectively, for since the meaning of any event lies in its consequences, human beings can never be sure of what they are doing until they have done it" (Brissett and Edgley 1990a: 203). Thus, "meaning is a continually

problematic accomplishment of human interaction and is fraught with change, novelty, and ambiguity" (Brissett and Edgley 1990b: 2). Moreover, "It is simply that whether we like it or not, plan it or not, want it to be or want it not to be, our behavior is expressive" [e.g. via clothing] (Brissett and Edgley 1990b: 4).

Dramaturgy is interested in both "discursive (speech and language) and nondiscursive (clothing, hair style, gestures – indeed, a myriad of objects that people use in their communication with others)" (Brissett and Edgley 1990b: 4–5). Thus, society does not simply determine what individuals wear and then hang clothes on unsuspecting persons and inert bodies. People, though they must act within certain culturally defined parameters, actively choose, get into, alter and show off what they wear. Any analysis must view individuals as conscious social actors who are actively and creatively involved in their own presentations and performances. Their selves and identities are expressed and negotiated within in an ever-changing sociopolitical force field. Such shifting, emergent and contingent forms of social life demand a dramaturgical approach.

(3) *Motives as Interpretive Accounts.* There are two ways to view the role of motives: as either causes 'in' individuals or as tools of interpretation "between" individuals. If people are meaning-generating and meaning-interpreting social actors, then it makes sense to view motives not only as triggers leading to action, but also as interpretive accounts of our own and others' behavior. According to Mills, "Rather than fixed elements 'in' an individual, motives are the terms with which interpretation of conduct *by social actors* proceeds" (1990: 207, original emphasis):

> We steer our lives one way or another using reasons and purposes not causes and effects. Motives become a part of acts, not a precursor to them, and their job is to put people into communication with one another about why they do the things they do. In this sense, human beings are neither rational nor irrational (with the appropriate push-pull terminology that accompanies either assumption) but rather *rationalizers* who engage in motive conduct during the course of their on-going activities (Brissett and Edgley 1990a: 203, original emphasis).

(4) *Social Life is Drama.* Brissett and Edgley ask whether "life *is* drama" or "life is *like* drama" (1990b: 32). I start from the premise that though it may be useful to sometimes regard "life as drama", in actuality "life *is* drama". Elsewhere, I have argued that self-presentation and stagecraft are not metaphoric mirrors of each other, but share an inherent sociopsychological identity and dynamic. Though social actors and stage actors have different motivations and purposes, at a fundamental cognitive and physiological level

they do the same thing (McVeigh 1997b: 35–59). This is probably "because ordinary social intercourse is itself put together as a scene is put together, by the exchange of dramatically inflated actions, counteractions, and terminating replies" (Goffman 1959: 72). "All the world is not, of course, a stage, but the crucial ways in which it isn't are not easy to specify" (Goffman 1959: 72), and the fact "that almost anyone can quickly learn a script well enough to give a charitable audience some sense of realness in what is being contrived before them" (Goffman 1959: 71) should alert us to how important acting is as a basic human activity and the potential of gleaning social scientific insights from it.

Though many observers have explored the affinities between the stage production and the everyday encounter, I feel that much can still be learned from acting since it offers a window into the complex interactions between society, self and the very nature of self.[7] The more quotidian forms of performativity – dramatizing, being affected, impersonating, imitating, mimicking, parodying, putting on airs, impressing others, telling white lies, etc. – are so ubiquitous that what we may learn about sociopsychological dynamics is easily overlooked. I am interested in the rhetorical strategems that "people employ, in endless variations, consciously and unconsciously, for the outwitting or cajoling of one another" (Burke 1990: 413).

In order to frame my arguments and illustrate the linkages between sociopolitical forces, subjectivity, self-presentation and the uses of material culture within the dramaturgical approach, I adopt Burke's exposition of the "five key terms of dramatism". Burke notes that "any complete statement about motives will offer some kind of answer to these five questions": *act* – what was done in thought or deed; *scene* – when or where an act was done, or the background or situation in which it occurred; *agent* – who or what kind of person did the act; *agency* – what means or instruments the person used or how an act was committed; and *purpose* – the "why" of an act (Burke 1990: 411, 1969). I utilize these "five key terms of dramatism" not as essentialist phenomena that can be neatly defined, but rather as analytic tools to organize my data and to promote my arguments throughout this book. My exploration of these terms is carried out within a local and particular context: the Japanese cultural milieu.

More specifically, in Chapter 3 I focus on how students learn (i.e. are socialized) about "acts" and how to "act". "Acts" may refer to large-scale and spatio-temporally clearly delimited events or to more mundane and seemingly insignificant micro-practices and minor activities (usually accomplished with little reflection by social actors) that are, as I argue elsewhere (McVeigh, forthcoming), just as important as ceremonials. Such "acts" may include washing, dressing and other examples of bodily management. The repetitive nature of such actions, performed on a daily basis, grants them a heavy socio-semantic load, and these highly patterned but inconspicuous practices qualify as micro-rituals. They form the behavioral bedrock upon which the more conspicuous rituals are built, and also function as socializing experiences. Or, to phrase it differently, the latter stitch together socio-psychological material into larger patterns which have already been woven through incessant spinning on a daily basis. Thus, ceremonials and rituals largely make sense to participants/observers because *le quotidien* activities have already made sense of them.

I treat "scenes" in Chapter 3 in an examination of schools as socializing scenes/situations. In Chapter 2 I provide a theoretical treatment of "agent" (in relation to self-presentation) and in Chapter 3 I discuss students as "agents". In Chapters 3, 4, 5 and 6 I explore the various forms of "agency" (uniforms, their accessories, "cute" objects). In Chapter 2 I discuss "purpose", not only in the sense of individual subjectivity but also in the sense of massive collective forces of statist and capitalist agendas which construct personal motivation. This "ultimate purpose" can be termed "economic nation-statism", or a hard ideological alloy formed from statism, national identity and consumerist capitalism (McVeigh, n.d.). If we agree that clothes "are seen as the outer skin of our personality and identity" and that they "clearly form part of an *extended* self" (Dittmar 1992: 41, original emphasis; cf. also Hall 1987), we should be able to ask why, or more to the point, how they have become so.

Even though the relation between state and dress is not deterministic or causal in any simplistic way, this does not mean that no relationship exists between them. What it does mean is that any investigation must accept that this relationship is composed of hierarchical state/society layerings, complex connections and less-than-obvious linkages. The purpose of this book is to delineate these layerings, connections and linkages. The self, its cognitive production and presentation, socializing institutions and material culture are all part of these layerings, connections and linkages.

This book, then, is not just about how statist and capitalist projects influence the way people dress; it is very much concerned with how these projects construct particular forms of subjectivity suited to productivist and consumerist economics, and in this sense, dress and its associated practices are tools in the construction of this subjectivity. There are, then, larger themes that this book addresses: How do public undertakings and private plans relate? How do collective endeavors shape personal projects? How are individuals embedded in institutions and how is ideology transmuted into intention? Much of the theoretical discussion about cultural psychology, dramaturgy and self-presentation builds upon earlier work (McVeigh 1997b).

Some Basic Definitions

A cultural psychological perspective that attempts to analyze how social-ization, subjectivity, self and its presentation, symbols, body, state, economic production and material culture all relate to each other can quickly become complex. Therefore, special attention is given to the key terms that I will use. These terms will be further clarified, elaborated and interlinked to each other in Chapter 2 and throughout this book, but some provisional definitions are provided here.

By *"material culture"* I mean objects that are produced and imbued with sociocultural meanings. Investigations of such objects may be called "the study through artifacts of the beliefs . . . of a particular community" (Prown 1988: 18). But besides being things designed, shaped and manufactured (i.e. its passive aspect), material culture has an active aspect which can be presented, received and exchanged in complex socioeconomic patterns. Moreover, and quite pertinent for my purposes, another example of the active side to material culture is how it is employed and deployed as a socializing instrument: things can be used by moral communities to instruct, inform and inculcate individuals since objects carry and convey a host of values, and in Chapter 3 I examine how schools – as agents of statist and capitalist hegemony—employ uniforms for socializing purposes.

Material culture, then, is not merely material.[8] Far from being semantically inert and symbolically sterile, material culture is laden with meaning, active, dynamic and tactically deployed by social actors and institutions. Indeed, a uniform is best thought of as a *"symbol"* – indeed, a "key symbol" – in Japanese society (cf. Ortner 1979). Disentangling the many threads of meaning which are woven and knotted around a key symbol is no small challenge. In my attempt to analyze uniforms, I will employ four properties of symbols as delineated by Turner (1967) which explain why symbols are effective for mobilizing, channeling and communicating people's conceptions about the social world. The first property is multivocality (or polysemy): one symbol can represent many things, pointing to various meanings. Dominant symbols have a "fan" or "spectrum of meanings". The second property is condensation: one symbol represents and unifies many diverse meanings, bringing together different ideas. This is often accomplished at the "nonconscious" level (see Chapter 2), where the different ideas that make up a symbol are associated with and interact with other ideas. The third property is ambiguity: a symbol has no single, precise meaning. Many individuals can and do use the same symbol in different ways. Thus, a symbol may accumulate additional meanings. The fourth property is the double aspect of a symbol: a symbol can be said to be composed of conceptual (ideological) and perceptual (sensory) dimensions which, via association, mutually define and reinforce each other, convincing an individual of the reality of a symbol's meaning. Seeing becomes believing, feeling becomes thinking, and vice versa (Turner 1967: 27–30), so that the material and the meaningful define each other. Throughout this book, I employ these four properties to analyze material.

As a symbol, a uniform may be approached from three angles, and again Turner is useful here (1967: 50–2, 292–6). The first aspect concerns the *exegesis of a symbol*: how the people who use a symbol explain its meaning (to themselves and researchers). In Chapter 3, in addition to my own investigations, I rely on the work of my Japanese colleagues who have conducted investigations and surveys into school and occupational uniforms. Though in some cases the small size of the samples and the statistical analyses are cause for caution in reaching any definite conclusions, these studies nonetheless offer valuable insights into the uses and meanings of uniforms in Japan.

The second aspect concerns how a symbol derives meaning from its *relationship to other symbols* in a complex of meanings (see Chapter 5). The third aspect concerns how people *utilize a symbol* in everyday action to do things, i.e. more to the point, how people use a symbol to make other people do, think, or feel certain things. This is the operational, practical and sociopolitical aspect of a symbol. In the most general sense, uniforms are used to socialize individuals (in schools) to accept basic sociopolitical processes (hierarchization, categorization and standardization) generated by statist and capitalist projects (Chapter 3). These three types of interpretation overlap to some degree, but if applied to a body of data they can be distinguished for practical purposes.

"State" is conventionally defined as a centralized polity based on non-kin relations that monopolizes and protects a well-defined territory, is held together by interlinked bureaucratic structures and controls technologies of communication (symbolic, ceremonial, transport, telecommunications, postal, coinage, etc.). Usually there are several nations or ethnic groups under a state's sovereignty. However, rather than considering state in the conventional sense, I will focus on *"statism"* and *"statefulness"* in order to highlight how modern, centralized political structures and projects have penetrated into everyday life and produced individual subjectivities that are attuned to the projects of modernity. In the next chapter I will have more to say about what I mean by these terms, but here I define statism as the ideology of deliberately disseminating statefulness and its acceptance by a populace. We must be cautious of terms such as "statism", which "is simply another label for one-sided political determinism" (Weiss and Hobson 1995: 8). Instead, I adopt a position espoused by Weiss and Hobson, who in their work about politico-economic transformation are "unashamedly state-centric but not determinist or reductionist" (1995: 9). Socializing bureaucratic structures (i.e. schools) play an indispensable role in producing and reproducing statefulness. Statism also means strong attachment or devotion to political institutions, ruling structures or governmental machinery, and implies compliance with state laws, directives, policies and procedures. These sentiments may range from lukewarm to fervent. Statism, however, gathers its enduring strength not only from surface ideologies (usually myths of national identity), but also from more or less unquestioned deep ideological sources bound up with modernity: social evolutionism, economic progressivism, positivism, scientism. Thus, as Barshay points out, allegiance to the state "almost sinks beneath the surface of consciousness, just as our awareness of 'nature' tends to become something of an abstraction, broken by intermittent sensation" (1988: xviii). Here it is also pertinent to note that by "state" I do not mean "nation"; the former means the territorial boundaries and political structures that a nation(s) has, while the latter designates a people or ethnos (who may or may not have a state).

Narrowly defined, *"capital"* means wealth – money, property, assets and other instruments of value – that circulates throughout a market-based economy, whose value accumulates in businesses and banks and is invested by owners, stockholders and other groups. Broadly defined, "capital" denotes the deeply ideological substructures that legitimate the capitalist system, including notions of a monetized economic system, market exchange and private property. It also means capitalists considered as a class.

There are different varieties of capitalism, and each capitalist society mixes capital, labor, market forces, ownership, the role of the state and central controls differently. For purposes of contrast: if the Anglo-American model emphasizes private ownership and private control, the Japanese model emphasizes private ownership, and at least among certain key "strategic" industries, state control. These official controls, however, are not explicit and often take the form of informal and unwritten "guidance". Moreover, this control originates not so much in central-planning organs but in its strong legitimization by nationalist sentiment and is therefore subtle in its operations and effects (hence, such control cannot be easily measured by conventional economic notions). Thus, in Chapter 2 I introduce Japanese capitalism as an ideology of economic nation-statism.

Admittedly, the connection between capital and dress uniformity may appear tenuous, and it is certainly not inherent. But I do believe a connection, as indirect as it is, does exist: dress uniformity disciplines minds and bodies for the planned, coordinated, regulated and organized accumulation of capital. It does this in schools and, to a lesser degree depending on occupation and gender, in the workplace.

By *"socialization"* I mean the processes by which both state educational structures and informal, everyday learning experiences construct knowledge forms (i.e. subjectivity and self). Many take the processes of socialization for granted. Accordingly, the immense amount of psychological work required to apprehend, deliberate upon, and then interconnect pieces of information with other knowledge is not recognized. In order to highlight the under-appreciated and invisible functioning of psyche, I distinguish between conscious and nonconscious processes in order to explain how individuals are able to ingest and digest the vast amounts of knowledge needed to navigate their social worlds. Socialization, whose occurrence is bodily mediated, constructs *"subjectivity"* (or mind or psyche) which has both conscious and nonconscious aspects, with the latter the more primary, fundamental and preponderant. The nonconscious requires attention here because it is within this sociopsychological sphere that so much of the labor of subjectivity must be carried out in order to legitimate, maintain and inform the more official, obvious and "visible institutions" of the socioeconomic and political order.

A product of the psyche's cognitive processes is the *"self"*. But selves are not innate; they are forms of knowledge that are constructed from the time of birth, change over time, and are continually reconstructed each moment. The self is what others tell us we are, and more complexly, it is what we tell ourselves we are. "The advantage of an idea of your self is to help you know what you can or can't do or should or should not do" (Jaynes 1990: 458); or phrased differently, it is social imperatives made personal. The self is what is presented to others (*self-presentation*) and to one's own awareness. Its expression is provisional, expedient and situationally defined.

By *"body"* I mean the physical *and* psychic structures of the human organism. Though our disciplinary language games and folk theorizings have convinced many of us to rely on dualistic and essentialized thinking (e.g. mind/body, psyche/soma, object/subject, sociology/psychology, self/other; mind/society; individual/collectivity; belief/behavior; knowledge/practice and mental/material, etc.), the body and mind are aspects of a unitary reality (i.e. not a union), a singularity that may be called a "somapsyche".[9] For my purposes, attention to the body is necessary because socialization is very much a bodily process, especially since our corporeality, senses and acts of consumption relate to material culture.

The body is a key target of sociopolitical operations and management, a fact that is not surprising since socialization is very much a process of learning via embodiment. The body is also an icon laden with social meanings. Indeed, it is very difficult to conceive the human body *sans* material culture, cultural management and historical change.[10] Bodies are made to stand, sit, bow, salute, placed at attention, line up, mobilized en masse and made to emit sounds appropriate to time, place, occasion and persons present. In Japan, some women will attempt to "stretch" their bodies by wearing high heels, and others increase their height even more by wearing platform shoes (some twice the weight of regular shoes) and add to the illusion of height by wearing long pants to conceal the thick shoes. Heads are made to face forward, eyes front, mouth shut, head still, stomach in, back straight, hands at side and the face should be either serious, expressionless, respectfully blank and not smiling (in Japan, during certain ceremonials and events; especially vis-à-vis superiors), or they must smile and beam with joy (in Japan, for customers, clients and patrons; especially vis-à-vis males if the social actor is female). Moreover, the body itself is treated with more long-range disciplines, such as complex regimes of dieting, exercise and training. In Japan, *esute* centers and practices (borrowed from the European *esthétique*), which are for both men and women, respond to the consumer demand for healthier and more beautiful bodies. *Esute* means "Anything that is intended to improve or change the body may be catalogued as *esute*: weight loss, facials, massage, exercise regimes, electrolysis, exfoliation treatments, herbal remedies, diet pills, and other elixirs" (Miller 1998).

A wide range of artifacts are put on the body, particularly the female body. It is something which clothes are hung on, draped over, strapped to, tied on, wrapped in, belted, buttoned on, or laced (and for a special type of socks worn by female students in Japan, glued on; see Chapter 3). Parts of the body receive meticulous treatment. Faces are painted, brushed, coated and colored. Hair is washed, shampooed, conditioned, cut, permed, colored, combed, brushed, pulled back, straightened, layered, sprayed and tied up in numerous ways. Nails are trimmed, filed and polished. Eyes are lined with pencil, enlarged and highlighted with eye shadow. Eyelashes are thickened, curled and lengthened with mascara. Eyebrows are trimmed, picked and penciled. Sometimes the color of the iris is enhanced or changed by contact lenses. The face is brushed, plastered, exfoliated and its defects concealed. Cheeks are contoured and powdered to give a matte look. Lips are colored, lined and glossed. Skin is cleansed, creamed, toned, tightened and moist-uerized. Ears are pierced, double-pierced and jeweled (and at an Osaka coffee shop, cleaned with a fiberscope inserted in the ear so the customer can watch on a video (Ida 1997)). Hands are washed, softened and gloved. Legs are shaved, waxed and perhaps slid into pantyhose. Feet are massaged, scrubbed and softened with pumice stones. Note should also be made of the numerous tools of material culture – mirrors, combs, brushes, curlers, sponges, pencils, towels, razors, shavers, creams, lotions, jells, deodorants, anti-perspirants, colognes, perfumes, waxes, sprays – that are used as tools to decorate, beautify and make the body ready for self-presentation/performance. There are more radical treatments for the body. Eyelid surgery is used to "Westernize" the eye shape by adding a fold above the eyes (temporary folds to the eyelids can be obtained by over-the-counter "eye glues" and "eye tapes" (Miller 1998: 12)).[11] The face itself is tucked, nipped and sliced. Other parts of the body are exercised, reduced, lifted, augmented and unwanted portions are suctioned out. Many women are socialized to believe that their bodies are somehow defective: in one survery it was revealed that half of all female high school students classified as thin by an international formula thought they were fat and 90 per cent wanted to lose weight ("Drive to be thin puts self-image at odds with standards", 1998).

Linking Students and State via Uniforms

In Chapter 3 I discuss student uniforms which I regard as key socializing objects in Japan's politico-economic order. A focus on students is necessary because of all the social costuming visible in Japan, student uniforms are the most commonly encountered and, with the exception of military and police uniforms, are more regulated than other types of material culture identity kits. Moreover, and significantly for my purposes, student uniforms should be viewed as powerful socializing components of material culture. As we shall see, student uniforms are not merely identity kits used in schools; rather, they are material components of a much larger, relatively predictable, project of macro-forces composed of corporate concerns and statist structures (economic nation-statism). In this chapter I describe how uniforms can be viewed as material markers of a three-phase life-cycle managed (uniformizing, de-uniformizing and re-uniformizing) and monitored by powerful politico-economic institutions. I also describe in Chapter 3 how the state attempts to deploy its totalizing effects through local socializing sites – i.e. schools – that prime students for future roles that are gendered, nationalized and geared toward capitalist production.

Though school uniforms are not unique to Japan,[12] it is worth noting the heavy symbolic weight school uniforms possess in Japan. Consider Mori's *Misshon sukûru zukan* (Picture Book of Mission Schools, 1993) which lists one hundred "mission" (i.e. Christian) high schools throughout Japan for women. For each school, a detailed drawing of the type of uniform worn at the school is presented, along with information about the school. Mori has also compiled *Tôkyô joshi kô seifuku zukan* (Women's High Schools of Tokyo Picture Book of Uniforms, 1985) which lists 160 schools divided by the wards (*ku*) of Tokyo. Similar in format to *Misshon sukûru zukan*, *Tôkyô joshi kô seifuku zukan* also provides diagrams of school badges along with commentary on each school's uniform. The book has a map of where the women's high schools are located (1985: 2) and lists nine Tokyo private schools without uniforms (1985: 36). Also, each school's "standard deviation score" (*hensachi*), used by prospective students to decide on which school their own academic abilities match, is listed (1985: 197).

Patterns of Dress Uniformity

In Chapter 4, I conclude the analysis of the three-phase life-cycle begun in Chapter 3. Then, I offer examples of patterns and practices of dress uniformity by discussing a "continuum of uniformity". Next, I explore the usages and meanings of uniforms among so-called "office ladies" and public transportation personnel, probably the two most conspicuous categories of uniform wearers after students in Japan (excluding police).

The "Cult of Cuteness" and Consumption as Counter-practice

For my own purposes, what is significant about cuteness is its profound involvement in consumption practices as a form of "resistance"; the "cult of cuteness", as a particular daily aesthetic that is strongly associated with women, counters the dominant "male" productivist ideology of standardization, order, control, rationality and impersonality. There are countless ways to express resistance (cf. El Guindi's examination of the veil in Arab culture (1999)), and I am certainly not arguing that in Japan cuteness is the only way. However, being cute is a very obvious way of expressing uniqueness, deviation, freedom, spontaneity, personality. In the words of a fashion photographer, "I want everyone to be different. And I definitely want businessmen to stop wearing their stupid suits" (Badtke-Berkow 1997). The point of Chapter 5 is to delineate the interrelated nature of two key aesthetic/ styles and norms/ethics: one being the "official ideology" of production/labor and the other an "anti-official ideology" of consumption/leisure. These two ideologies have implications for activity in daily life, styles of object/clothes, socioeconomic relations and sociopsychological dynamics, and, both being products of Japan's consumerist capitalism, feed off each other. Thus, productivist demands and diligence ironically bolster consumerist desires and dreams and vice versa.

The groundwork for Chapter 6 is laid in Chapter 5, in which I explore the everyday aesthetics of cuteness. This aesthetic permeates every aspect of Japanese culture and is a complex, paradoxical commentary on sociopolitical relations. This is because, on one hand it reinforces vertical relations, in particular, male/female bonds (and master/student, junior/senior, parent/child bonds), but on the other hand, it strengthens the notion that those in inferior relations require and need care and empathy from those in authority. Those on top are obligated to bestow favors and benefits to those below (this is particularly evident in gender relations). Thus, I will give examples of how authority figures – whether in the form of individuals and institutions – go to great efforts to associate themselves with "soft" images. In Chapter 6 I continue the discussion initiated in Chapter 5, illustrating how the ethics of the cute aesthetic are embedded and implicated in consumerist acts.

Notes

1. Cf. Hendry ("Wrapping of the Body", 1993: 70–97).
2. Other stereotypes involving material culture come to mind: Japanese tourists weighed down with cameras, wearing hats and led by female guides holding flags, samurai swordsmen and fleshy sumô wrestlers in loincloth.
3. Suffice to say, regulated dress of some sort has a long tradition in Japan (as elsewhere). As early as the seventh century when the *ritsuyryô* system of statecraft was adopted from China, court officials were required to wear certain clothing. Prince Shôtoku, following Chinese conventions, initiated a system of twelve court ranks (*kan'i jûnikai*) that dictated the color of headdresses and clothing. Both the Taihô Code of 701 and Yôrô Code of 718 mandated clothing, headgear and accessories for visitors to the court. Special dress for ceremonial occasions were called *raifuku*; those who came to work at the court on a regular basis wore *chôfuku*, and scholars and officials without rank wore *seifuku*. In later centuries, the *chôfuku* for men became the *sokutai*. For women, the *raifuku* and *chofuku* would develop into the *karaginumo* and the *uchiki*, which eventually became lady's ceremonial court dress or the "12-layered garment" (*jûni hitoe*). By the fifthteenth century, the *hitatare* of the lower-ranking warriors became adopted by higher-ranking warriors. This piece of clothing was simplified into the *kamishimo* during the Edo period (1603–1867), while the *raifuku* was worn for important occasions. For women, the most important clothing for ceremonials from the Kamakura period (1185–1333) until Edo was the *kosode*. During the Edo period, the authorities implemented strict sumptuary laws. Massive changes in clothing and self-presentation occurred during the early Meiji period (1867–1912), when state authorities issued regulations that men must cut their topknot and adopt a "Western" style. Though many women also cut their hair, the authorities eventually prohibited such practices.

4. The relatively specialized usage and strictly enforced dress codes of kimonos arguably qualifies them as "uniforms". For an anthropological treatment of kimono, see Dalby (1993).

5. Changes in equipment or attire for the martial arts is noted in the media. See "New face mask takes blinkers off kendo" (1998), especially if such changes are felt to alter the "traditional" aspect of the sport (e.g. Yato 1997 and "Intl judo body OK's colored uniforms", 1997).

6. Symbolic interactionism can be traced to important thinkers such as James (1890); Cooley (1902); Peirce (1934); Dewey (1922); Park and Burgess eds. (1921); Simmel (1909); Mead (1910, 1934, 1938); and Blumer (1931, 1969). It has inspired and shaped many intellectual currents (negotiated order, political studies, feminist research, phenomenological, everyday life sociology, ethnomethodology, discourse analysis, role-identity theories, contextual interactionism and social constructionism), and it has been used to fruitfully investigate a wide range of subjects (see Denzin 1992, especially xiii–xviii, 1–21). Its impact has been both topic-related and methodological.

7. E.g. Burke (1966); Burns (1972); Durignaud (1973); Evreinoff (1927, 1990); Geertz 1980; Goffman (1959, 1974, 1990); Hare and Blumberg (1988); Lyman (1975); Mangham and Overington (1990); Schechner (1977, 1982, 1985, 1988, 1992); Schechner and Appel (eds 1989); Schechner and Schumar (eds 1976); and Turner (1967, 1969, 1974). See especially the volume edited by Brissett and Edgley (1990b). See Turner (1990) for a concise analysis of "role theory".

8. However, for articles on the more material aspect of uniforms, see "The End-Use Properties of Textiles Fabrics and Accessory in School Uniforms (Isobe and Eguchi 1996) and "Climatological Research on Clothing of Uniforms" (Yoshida, Egawa and Yokoyama 1989).

9. The literature on the body is immense and growing and I will not attempt a review here. However, Lock (1993), Scheper-Hughes and Lock (1987), Shilling (1993) and Turner (1984, 1991) offer useful recent reviews.

10. As an example of changes in body perceptions, note that "When four women appeared on a calisthenics show in sleeveless shirts and shorts, the nation was shocked. Four decades later, women on the show wear skin-tight Spandex" (Matsuzaki 1997).

11. As for "Westernizing" Japanese physical traits, Miller points that we should be wary of reading too much into the interpretation that such practices are motivated by a "racist beauty ideology that denigrates Asian physical appearance": "Wouldn't that be confounding the rejection of older Japanese models of male identity, particularly the salaryman, with a rejection of ethnicity? When American Ravers or Cyberpunks appropriate non-western forms of body modification, such as genital piercing or tattooing, we don't hear anyone accusing them of trying to turn themselves into New Guinea highlanders, or Berber nomads" (1998: 14). Cf. Flannery (1997) and Onozuka (1996).

12. For a discussion of school uniforms in Taiwan, see Strawn (1999). In the United States, school uniforms are not unheard of, and many believe they should be worn. See "N.Y. education board urges uniforms for schoolchildren" (1998).

2

The Dramaturgical Approach: Linking Subjectivity, Self-Presentation and the State

Burke writes that "any complete statement about motives will offer some kind of answer to these five questions: what was done (act), when or where it was done (scene), who did it (agent), how he did it (agency), and why (purpose)" (1990: 411). In order to delineate the theoretical framework of this book, I divide this chapter into five major parts corresponding to these aforementioned questions. I first explain and explore the notion of "scene", paying particular attention to the Japanese specificities of "scene". Next, I will examine "agent" (social actor) from a cultural psychological perspective, dissecting subjectivity, nonconsciousness and the features of consciousness (especially the self and its various modes of presentation). Then, I treat "act" (practice) and "agency", the latter meaning, for my purposes, clothes and material culture. For reasons of argument and convenience, I save "purpose" or the intention of social actors – the "why" of their actions – for last. Purpose is a rather broad concept in my adoption of Burke's scheme, and it designates the source of an individual's ideas, aims, plans, goals and motivations formed from sociopolitical and economic processes.

Two caveats are in order. First, these concepts are admittedly not always clearly distinguishable and easily merge into each other (e.g. acts often constitute scenes, acts are an inherent component of agents, scenes can be utilized as a form of agency). But in this work I hope to display the usefulness of these concepts as hermeneutic tools. The second caveat concerns "purpose"; though the subjectivity and intention of an individual *originates in and is shaped by* sociopolitical and economic structures and their legitimating ideologies (both explicit and implicit), a social actor's psyche cannot be *reduced to and explained away by* such collective processes and tenets. There is no one-way, deterministic relationship between society and subjectivity, and hence it is impossible to predict how a person will interpret and reinterpret the innumerable conflicting, contrasting and diversifying socializings, resocializings and desocializings to which he or she is exposed.

Part One: Scene

A "scene" is the background or situation in which an act or practice occurs. But backgrounds and situations are socially designed, manipulated and shaped by local understandings of human nature, social dynamics and cultural preferences. Moreover, scenes, whether educational, occupational, or kin-related, are embedded in larger sociopolitical systems and are linked (some more firmly than others) to politico-economic projects.

The Role of Observing Others

In order to ensure that everyone properly presents his or her part, the *seken*, a generalized audience, or, perhaps more ominously, a sort of omnipresent social spook, keeps an eye on everyone. Literally, the word means "in the world", but may be translated as public, the world, community, people, or society. Lebra defines the *seken* as "The surrounding world of community consisting of neighbors, kin, colleagues, friends, and other significant persons whose opinions are considered important" (1984: 338). What one does, says, wears and how one wears something, are carefully observed by the *seken*, and one's appearance or reputation is called *sekentei*. Ideally, one should conform to the *seken-nami* (average, ordinary standard of *seken*) to avoid "talk of *seken*" (*seken-banashi*). The *seken*, which may be described as a normalizing gaze, constantly observes one's actions and appearance, as does *hitome* (literally, "the eyes of people"), often translated as "notice", "observation", "attention", "public", or sometimes "public gaze" or "sight (eyes) of the world".

Another related word is *hitomae* (literally, "in front of others"). *Hitomae o habakarazu* (literally, "without being diffident towards others") means "without regard to decency" or "openly"; *hitomae o habakaranai* (literally, "not being diffident towards others") means "to be free before others" or "ignore the presence of others"; and *hitomae o tsukurou* means "to keep up appearances". Many associate *hitome* and *hitomae* with giving speeches and the anxiety of speaking in front of others, ceremonies, being polite and more specific practices concerned with civility, such as not littering, not talking loudly on trains, covering one's mouth when yawning and "not doing silly things in public". According to some Japanese, *seken, hitome and hitomae* are associated with being uneasy, worrying about the opinions of others, being shy, being tense, being evaluated by others, and "the feeling of being surrounded by many people". And according to some, these terms, especially *seken*, are all "very Japanese".

Dictionaries translate *seken, hitome* and *hitomae* as "public", but this translation, while perhaps sometimes appropriate, fails to capture the nuance of "being watched". In a sense, then, *seken, hitome* and *hitomae* are the counterpart of performers and presenters of selves. Other similar terms are *shû-i* (environment, surroundings, neighborhood) and "those around one" (*mawari no hito*).

In Japan, self-presentations occur in reference to four key terms that demarcate a sort of sociopolitical geography. These terms, *uchi/soto* (internal/ outside) and *ura/omote* (hidden/exposed), describe social categorizations and are used in countless terms and expressions (Bachnik 1992, Bachnik and Quinn 1994, Doi 1986, Ishida 1984, Johnson 1980, Lebra 1976, McVeigh 1997b). But despite their cultural specificity, the use of these notions deeply resonate with interactional practices elsewhere, and as I define their meanings below, I compare them to observations about social life made by Goffman in order to avoid essentializing Japanese culture.

The first categorization is *uchi*, which means inside, internal, informal, familiar, concealed, or private and is used as an adjective to refer to oneself, family, house, group of playmates, workers, school, or company. It can also denote bounded, nearby, enclosed, concave, dark, domestic, casual, comfort-able, indulgent, free, secret, primary, privileged, special and sacred (Quinn 1994: 53). The second categorization is *soto*, which means out, outside, nondomestic, public, exposed, or others, and is often associated with strangers, "them", customers, secondary, the less known, and secular (Quinn 1994: 63–4). The third categorization is *omote*, which means front or what is visible. *Omote* may refer to anything exposed to public attention and sometimes implies dramatized, dignified, formal, or rigid and appears in phrases such as *omote o tateru* ("putting up a front"), *omote o tsukurou* ("keeping up appearances") and *omote o haru* ("keeping up a façade"). Buruma notes that in Japan, "consensus may often be a public façade, but then façade counts for a great deal in Japanese life" (Buruma 1984: 221).

Compare *omote* with Goffman's "front": "that part of the individual's performance which regularly functions in a general and fixed fashion to define the situation for those who observe the performance. Front, then is the expressive equipment of a standard kind intentionally or unwittingly employed by the individual during his performance" (1959: 22). Goffman describes two types of "fronts". The first is "setting", which involves "furniture, décor, physical layout, and other background items which supply the scenery and stage props for the spate of human action played out before, within, or upon it". The second is "personal front", which involves "items that we most intimately identify with the performer himself and that we naturally expect will follow the performer wherever he goes". This may include "insignia of office or rank; clothing; sex, age, and racial characteristics; size and looks; posture; speech patterns; facial expressions; bodily gestures and the like" (1959: 23–4). The second type of "front" is directly linked to self-presentation as it relates to uniform dress.

The fourth social categorization is *ura*, which means back, reverse side, but may refer to anything hidden from public attention, privately allowed and sometimes implies practical, efficient, informal, or flexible. Compare what Goffman writes about the "backstage", or the area or activities that are suppressed because they might discredit the fostered impression. The back region is "defined as a place, relative to a given performance, where the impression fostered by the performance is knowingly contradicted as a matter of course". Thus, "It is here that the capacity of a performance to express something beyond itself may be painstakingly fabricated; it is here that illusions and impressions are openly constructed" (1959: 111–12). And, "Since back regions [*ura*] are typically out of bounds to members of the audience, it is here that we may expect reciprocal familiarity to determine the tone of social intercourse. Similarly, it is in the front regions [*omote*] that we may expect a tone of formality to prevail" (1959: 128).

According to Lebra (1976), social life in Japan can be categorized into "three domains of situational interaction" which result from permutations of the four terms discussed above (one permutation, the *uchi–omote* situation, does not occur; cf. Table 2.1). The first domain is *uchi–ura*, or intimate situations, in which people – usually among family or close friends – express feelings of togetherness, belonging, emotional attachment and spontaneity. Free from the observing eyes of others (*hitome*) and relatively protected from *seken*, status, position and rank are de-emphasized, so that styles of self-presentation are usually informal.

The second domain is *soto–omote*, or ritualized situations. Situations that call for ritualized behavior range "from the extremely structured situation, such as a ceremony, to the undefined, accidental situation, such as an unexpected encounter with an acquaintance on the street, from play scenes to work scenes" (Lebra 1976: 120). Knowing how to navigate one's way through a ritualized scene comes from having acquired a "sense of ritual": "It is through a socially acquired sense of ritual that members of a society know how to improvise a birthday celebration, stage an elaborate wedding, or rush through a minimally adequate funeral" (Bell 1992: 81). Unlike intimate situations, the weighty presence of *seken* is felt, as are hierarchical distinctions. Thus, there is a conscious self-monitoring of bodily movement and positioning, posture, gestures, countenance, style of speech (formal and honorific) and of course, dress and personal adornment. Ritualized situations often involve group entry or exit rituals or some change in the group structure, thus everyone must be on their best behavior in order to handle any unforeseen unpredictability. This is why so much of ritualized scenes is scripted, even pre-scripted; if everyone knows their part well, there is less chance of faux pas or someone forgetting his or her lines and causing loss of face.

Intimate and ritualized situations and scenes complement and balance one another. "Since back regions are typically out of bounds to members of the audience, it is here that we may expect reciprocal familiarity to determine the tone of social intercourse. Similarly, it is in the front regions that we may expect a tone of formality to prevail" (Goffman 1959: 128).

The last domain is *soto–ura*, or anomic situations. Compare anomic situations to what Goffman labels the "outside": "It would seem reasonable to add a third region, a residual one, namely, all places other than the two already identified" (1959: 134–5). Whereas intimate-familiar situations involve only "insiders" and ritual-formal situations involve "outsiders" but require maintaining face while following certain rules, there are many times and places when a person treats someone as an outsider but does not feel any need to maintain face since there are no rules with which to comply; for example, commuting, taking public transportation, shopping, or any other activity that requires moving among strangers, unknowns and crowds. Though most Japanese are certainly orderly and polite in a perfunctory sort of way, in Japan the aforementioned situations do possess a degree of "asociality" characterized not by discourtesy but by inattentiveness. It often seems as if public space in Japan is a socially ambiguous "betwixt and between" territory one must put up with, rather than a socially valued space with its own *raison d'être* (McVeigh 1998a). This asociality is expressed in many ways. For example, a sign near an apartment complex in my neighborhood reads: "You Are Being Observed by a Video Camera: Urinating in the Street Is Prohibited and Is a Minor Offense Against the Law." I do not, however, want to stress the asocial character of public space in Japan too much, since, as I will illustrate later, public space in Japan certainly possesses its own code of behavior and a certain performative value utilized by uniformed students, as well as others.

A Unitized Society

All societies, of course, have socially instituted and regulated groups, or what may be termed "units": a basic structural unit of a larger system which is capable (to a relative degree) of functioning independently and is mission-oriented (again, to a relative degree). However, the argument can certainly be made that some societies are more "unitized" than others. In highly unitized (or perhaps cellular) societies, the walls between different groups are higher and thicker and the gaps between units more anomic. Thus, spaces outside units are socially de-emphasized and more attention is given to involved entry and exit rituals. For example, in Japan, predetermined and carefully choreographed practices of civility (*aisatsu*) uphold *omote* (i.e. fronts), thereby strengthening internal cohesion (*uchi*) vis-à-vis the outside (*soto*) and facilitating traffic between different groups (and constructing, it might be noted, a rather different notion of civil society if compared to North America). A neutral perspective or forum in which one can interact with others is not emphasized. Rather, there is a continuum between exposed settings in which one is observed, and private situations in which one is removed from the gaze of outsiders. One is either moving betwixt and between groups through non-places or firmly situated within groups, among intimates or more relatively formal settings (school, workplace, etc.). In this sense, then, Japanese notions of publicness stress group-orientedness, but not necessarily freedom from the group, a protective zone within which the individual is secure as idealized in many Euro-American societies. In these societies the public is often regarded as an area that may be used to mediate disputes, defend rights, effect political changes, or facilitate social exchanges, wanted and unwanted. It is essential to point out that the third meaning of public (autonomous) may conflict with the second meaning (official) as noted above: i.e. the public may be utilized by an individual as an institutional buffer in the face of state infringement (at least ideally).

In societies that are less unitized, not as much attention is given to entry and exit rituals, since a "public" or neutral zone exists – with an abstract set of rules that apply to all groups – between more permeable units. In such societies, social frontage and façades, though certainly not absent, receive less maintenance (McVeigh 1998a). But whether a society is unitized or less so, codes of etiquette are necessary to ensure that interactions do not cause loss of face: "Civility is the condition necessary for someone's performance to be welcome" (Pin and Turndorf 1990: 179).

Certain units under the right conditions can readily adopt the characteristics of "total institutions"; these "are institutions purportedly established the better to pursue some worklike task and justifying themselves only on these instrumental grounds: army barracks, ships, boarding schools, work camps, colonial compounds, and large mansions from point of view of those who live in the servants' quarters" (Goffman 1961: 5). However, units are not necessarily always highly mobilized and their task is not necessarily clear.

Indeed, members of a unit may subvert, alter, or even invert their group's stated or mandated mission.

In Japan, units are significant for socializing, productive, consuming and reproductive practices. They instill the virtues and vices of mutual surveillance and "collective responsibility" (*rentai sekinin*). For the sake of argument, we can picture a vast array of units that make up the organizational tissue of a much larger sociopolitical organism, the sociopolity known as Japan. Though each unit may have its own *raison d'être*, traditions and objectives, they are all ideo-institutionally tied to varying degrees to the projects of economic nation-statism. A host of situational variables determines which units are privileged over others, but for the sake of convenience, we can talk of five basic types: (1) educational; (2) occupational and workplace; (3) familial; (4) neighborhood; and (5) non-kin intimates.

Here I should note that rather than translating *shûdan* as "group", I prefer "unit", which has a less abstract, more concrete sense, and carries the connotation of being one component in a larger system which has its own mission or project (e.g. school, education system, corporate culture, nation-state, etc.). That is, *shûdan* often means an institutionally-required grouping. Also, from contextual usage within school culture, *shûdan* denotes not so much a conceptual "groupiness," but rather a practical purposefulness. Moreover, a group often connotes an assembly of people who came together willingly, whereas a unit is put together by someone else (cf. *shûdan ni awaseru*; to "be put into a unit").

As units, schools are held together as moral communities through their own school tradition or customs (*kôfû*; sometimes "school spirit"), school song (*kôka*), school rules (*kôki*), school regulations (*kôsoku*) and school precepts (*kôkun*). At the subunitized level, schools are divided into home-rooms (*homurûmu*; probably the most important organizing unit for students), grades (*gakunen*) and classes (*gakkyû* or *kumi*), which are in turn subdivided into small groups called *han* (usually five to ten students) for specific tasks. All this slicing and dicing into groups allows smooth administrative functioning and instills within students the sense that they are always being eyed, and it is within schools that students learn "group living" (*shûdan seikatsu*), practices that shape sentiments of inside/outside later in life (e.g. workplace, national identity). Consequently, "Japanese schools teach a buttoned-down sense of time and space not unlike what one finds in the military" (Rohlen 1983: 316).

As units, companies (especially the bigger ones) express and codify their identity through company traditions and customs (*shafû*). New employees acquire a knowledge of company regulations (*shasoku*) and perhaps recite company precepts (*shakun*) on a daily basis during "morning ceremonies" (*chôrei*). At company events (*shanai gyôji*) the company anthem (*shaka*) might be sung. Besides the usual organizing units of departments and divisions, the latter are sometimes divided into "total quality control" groups (ten to fifteen individuals).

As self-contained units, kin groups (often the nuclear family) and households also have their own family traditions and customs (*kafû*) (that traditionally all good daughters-in-law in Japan's patrilocal culture were expected to learn). Moreover, families might have their own family precepts (*kakun*), and for some families, a family crest (*kamon*).

Neighborhood associations may also be understood as units. Variously called *chônaikai* (town-block associations; or *chôkai*), *jichikai* (self-government associations; or *han*) or in rural areas, *burakukai* (hamlet associations; or *kukai*). These organizations are made up of a few dozen households, are semi-compulsory, are usually male-dominated, have as their basic unit of organization not the individual but the family, and engage in a host of neighborhood-related activities (community gatherings, festivals, street cleaning, anticrime measures, disaster drills, safety prevention drives, donations for community causes, state-encouraged saving campaigns, etc.). "There are only seven municipalities in Japan without such associations" (Sugimoto 1997: 248).

As for non-kin groups, various societies, circles and associations might qualify as units depending on their degree of formalization. School sports teams and clubs perform a key socializing function, and membership is mandated at most schools. Clubs also play an important socializing role at the university level for many students. Moreover, though ostensibly less formalized and voluntary, one's circle of friends or *nakama* (mates, fellows, or comrades) may function as units in how they check untoward behavior.

In order to ensure that unit members acquire a cooperative attitude, individuals must know the group's rules, and this entails an emphasis on resocialization when joining a unit. This is why, more than just a matter of acquiring practical information, knowing the right way to do something signals one's level of loyalty to a unit. The acceptance of a certain way of doing things, often different from the way the same thing is carried out in another group, acts as a barometer of one's affiliation to the unit and acceptance of its mission. This is why the authoritative gaze within a unit is directed to the details of how one behaves.

At this point, it is useful to reintroduce Lebra's three domains of situational interaction and illustrate how they relate to units (Table 2.1).

Evidence of the importance of units is revealed in the oft-cited idea that Japanese society is comprised of "compartmentalized spheres of activity" (Benedict 1946: 137). This tendency to compartmentalize resonates with

Table 2.1. *Three Types of Situations/Scenes as They Relate to Units*

	omote: front of unit	*ura*: back of unit
uchi: inside unit	–	(1) intimate scene: lack of formality
soto: outside unit	(2) ritualized scene: entry/exit formalities or space between units change in unit structure	(3) anomic scene: asocial

Source: Lebra (1976: 112), with my modifications.

Nakane's discussion of "frame" (*ba* or *bamen*) (1970: 1–5) which is defined by Edwards as "a locality, an institution or a particular relationship which binds a set of individuals into one group" (1989: 137). Indeed, according to Edwards, framing social reality into a series of predefined stagings which require appropriate displays of self is a "basic approach to experience" which finds expression in other spheres of Japanese life (1989), such as in the traditional theater, where maintaining a *mie*, or "dramatic pose", is appreciated.

In addition to the less well-defined situations and scenes, mention should also be made of social arrangements designed to cultivate or stage the appropriate "atmosphere" or "mood" (*funiki*). From the perspective of a social actor, this concerns presenting one's self in the appropriate manner, or as they say in Japan, "appropriate to TPO" (time, place and occasion). Such presentations of self involve dress (uniforms, formal wear or informal clothes), bodily movements (sprawled out on a chair, relaxed posture, or bowing) and other personal adornment (flashy jewelry, tasteful accessories or make-up), i.e. one doesn't wear casual wear to an important job interview any more than one dons the wrong costume on stage.

The concern with being watched and for being properly uniformed appears to resonate with the view that social life is a stage and individuals should wear costumes. Indeed, the idea of being uniformed appears to be well received in Japan. In the words of one commentator, young workers "prefer what he calls 'performance' work, meaning wearing flashy uniforms and seeing the workplace as a sort of 'stage'" (e.g. gas stations, convenient stores, delivery services) (Inside the Weeklies: "It's tight times for part-time workers", *Japan Times*, 15 January 1994: 19). Though the notion that "society is a stage" where all have costumed parts to play is certainly present in Euro-American societies, Japanese society strongly emphasizes this way of thinking in many (but not all) contexts.

Part Two: Agent

This refers to what person or kind of person performed the act and for my present purposes is interchangeable with "social actor". Students, housewives, "office ladies" (secretaries), blue-collar workers, white-collar workers, police, military personnel, guards and various service personnel are all different kinds of persons, each type with their own accouterments. Their appearance and actions are determined by various attributes – age, occupation, socioeconomic class, gender, state membership (i.e. citizenship) and ethnic/cultural identity, which, taken together, also constitute what kind a person an individual is. Agents can also be characterized by the kinds of roles they have been influenced by *and* to which they aspire. After discussing the Japanese perspective on the meaning of socially ideal "parts" and appearance, I treat the cultural psychological nature of being an agent.

"Parts" and "Likeness"

In Japanese, a "part" (of something larger) is a *bun*. Thus, one's self is a *jibun*, or "self part". One is taught "to know one's *bun*"; "to adhere to one's *bun*"; "not to disgrace one's *bun*"; and to take seriously "the *bun* that one takes". The concept of *bun* is closely related to "occupying one's proper place" in the social order (Lebra 1976: 67). Lebra delineates three implications of this concept "which all derive from the image of society as an organic whole, individuals being part of that organism": (1) each individual is conceived as a fraction. A person's identity is derived from being a part of the whole; (2) *bun*-holders are interdependent; and (3) everyone belongs to the group in some capacity and claims a role. Thus, everyone should have a socially sanctioned *bun* (1976: 67–8). Each *bun* possesses a predetermined set of normative ideals and material accouterments, and being mature often means expressing the essence of one's *bun* by donning the socially sanctioned attire. In order to denote how a *bun*-holder should behave, the auxiliary adjective -*rashî* ("like") is sometimes suffixed to nouns, so that a "woman-like woman" (*onna-rashî josei*) is a "feminine woman" or a "student-like student" (*gakusei-rashî gakusei*) is a "studious student". Also, a person who expresses his or her individuality has *jibun-rashisa* (literally, "self-likeness"; *rashisa* is the nominalized form of *rashî*) (cf. a section called "About 'rashisa'" in Ôya (1995: 53)). In Japan, "everybody is dressed for his or her part" (Buruma 1984: 70). These parts – the most obvious being worker, father, mother, teacher, student – all demand appropriate dress and behavior. "Appropriate uniforms – including the standard "salaryman's" suit as well as special outfits for golf, tennis, hiking – all help people get into their roles.

Whatever the activity, it is expected that one will be wholeheartedly engaged and do his or her best" ("The Twain Meet: In Japan, many parts to play", 1994). There are many ways to get into a role, but wearing the appropriate clothes is the most common.

In Japan, given the sharp distinction between backstage/inside and front/outside, it is not surprising that there is great concern with forgetting one's lines and "stage fright" when positioned/performing in the latter social space. Thus, in Japan, shyness, shame and embarrassment are often associated since ethics are so closely related to etiquette and morality with manners. Terms that convey such meanings are *hazukashî* (shy, embarrassed, ashamed); *tôwaku suru* (embarrassed, perplexed); *komaru* (embarrassed, awkward, confused, even not knowing what to do, though it can also mean worried, troubled, or annoyed); *uchiki* (shy, bashful, reserved); and *tereru* (embarrassed, awkward). Linked to these concepts are notions of "face" (*kao, mentsu, menboku*) and reputation (*taimen, teisai*), which are often glossed as honor, dignity, or self-esteem. But as Lebra makes clear, such words fail to "fully convey the self's sensitivity to interactional immediacy and vulnerability entailed in the Japanese terms" (1992: 106). Wearing attire appropriate to one's social position (school uniforms, occupation-specific clothes, feminine or masculine apparel, etc.) places one in one's position, thereby preventing one – and others – from losing face.

Subjectivity and Its Features

In this section I discuss subjectivity and its related features, which include nonconsciousness, consciousness, selves (and a word that I use interchangeably with roles), aspects of selves and their different modes of presentation. I will start with the most inclusive and misunderstood feature: nonconsciousness.[1] This aspect produces the other features of subjectivity, though it is itself constructed and modified through a lifetime of socializing and resocializing experiences. Here it is pertinent to point out that much, if not most, of what we learn we do so nonconsciously, and that covert cognitive processes are incessantly reworking information. Ordinarily, the nonconscious, constituting the very fabric of mind itself, is *directly* unknowable, though it can be *indirectly* known through its products.

The next feature is consciousness, which is a small fraction of cognition.[2] As a cognitive process, consciousness usually kicks in when our environment confronts us with novel problems that preprogrammed and scripted behavior cannot adequately handle (such as being embarrassed or losing face). "For men live in immediate acts of experience and their attentions are directed outside themselves until acts are in some way frustrated. It is then that awareness of self and of motive occur" (Mills 1990: 208). As I will discuss below, the hindering of unmindful and routinized activity (cf. "reactivity" in Jaynes 1976) often causes rupture between spontaneous and more directed forms of self-presentation. This is why "under some circumstances in everyday life the actor becomes, is, or is made *aware* of an actual or potential discrepancy between his 'real' and his 'projected' selves, between his 'self' and his 'character'" (Messinger, Sampson and Towne 1990: 74, original emphasis).

There are a number of important features of consciousness, but for my purpose only two deserve attention: spatialization and the self.[3] Spatialization – an internal, "introspectable mindscape" built up from linguistic metaphors and visible with the "mind's eye", may be thought of as the inner psychological stage upon which another related feature of consciousness – the self – performs. Because in addition to being presented to others (see below), we present selves and different roles to ourselves within our consciousness:

> The same theatricalizing genius is at work in us when we recall the events of our past (no matter whether it is the events of yesterday or of 10 years ago). We cause these events to unfold again before our mental eyes. In other words, we compose a historical play, monodramatic in character. We stage it, and we ourselves appear in it as spectator and critic (Evreinoff 1990: 423).

After all, an individual "'plays a role' not only when he is seen by others. He continues to 'act' even when he is alone, when he is left entirely to himself. Moreover, he is at such moments not only a 'player,' but also a 'playwright' and a 'stage director'" (Evreinoff 1990: 422).

But from where does the belief in mind-space – or what may be called the "inner forum" or "theater of the mind" (Brissett and Edgley 1990b: 16) – and the self come? In the next section I answer this question.

The Self as Socially Constructed "From the Outside-In"

The theoretical issues involved in the construction of consciousness and the self are complex and I have discussed them elsewhere in more detail (McVeigh 1995a, 1997b), but in the most simple terms its construction begins in infancy, when the world of social others "commands" (here "command" denotes watches/monitors/influences/controls/observes) and establishes a socializing field which gradually convinces us to believe in the various features of consciousness (especially a "mental space" in which a body-controlling self dwells).

Basically, beginning in infancy an individual is socialized by four modes of command which are built by active agents (those doing the commanding) and passive recipients (those being commanded) who together spin a web of complex and co-constituting processes, the first three of which should be readily appreciated: (1) others command individual; (2) others command other (as observed by oneself; here "oneself" does *not* mean "self" but a person who is being socialized to have a self); (3) individual commands other. The last mode, (4) individual commands oneself, results from and rests upon the other three processes and in itself constructs a form of identity that I refer to as the "self" (Table 2.2). All four processes continue through one's life during later socializings and re-socializings, even after one possesses a self.

Table 2.2. *Four Modes of Observation*

| | | Active Agent in Control | |
		Oneself Observes	Other Observes
Passive Recipient under Control	**Other**	(3) individual commands other	(2) others command other
	Oneself	(4) individual commands oneself	(1) others commands individual

My explication is a simplification, of course, but a necessary step for understanding the complex formation and sociopyschology of the self. The key point to keep in mind is that acting and being acted upon eventually construct the self, a key feature of consciousness, and here, it should be emphasized, the self is *not* consciousness but rather an object of consciousness (or more metaphorically, an object of the "mind's eye"). Here I should also emphasize that there is nothing deterministic about the relationship between society and self. Because psyche is a chaotic but creative confluence of experiences, subjective spaces are able to form within which suspicions, doubts, questions and perhaps a touch of cynicism, emerge, criticizing, challenging, resisting and contesting dominant sociopolitical arrangements (or at least one's immediate situation).

Remember that we are socialized to believe in a type of "space" "inside" our heads: just as we learn to navigate our bodies (or are ordered about) through physical space, we are socialized to imagine a self that vicariously moves about "in" our minds, i.e. we are socialized to have a psychologized form of identity that dwells in our inner subjective world which is analogous to the "outer" social world of others. The self is socially constructed via analogy to the body and its observable behavior. But if we introspect and visualize our "selves", sociopsychological dynamics become more complex and intriguing. This is because we learn to imagine our selves in the same manner that we conceptualize our persons and bodies, as an active subject in control (agent) and as a passive object under control (patient) (Table 2.3). Because the self is formed in a complex matrix of social relationships the self acquires both an active and a passive facet, and just as a person can be viewed as either an agent (observable doer) that acts and possesses bodily control or as a patient (observable receiver of action) upon which others act and is under bodily control, so the internalized form of identity called "self" may be conceived in active or passive terms (cf. Jaynes 1976: 62–3).

Thus, as Jaynes (1976) argues and as I have illustrated elsewhere (McVeigh 1995a, 1997b), the self has two facets, an "I" and a "me". The "I" is the active subject which governs and the "me" is the passive object which is governed. The "I–me" aspects of self are not innate psychological structures, but rather are constructed through a person's socializing experiences and practices of being treated as an agentive ("I") and passive recipient ("me") of social action.[4] There is nothing stable or structural about the "I" and "me" relationship and it is always in a state of constant flux. The two sides of the self may be understood as "psychological" (the feeling of being an agent or recipient of action) or as "sociological" (person as observable doer or receiver of action from others in the observable world. Admittedly, the relations between the "I–me", person/body and others can become exceedingly complex, but here I am only delineating the nature of the problem. In any case, the four aforementioned processes that build a self eventually are transformed into: (1) others command self; (2) others command other (as observed by oneself); (3) self commands other; and (4) self ("I") commands self ("me"). Table 2.3 diagrams the relation between society, individual, self, its modes of presentation and the stages of self construction.

Table 2.3. *Stages of Construction of Self*

(1) Society → Individual
(2) Society → Individual → Self
(3) Society → Individual → Self → ("I" ↔ "me")

How do the "I" and "me" relate to each other? Basically, there are two ways – or modes of self-presentation – in which the "I" and "me" interact. The first may be called "coupled" and describes social roles in which the "I" and "me" are joined, i.e. there is no role distance between one's two facets of self when an individual "is being oneself" (cf. Goffman: "the performer comes to be his own audience; he comes to be performer and observer of the same show" (1959: 80–1)). The second way may be called "distal" and describes social roles in which the "I" and "me" are separated by role distance, i.e. one "is not being oneself" and is acting on stage, lying, or deceiving someone. In this mode of self-presentation, the "I" monitors and manages the "me". Here it might be noted that stage fright, whether theatrical or social, are sociopsychologically the same. They occur when one's "I" cannot artfully manage one's "me", when a coupled role becomes de-coupled. There are many situations when a wedge emerges between the "I" and "me", creating what may be called a "virtual self". Goffman explains what happens when an individual must perform a role he or she feels less than enthusiastic about:

> The image of him that is generated for him by the routine entailed in his mere participation – his virtual self in the context – is an image from which he apparently withdraws by *actively* manipulating the situation. Whether this skittish behavior is intentional or unintentional, sincere or affected, correctly appreciated by others present or not, it does constitute a wedge between the individual and his role, between doing and being. This "effectively" expressed pointed separateness between the individual and this putative role I shall call *role distance* (1990b: 103, original emphasis).

Another way to phrase the dynamics between "I" and "me" is to view presented personas as either "expressed" (or "self-expressed") or "performed" (or "self-performed"). The former designates the joining of the "I" and "me", so that the distance between the "I" and "me" is collapsed. Subjectivity produces a mode of self-presentation of spontaneous roles. The latter designates the de-coupling of the "I" and "me". Subjectivity produces a mode of self-presentation of controlled roles in which we play our ideal selves in front of others (cf. Pin and Turndorf 1990). In the words of Goffman, "an individual may be taken in by his own act or be cynical about it" (1959: 19). Such distancing often occurs during ritualized situations: "The formalization of ritual often appears to involve a distancing within actors of their private and social identities" (Bell 1992: 216; cf. Tambiah 1979: 124–5) (Table 2.4).

The distinction between coupled/distal roles corresponds to an observation of Goffman's about the "sincere and cynical continuum": "At one extreme, the performer [social actor] can be fully taken in by his own act; he can be sincerely convinced that the impression of reality which he stages is the real reality" (1959: 17). "To embrace a role is to be embraced by it" (Goffman 1990: 102). Being sincere characterizes, one imagines, everyday social

Table 2.4. *The Production of Selves/Roles and Their Modes of Presentation*

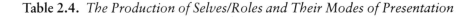

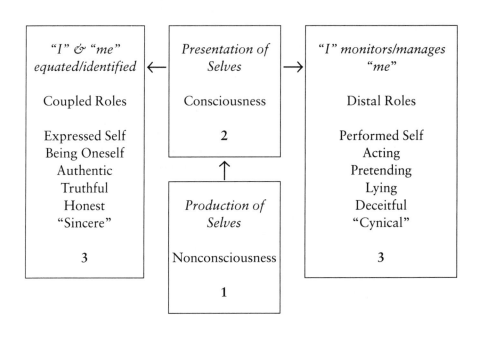

"I" & "me" equated/identified ←	Presentation of Selves →	"I" monitors/manages "me"
Coupled Roles	Consciousness	Distal Roles
Expressed Self	2	Performed Self
Being Oneself		Acting
Authentic	↑	Pretending
Truthful		Lying
Honest	Production of	Deceitful
"Sincere"	Selves	"Cynical"
3	Nonconsciousness	3
	1	

interaction in which we present selves of which we are convinced. "But at the other extreme, we find that the performer may not be taken in at all by his own routine" (Goffman 1959: 17). Being cynical is necessary for the theater, lying and other forms of deception. There are different degrees of coupled roles ("I" & "me" joined) and distal roles ("I" & "me" separated) depending on the purpose of self-presentation, and hence they should be viewed on a continuum (Table 2.5).

Admittedly, the theoretical framework that I have introduced above (as illustrated in Tables 2.4 and 2.5) is somewhat abstract (though throughout this book I offer concrete examples of the different modes of self-presentation).

Table 2.5. *Continuum of Modes of Self-Presentation*

Coupled Roles ←	Modes of Self-Presentation →	Distal Roles

Being Oneself ← Affected ← Mimicking → Impersonating → Acting

Moreover, this framework is idealized; not only do the different modes of self-presentation exist on a continuum, but each mode contains elements of the other. There is no such thing as a "pure" coupled or a distal role since an actual instance of presentation of self may rest upon different levels of intentionality. For example, when an actor on stage presents a performed self ("character"), elements of an expressed self (e.g. personal style, artistic dedication, genuine emotion) surely bolster/authenticate/facilitate the performed self to some degree. In other words, "being oneself" ("self-expressed") and "acting" ("self-performed") are intimately bound up with each other and can only be sharply divided for analytical purposes; my conceptual framework does not do justice to the multilayered, multi-intentional, subtle and dynamic interrelationship between the "'I'-monitors-'me'" and "'I' & 'me' equated" modes of presentation.

Part Three: Act

Within the dramaturgical perspective, "act" designates what took place in deed (or, as I will sometimes phrase it, "practice") or thought (see below). The meaning of "act" is rather broad, and subsumes the vast array of productive and consumptive practices that are woven together to form the complex pattern of consumerist capitalism, such as schooling, training, manufacturing, office work, commuting, shopping (for necessities and enjoyment), social interaction, eating out, entertainment, vacationing and other forms of labor and leisure. Thus, "act" to a large degree includes *le quotidien* and micro-practices that are the building blocks of the more salient, obvious activities and include common courtesies, bodily management and daily routines to make oneself presentable, e.g. bathing, grooming and for my purposes, covering, dressing and decorating one's person.

Though we conventionally think of "act" as something visible, objective and bodily, I contend that many acts are also invisible, subjective and mental. Thus, the much-theorized relation between society and mind should be thought of as a unity, not a union, i.e. a sociopsychological reality, not a layering of the social over the psychological (McVeigh 1997b: 21–34). Selves and self-presentations, then, with all their complex interactions of active "I" and passive "me", are sociopsychological "acts". Below I illustrate this point by discussing modes of self-presentation in Japan.

Subjectivity as Social Practice

Though the presentation of "expressed selves" (coupled roles) and "performed selves" (distal roles) is universal, the weight and significance each culture assigns to one mode of self-presentation varies, and particular local sociopolitical pressures and structures will contour how and when these self-presentations occur. As I already explained above ("Scenes"), Japanese social life can be understood as comprised of three types of social interaction (being socially problematic, the "anomic" situation is exempt from the present analysis). Two types clearly correspond to (or produce) the two modes of self-presentation.[5] The first is the *uchi–ura* (inside/back) which occasions the expressed self: one plays a fairly relaxed, spontaneous, natural and revealed role towards one's family, friends, classmates and colleagues. Such a persona is marked by informal and nonhonorific speech. One is safe from *seken* and observing others. *Honne*, meaning one's true thoughts, private feelings, or honest opinions, is often associated with the expressed self. The second is the *soto–omote* (outside/front) which occasions the performed self: one plays a fairly solicitous, circumspect, staged and guarded role towards non-kin, non-intimates and those with whom one is engaged in a ceremonial situation (interviews, first meetings, formal gatherings, weddings, funerals, rites of passage, etc.). Such a persona is marked by formal and honorific speech. The presence of *seken* and observing others are clearly felt. *Tatemae*, meaning agreed-upon policy, predetermined consensus, or the rules of the game at hand, is often associated with the performed self.

A sense of what *tatemae* denotes is evident in the word's literal meaning: the "framing of a house" or a "framework-erection ceremony". The implication is that fundamental principles or a working agreement that sets parameters of sociopolitical negotiating have been established. Compare Goffman's "working consensus", for which a person

> is expected to suppress his immediate heartfelt feelings, conveying a view of the situation which he feels the others will be able to find at least temporarily acceptable. The maintenance of this surface of agreement, this veneer of consensus, is facilitated by each participant concealing his own wants behind statements which assert values to which everyone present feels obliged to give lip service (1959: 9).

Tatemae are attempts to keep egoism in check. But this does not mean that the Japanese regard morality as the mere following of form for form's sake since how one feels internally is just as important as how one behaves externally. Appearance is more than just good form since it announces one's commitment to the idea that the social reality at hand is legitimate. Members of a unit with a clear mission are expected to assist in maintaining group solidarity, and they should especially help in the erecting of fronts (*omote*) vis-à-vis the outside (*soto*). An individual is judged on the degree to which he or she attempts to support social propriety and amiable feelings. This is why appearances count so much in Japan: people may think or feel whatever they want, but not providing a good rendition of one's assigned social role – via clothing, grooming and deportment – is not excused. Such a theory of self-presentation is not unique to Japan, of course, but it is certainly emphasized in this society.

If a politically and economically complex society lacks a culturally sanctioned sphere where an individual's opinions, interests, or self may be readily expressed before a collectivity that safeguards such expressions, then certain social practices will be needed to facilitate exchanges. In Japan, because non-places are so common, *tatemae* is employed to construct a type of publicness, and thereby serves a similar function as public institutions do in Euro-American societies, i.e. *tatemae* serves as a collectively agreed-upon neutral or buffer area where the individual is, in at least a certain sense, protected from others. Staged formalities erect dense walls of rituality (*aisatsu*; usually inadequately translated as "greetings", but meaning numerous sociolinguistic practices), taking the place of an impartial public arena.

Part Four: Agency

An examination of "agency" answers what kinds of means or instruments are used in dramaturgical analysis. This is where material culture comes in, specifically uniforms, but other objects that supplement dress uniformity may be included under this category. "The uniform is a dramaturgical device which provides a symbolic medium for interaction" (Joseph 1986:71). Moreover, any form of material culture that criticizes, critiques, controverts, subverts, evades (even if only temporarily), or ironically comments on dress uniformity (i.e. the official code) may be included under agency. An examination of agency is also highly significant for another reason: it points to the actual objects and tools that socialize individuals to accept – even if to a limited degree – the official dictates about appropriate self-presentation.

One's appearance may be thought of as a form of agency since it is often utilized by a social actor for purposes of impression management: "One's appearance commands the gaze of the audience" (Stone 1990: 141). And in Japan, where everybody is socialized to take their assigned roles seriously, appearances carry great import because they announce so much information about an individual from an observer's point of view. Regulated dress is expected in a cultural milieu that places great emphasis on performed roles and unit affiliation. Furthermore, we should expect dress uniformity and conformity where distal roles are encouraged. Thus, the Japanese social landscape is peopled with identically clad kindergarten toddlers with yellow caps, oversized backpacks and various accouterments for the day dangling from their person; male students in military navy blues and female students in sailor uniforms; white-gloved public transportation workers; ultrapolite "elevator girls" costumed in snappy suits and heavy make-up; prim and neatly attired "office ladies" in their company-specific uniforms; security guards with their pseudo-military uniforms; housewives in slippers and aprons decorated with appliqué; and dark-suited white-collar workers carrying briefcases. Even sanitation workers, in helmets and brightly colored suits, are neatly uniformed.

As a form of agency, uniforms fulfill two basic interrelated purposes. First, they act as socializing instruments because they are used to instill a sense of solidarity, *esprit de corps*, identification with a particular unit, or identification with some figure. An example of how donning uniforms indicates solidarity can be seen in a newspaper picture of children wearing mock space suits who gathered in the town hall of astronaut Mori Mamoru's hometown to watch the televised liftoff aboard the Space Shuttle Endeavor (JT 14 September 1992: 2). Another example of national solidarity is how, during the 1998 World Cup, All Nippon Airways flight attendants wore replicas of Japanese soccer shirts over their regular uniforms and distributed "Rising Sun flags to passengers to wave during the matches". Passengers also received headbands with "win at all costs" emblazoned across them in Japanese, "as well booklets detailing players of the national squad and of the teams that Japan will be competing against". Japan Airlines redesigned the livery of fifty-eight aircraft to include the slogan "*gambare*! (Go for it!), Japanese World Cup soccer team" ("Airlines kick in with special Cup flights", 1998). And window washers demonstrated their support by wearing the uniform of the Japanese team and "soccer balls attached to their work helmets" ("Sky-high pride", 1998). Uniforms also inculcate, via design, the importance of age distinctions and sex-specific differences and encourage genderizing and its many concomitant norms. The second purpose of uniforms as agency is as material cultural markers; they identify and position social actors in various hierarchies, units, occupations and gender categories.

> One's identity is established when others *place* him as a social object by assigning him the same words of identity that he appropriates for himself or *announces*. It is the coincidence of placements and announcements that identity becomes a meaning of the self, and often such placements and announcements are aroused by apparent symbols such as uniforms (Stone 1990: 143, original emphasis).

As identification markers, uniforms have two functions: one function is aimed at members within the group, and the other is aimed outside the group.

Internally, uniforms act as badges of membership for individuals belonging to or in some way affiliated with a school, company, or occupation (*uchi*). There is also a clearly politicized use of uniforms, as when authorities utilize them for control, as barometers of an individual's level of commitment. Uniformed dress is a way to express one's character, or at least one's level of commitment to the dictates of the group. The body, when draped in formalized attire, is treated as a politically encoded, meaning-carrying icon. Its appearance is the visible expression of the moral system (Bourdieu 1977, 1990).

The second function of uniforms is for those outside the group (*soto*). Outsiders may rely on uniforms as a means of quick and convenient classification, as a way of knowing who does what, of what role a person performs and in this sense uniforms act as a type of *tatemae*, an agreement about what appearances signify. How one looks is essential for social order, because by observing a person's appearance, others are able to calibrate their treatment of that person: male? female? student? housewife? blue-collar worker? white-collar worker? company president? police? military personnel? What type of *rashisa* ("likeness") does this person express? Uniforms can also be used to impress others and to gain the attention of outsiders. This is why, according to Buruma, people in Japan do not only wear the correct dress; they do so with great concern and thoroughness. This is why "life in Japan seems highly theatrical to the outsider". This is why "No Japanese cook worth his salt would want to be seen without his tall white hat; 'interis' (intellectuals) sport berets and sunglasses, like 1920s exiles on the Left Bank of Paris. And gangsters wear loud pin-striped suits over their tattooed bodies. In brief, everybody is dressed for his or her part" (1984: 70).

Part Five: Purpose

Above I introduced the notions (*bun, -rashî, uchi/soto, ura/omote* and *seken*) which constitute a subjectivity encouraging people to clothe themselves in the appropriate apparel. But from where does this subjective substructure ultimately come? What shapes scenes? What motivates agents? What prompts acts? And what utilizes different forms of agency? In this part I examine the forces that configure scenes, socialize agents, provide the "why" of acts and determine the uses of agency.

The Politico-Economic Environment of Japan

The aforementioned questions can only be answered in the most general terms, and any explication runs the risk of sounding monolithic and overly abstract. But for my present purposes, a measure of generalization should be acceptable. In any case, Japan's manifold codes of regulated dress – particularly in schools (socializing and training sites) and workplaces (sites of production) – are rooted in the massive rationalizing projects of state interests and economic concerns, as well as allied "isms" of modernity, such as social evolutionism, scientism and positivism. And according to the conventional wisdom about Japan (i.e. the "Japan, Inc." argument), state bureaucracies and commercial enterprises are highly integrated and mutually work in tandem, driven by economic nation-statism. More concretely, Japan's economic nation-statism takes the form of the "capitalist developmental state", a type of politico-economic system forged in the late nineteenth century as Japan attempted to "catch up and surpass the West" (*oitsuki oikose*); become a "rich nation with a strong army" (*fukoku kyôhei*); and "increase production, promote industry" (*shokusan kôgyô*).[6] The search and use of overseas technology in order to maintain the power of domestic elites and to build a strong state and a respectable nation that would be respected internationally is reflected in slogans such as "Japanese spirit, Western skills" (*wakon yôsai*) and "Eastern morality, Western technology" (*tôyô dôtoku, seiyô gijutsu*). Though such slogans may now sound out of date, their spirit at least has been institutionalized in state structures and economic practices that in no small measure shape everyday practices. Johnson uses the term "developmental orientation" to highlight Japan's politico-economic phil-osophy (as opposed to the American model of "regulatory orientation"). Developmental orientation assumes that the state is more involved in the market, concerning itself with plans, goals and specific outcomes, whereas regulatory orientation assumes that the state's laissez-faire approach to the market is ideally impartial and concerned with procedural matters (Johnson 1982: 18–19). In their pursuit of economic security, the Japanese did not so much alter capitalism; rather, they innovated it.

In order to accomplish economic nationalist projects, Japan's elite have diligently developed their nation's industries, advanced its economic interests abroad and carefully cultivated its human resources. In order to accomplish these goals, social cooperation, collaboration and coordination, at least from the elite point of view, should be the order of the day. During the Meiji period, Japan's educational system was designed to inculcate these values. More specifically, students (who were primarily viewed as future workers, not learners) were socialized to accept the demands of rationalization: (1) hierarchy, (2) social categorization, and (3) social standardization. It is only natural that such a "strategic schooling" would require students to wear uniforms. This term is inspired by Huber's (1994) "strategic economy" which views the state in league with elite economic interests, integrating, building hierarchies and in general, ordering the relations between governmental organs and commercial enterprises. Thus, the current Japanese state's profound involvement in educational affairs is not just an institutional remnant from Japan's ultra-nationalistic and militaristic period. The bureaucratic elite's concern for "guiding" education has much deeper historical roots, and is part of a fundamental political philosophy about the role of the state in individual intellectual and moral development.

Conventionally defined, a state is a non-kin-based political system with centralized bureaucratic institutions which have power and authority over large populations living within clearly defined territorial boundaries. However, as Mitchell points out, "The customary Weberian definition of the state, as an organization that claims a monopoly within a fixed territory over the legitimate use of violence, is only a residual characterization. It does not tell us how the actual contours of this amorphous organization are to be drawn" (1991: 82). In other words, the state is not just "political institutions", "power centers", and "legal systems"; it is also "unquestioned assumptions", "substructural knowledge", and "bureaucratized subjectivity". The socio-politicized atmosphere of nation-states should be described in terms of "stateness" or "statefulness" (processes and properties) as well as systems possessing something called "state" (institutions and organs) (cf. Zelinsky's discussion of "statefulness" (1988: 8)). Moreover, where the state ends and society begins is highly problematic. Indeed, according to Pierson, "Disengaging state and society proves to be a more or less impossible task" (1996: 93), a notion that resonates with Althusser's "ideological state apparatuses" (1971), Foucault's "discourse" (1979) and Gramsci's "hegemony" (1971), as well as the latter's concept of "the integral state" (*lo stato integrale*) or the state in its "inclusive sense" (1971). As Weiss and Hobson phrase it, we should be concerned not so much with how a state exercises power *over* society, but how it exercises power *through* various social forms (Weiss and Hobson 1995: 168).

Therefore, for my present purposes, I propose three sociopsychological aspects of "state" in order to illustrate just how deeply subjectivity is colonized by and for politico-economic projects. Briefly, these aspects are (1) state core structures: central bureaucracies administered by elected or selected/appointed officials; (2) state parastructures: organizations with quasi-state core structure status; and (3) state substructures: deep cognitive and affective patterns underpinning all sociopolitical arrangements and the institutions usually relegated to "private society". State substructures are a type of statefulness that is motivated by unquestioned assumptions and possesses a large degree of taken-for-grantedness (e.g. the inherent benefits of social evolutionism, scientism, rationalism, positivism). In the case of Japan, notions discussed above (*seken, uchi/soto, ura/omote, honne/tatemae*) qualify as state substructural knowledge. In this sense, state substructures may be described as the "deep ideology" or "invisible institutions" that animate social life ("surface ideology" are the more explicit "isms" of political life and "visible institutions" are the more obvious forms of state, such as organs, parties, security forces, etc.). Here it should be obvious why I discussed the role of the nonconscious above in "Part Two: Agent", since this is the component of psyche in which the socializing forces of the state construct "background expectancies", and transmute institutional imperatives into individual ideas and official projects into personal programs of behavior.[7]

These three manifestations of statefulness are actually aspects of a single social and politico-economic reality. Because they are co-constituting, no one aspect is necessarily more basic than another. However, though the three aspects are intimately bound up with one another and the boundaries between these different forms of statefulness are not always clear, they can be teased apart for certain analytical purposes. It must be emphasized that they are mutually co-constituting realities. My tripartite scheme attempts to link self with macro-level collectivities, individual with institutional structures and subjectivity with sociopolitical arrangements. I make these distinctions about the meaning of "state", not to provide a taxonomy of political structures, but rather to demonstrate the depth and extensiveness of "statefulness". Thus, by using the term substructural, I want to dismantle the dualistic paradigms (i.e. state/society, ideological/intentional, public/private) that conceal the relationship between sociopolitical structures and self-conceptions, collectivities and subjectivities. Dualistic thinking is encouraged by our everyday conception of the person as possessing an internal life ontologically distinct from the external world of things, others and objects. This mythology, as pointed out by Mitchell, is actually part of a whole range of dualisms that, like an intellectual house of mirrors, reflect and confirm each other: mind/body; ideas/material force; meaning/material; ideological/material; consciousness/behavior; words/action; coerced/free; hidden/observable; superstructure/base; persuading/coercing; state/society. These dualisms produce a "metaphysical effect" which convinces us that power originates "outside of local life, outside actuality, outside events, outside time, outside community, outside personhood" (1990: 569). According to Mitchell, the state should be analyzed as a "structural effect"; "That is to say, it should be examined not as an actual structure, but as the powerful, metaphysical effect of practices that make such structures appear to exist" (1991: 94). My purpose in proposing the notion of the substructural state is an attempt to account for the state's "metaphysical effect".

It should be noted that no national-level organ in Japan (except for the military and police) stipulates that uniforms must be worn. Nevertheless, highly regulated attire pervades Japan's social landscape. This is because state power so thoroughly permeates ostensibly non-state spaces and practices, that there is no obvious need for officialdom to order the donning of uniforms. This is especially true in educational and economic endeavors.

The State as *Seken*: The Political Economy Behind the Official Gaze

Above I introduced the concept of *seken*, a powerful gaze that exerts its normalizing effect within the family, school and workplace. The ubiquity of statefulness ensures that multiple *seken* exist and that overlapping socio-political and economic hierarchies emit similar messages about standards, values and mores which ideally should be encoded and expressed through proper self-presentation (e.g. clothes). Here I want to contend that the state and its allied capitalist interests may be regarded as the ultimate source of the "official gaze" or *seken*. As ubiquitous normalizing presences, the various *seken* are institutionally deployed by the three types of interlinked statefulness introduced above. This deployment is multilevel, elaborate and complex, but there is a high degree of ideological agreement among the many *seken* produced. Thus, overlapping gazes interact and an individual is always a member of multiple *seken*.

A brief delineation of the deployment of *seken* is in order. The state core is composed of Japan's national Diet, twelve main ministries and other organs. State core structures encourage the production of *seken* in order to accomplish their general goals of economic nation-statism. The upshot is that different state structures – indirectly and not always visibly – build overlapping hierarchies that share the same basic ideology of economic growth. For example, the Ministry of Health and Welfare manages medical, bodily and family affairs, while the Ministry of Labor oversees the workplace. The National Public Safety Commission and the National Public Agency (both in the Prime Minister's Office) oversee district police bureaus, prefectural police headquarters and the Tokyo Metropolitan Police Department, which in turn oversee police stations, substations and the ubiquitous *kôban* or "police boxes" (which might literally be glossed as "traffic guard"). The word for "police", it might be noted, is *keisatsu* (roughly and literally, "instruct and judge") and for "police superintendent", *keishi* (roughly and literally, "instruct and observe").

For my present purposes, it is the Ministry of Education (*Monbushô*) that deserves special mention, since it administers schools, sites where uniforms are usually mandated. Ministry of Education officials are charged with the task of administrating education, moral development, cultural activities, scientific progress and religious matters. Like officials in the other ministries of Japan, theirs is an activist, goal-oriented mission. Attention to the bureaucratese of Ministry of Education officials furnishes a sense of how they view their calling. The most common word encountered in official discourse is "guidance" (*shidô*), though it often denotes more of a sense of actively directing or strongly persuading others (*shidô* is part of the term used by all ministries in the term "administrative guidance"). This term suggests the administrative atmosphere, radiating from the state's top/center to the lower levels/periphery, that encourages the production of units (primarily schools) and *seken* within schools.

The Ministry of Education does not enforce specific regulations concerning uniforms. These are decided by prefectural and municipal boards of education (whose members are appointed by local government officials, not elected by the public). Nevertheless, the Ministry of Education, along with other ministries and business interests, ensures that an atmosphere – or scenes – laden with official gazing is maintained, so that donning a student uniform is a disciplinary practice linking the individual with the state and its allied economic interests. The practice of putting it on every day reinforces a host of associated values that maintain the rationalizing projects of the state and its economic interests. This is not to say that those who wear uniforms completely and always agree with these rationalizing projects, but wearing a uniform is a sign that one at least is playing his or her role in these projects *to some degree* or at least is learning about the official ideology of hierarchization, categorization and standardization.

State parastructures are quasi- or semi-state organizations, such as *gaikaku dantai* (variously translated as "affiliated organizations", "auxiliary organs", or "semiprivate organizations"), special corporations (*tokushu hôjin*), some public service corporations, nonprofit enterprises (*shadan hôjin* (incorporated associations) and *zaidan hôjin* (foundations)), which are all institutionally and tightly tied – and sometimes controlled by – the state core, indicating the density of state/society networks and the cohesion of public projects and personal agendas in Japan. Many of these parastructural organizations are educational in purpose and directly affiliated with the Ministry of Education.

Though further removed from the controls of the central bureaucracies than parastructures, state substructures, however one wishes to categorize them, are in one way or another and to differing degrees tied to the central bureaucracies of the state core despite their official designation as "private". Examples of state substructures are private corporations and incorporated businesses (governed by the Commercial Code and taxed and regulated by the Ministries of Finance and International Trade and Industry) and incorporated private associations, nonprofit incorporated foundations and families (governed by the Civil Code and monitored by the family registration system).

How does Japan's educational system fit into this complex system of three forms of states? State (*kokuritsu*) and public (*kôritsu*) schools are clearly parts of the state core.[8] But private schools (*shiritsu*) also fall under the Ministry of Education's bureaucratic gaze though they are not as directly under its administration as state and public schools. Legally, they are designated educational foundations (*gakkô hôjin*), though they must still adhere to centrally devised bureaucratic regulations.

Another way to grasp the concreteness of the normative pressure of the official gaze is to note the units in which it makes its presence felt: in classrooms, offices, factories, families and neighborhoods (McVeigh 1997c, 1998b). The socializing significance of units is important for their "mutual surveillance within small groups" (Sugimoto 1997: 245–7). "Instead of vertical control, the system counts upon a kind of horizontal control where the policing of people of the same status in a small unit – classmates, work colleagues, or neighborhood acquaintances – makes it difficult for them to diverge from the standard expected" (Sugimoto 1997: 249). Consider neighborhood associations (*chônaikai*), which blur the line "between voluntary dedication and state manipulation" (Sugimoto 1997: 249). These semicompulsory organizations are used to channel information, organize state-encouraged fund-raising campaigns and cooperate with local state bodies for a host of activities (Sugimoto 1997: 248). Though such organizations certainly bring people together, their unitized nature is revealed in how their boundaries are clearly delimited; they are inward oriented rather than outward in perspective and their missions are usually task-specific. This has implications for civil society. Recall that in "Part One: Scenes" I discussed how in Japan there is a clear separation between formal/ritualized situations and informal/intimate situations. This separation strongly encourages a sort of polarization between "outside" public situations in which the gaze of *seken* intently scans and "inside" private situations in which the gaze of *seken* is not as focused. Such forms of visuality discourage the formation of "impartial spaces" (i.e. civil society) in which individuals move about relatively freely, temporarily unconnected to social structures. This social polarization also encourages a rather theatricalized social existence evidenced in ritualized behavior, practices of etiquette (*aisatsu*) and appropriate dress.

Notes

1. Here, it is worth noting that the "unconscious" (I prefer the less Freudian-sounding "nonconscious") has been one of the great leitmotifs of our intellectual past, manifesting its ghostly presence in very corner of the edifice of Western

intellectual history. The list of relevant works is too long to cite here, but see Whyte (1978). Recent work in cognitive science strongly supports the premise that most thinking occurs nonconsciously, e.g. see Lewicki (1986).

2. My understanding of consciousness relies on Jaynes, who argues that, rather than an inborn neurological capability, consciousness is culturally constituted and historically specific (1976).

3. Other important features of consciousness are: (1) excerption: selecting information to which attention is focused; (2) narratization: constructing meaningful accounts based on perceptions and daily events; and (3) conciliation: assimilating new perceptions and experiences into previously learned schemas (Jaynes 1976: 59–65).

4. My thinking on this topic is related to, but in some respects differs from, Mead's (1934).

5. My use of expressed/performed selves resonates other works on the Japanese self, e.g. Bachnik's "personal emotions/social constraint" (1992); Rosenberger's "discipline and distance/spontaneity and intimacy" and personal productivity, personal accomplishment, harmony and affection and pure impulse (1989); Lebra's "empathetic self" and "presentational self" (1992).

6. Samuels begins his book about Japanese "technonationalism" by noting that when he was once asked to put in one word what makes Japan tick, he answered "insecurity". "This pervasive anxiety – what the Japanese refer to as *fuan* – helps to mobilize millions of people each day" (1994: ix). This anxiety is generated by a general perception that Japan is a poor country surrounded by enemies. General insecurity is one of the prime ingredients of what has become known as the "capitalist developmental state".

7. Cf. Scott and Lyman: "By background expectancies we refer to the those sets of taken-for-granted ideas that permit the interactants to interpret remarks as accounts in the first place" (1990: 226).

8. *Kokuritsu* is conventionally called "national" but I believe that the original meanings of "nation" and "state" should be maintained for the sake of clarity.

3

Learning to Wear Ideology: School Uniforms

Introduction: Uniforms as Material Culture Markers in the Life-cycle

Most nursery schools, kindergartens, elementary, middle and high schools have student uniforms (*gakusei fuku*) (or at least regulations about attire). Uniforms are intended to provide order, discipline and solidarity within a school. Other examples of material culture that express "school spirit" (*kôfû*) are school pins (*kôshô*) and, of course, school uniforms (*kôfuku*). Likewise, nursery schools, kindergartens and some elementary schools mandate *seibô* (school cap; literally, "regulation cap"). Some women's universities and junior colleges have uniforms or at least regulations about "ladylike" dress (see McVeigh 1997b).[1]

School uniforms were first introduced in Japan to the Gakushûin (Peers' College) in 1879, and by the mid-1880s other schools adopted uniforms modeled after European military uniforms. In 1885 a kind of satchel (*randoseru*), still carried today by young students, was introduced to students at Gakushûin. Mori provides a thumbnail sketch of female uniforms. Through the decades, women's uniforms underwent a variety of changes. In the late 1880s, they wore maroon *hakama* (a long, divided skirt). Frequent changes in how young women attending school should be uniformed reflected the controversies concerning the role of women in Japan's rapid modernization: "in less than thirty years, from early mid-Meiji, female students' clothes changed more than five times . . . it started with the kimono, then moved to men's *hakama* with short hair, back to kimono, then to western style long skirt, then women's *hakama* (*onna bakama*), and kimono again" (Toyama 1997: 5).

Beginning in the Meiji period, uniforms were associated with being "frugal and courageous" (*shitsu jitsu gôken*) for young men, while for young women, they were associated with being "good mothers of a nation at war" (*yoki gunkoku no haha*) (Uchino 1995: 56). Due to the influence of the Russo–Japanese War (1904–1905), "sailor uniforms" became popular among both male and female students. Hoshino attempts to put discussions about uniform reform in historical perspective and discusses how reforms at a Hokkaidô higher women's school (*kôtô jogakkô*) in 1940 led to a change from skirts to pants. The result: less colds, increased attendance and more active students (1994: 4–5). In the 1930s, gym clothes, skirts and short sleeves were popular, and during the war, "sailor" tops and pants with elastic at the ankles were adopted for easy movement for work in factories. In the 1950s, the "sailor uniform" (with skirts) became standard at many schools (with different colors depending on one's grade), and by the mid-1980s, the skirts of "sailor uniforms" became shorter (Mori 1985: 200–1).[2]

Schools uniforms are more than just standardized clothing; they are symbolic lightening rods often implicated in debates and discussions about ethical issues and human rights (particularly those of women uniformed as "office ladies" and children uniformed as students) and their violation; the right of self-determination (*jiko kettei-ken*); school rules; "student management syndrome" (*seito kanri shôkôgun*); paternalism of and interference from schools and teachers; sexual discrimination; parental right to decide on educational matters; freedom (or lack thereof); responsibility; stifling of self-expression; the "disappearance of individuality" (*bokkosei*) (e.g. Aikawa 1994; Nakagawa 1994; Ôya 1995; Taniguchi 1995; Uchino 1995; Watanabe 1994); and school violence ("Readers' Forum: Can school uniforms effectively curb juvenile violence?" 1998). In one individual's opinion, uniforms are a type of "persecution", and wearing "those totally unbeautiful and stuffy uniforms is nothing but sheer violence" ("To hell with school uniforms!" 1997). Aided by the Japanese arm of Defense for Children International and the Japan Federation of Bar Associations, Japanese students told members of the UN Commission on the Rights of Children in Geneva that uniforms may violate the Convention on the Rights of the Child since they suppress an individual's right of self-expression ("Japan school uniforms under fire", 1997). Some are self-conscious of what those outside Japan think about uniforms and note that non-Japanese consider uniformed students to have an odd appearance (Ôya 1995: 53).

How can wearing uniforms – such a widespread, mundane and "commonsensical" practice in Japan and yet so charged with diverse meanings – be discussed in such a way that some interpretive order and understanding can be injected into an analysis? To begin with, students are agents, and uniforms are the agency through which the official ideo-institutional forces construct subjectivities. Also, I suggest that an appreciation of the life-cycle, which is in no small way driven by, ordered and configured by massive political and economic institutionalizing forces, will provide a useful conceptual framework. For many individuals in Japan, the socializing life-cycle can be viewed in three phases. The first phase is one of socialization received after leaving family, entering the outside world and being integrated into the culture of preschool, elementary, middle and high schools and being instilled with the concomitant norms and values, both explicit and hidden. The second phase is one of leaving secondary school and entering: (1) university (*daigaku*) or junior college (*tanki daigaku*), (2) another type of post-secondary institution such as special training colleges (*senshû gakkô*), colleges of technology (*kôtô senmon gakkô*), or miscellaneous schools (*kakushu gakkô*), which for the sake of convenience I will call "vocational schools", (3) being directly inducted into the labor force, or (4) becoming unemployed. The third and final phase is becoming an adult worker and, almost always, a husband/father or wife/mother. This three-phase life-cycle is to a large degree regulated and managed by the state (educational institutions) and economic interests (capitalist corporate culture).

About two-thirds of new high school graduates enter university or some other post-secondary educational institution noted above (the other third falls into category (4)). Thus, the life-cycle of a significant number of Japanese can be understood as beginning with socializing practices that: (1) "uniform-ize", followed by practices that (2) "de-uniformize", and ends with practices that (3) "re-uniformize".

> Life must be viewed as a continuous socialization, a series of careers, in which old identities are sacrificed as new identities are appropriated, at which old relations are left behind as new relations are joined. Each critical turning point of life is marked by a change of dress, and, ordinarily, the new upcoming "game" is rehearsed prior to the entry upon the appropriate field of play (Stone 1990: 158).

For a large number of Japanese, then, uniforms function as material markers in a general life-cycle (Table 3.1). This life-cycle, however, has some interesting variations, and later (Chapter 4) I will look at how gender modifies the cycle for female students at a women's junior college. For organizational purposes, this chapter is divided into five parts: First Phase: Uniformize; "Being Observed During the Uniformization Phase"; "Uniforms as Objects that Socialize"; "What Students Think of Uniforms"; "Self-Presentation and Uniforms"; and "Gender Differences". I examine "Second Phase: De-Uniformize" and "Third Phase: Re-Uniformize" in the next chapter.

First Phase: Uniformizing

The Sociopsychology of Uniformizing

The first phase of uniformization starts with a child leaving home and entering the highly regulated and routinized world of school culture (Hendry 1986).

Table 3.1. *Uniforms as Life-Cycle Markers*

First Phase ⟶	Second Phase ⟶	Third Phase
Uniformize	**De-Uniformize**	**Re-Uniformize**
Ages 3–18;	*Ages 18–22;*	*Ages from 22;*
Socialization after Leaving Family and Entering the Outside World and School Culture	Post-Secondary Education: Period Between Studying and Working	Graduating and Becoming an Adult Worker, Husband/Father or Wife/Mother

This phase begins the long socialization process that constructs a subjectivity that will eventually be able to cooperate with others, absorb vast amounts of academic knowledge in a relatively disciplined manner, and then understand and work within regimented and rationalized socioeconomic structures. But even before a child begins school, he or she has already been woven into, and in turn starts to weave, a complex sociopsychological fabric.

In order to discuss the relation between identity and dress, Stone builds upon Mead's (1934) thinking on the emergence of self. Mead theorized that there are basically two socializing activities, "play" and "games". The former is early socialization and the latter any form of later socialization. Play occurs when a young child learns social roles by acting out a society's institutionalized and accepted roles. "Playing the role of the other requires that the player *dress out* of the role or roles that are acknowledged to be his own" (Stone 1990: 154, original emphasis). Play is the donning of costumes and is a socializing exercise in which a young child's self begins to be separated into an "I" and a "me", the latter the target role that a child is attempting to imitate: "Acting out of role implies that one appear out of role. Play demands that the players leave themselves behind so to speak. The players may do this symbolically by doffing their ordinary dress and donning extraordinary dress so that the play may proceed" (Stone 1990: 154).

The second socializing activity, which builds upon and emerges from "play", is the "game", or taking the role of the "generalized other" (or perhaps a "team"). During a game a person "dresses in". A child has clearly learned the difference between the self as active agent ("I") and the self as passive ("me") and between coupled and distal roles. Thus, if the child "play-actor is costumed", the more mature child and adult "team-player is uniformed" (Stone 1990: 157). "Growing up is dressing in" (i.e. into roles)

(Stone 1990: 158). In Japan, "dressing in" outside the home begins at the pre-elementary level. Some, though not all, nursery schools and kindergartens are stricter than others and stipulate the wearing of uniforms. As a rule, elementary, middle and high schools have uniforms. A young student who wears a uniform does not necessarily learn to wear a *specific type of uniform* later in life (certainly not a school uniform), but he or she does learn about a *general sense of dress uniformity* and its social significance of conformity and standardization.

It is worth briefly describing several important organizational features of schools, since these are the bounded spaces/scenes/situations in which students (as agents), via the agency of uniforms and related accouterments, execute acts and practices.

Schools as Training Units

Since the Meiji period, Japan's statist and capitalist elite have regarded schools as vital to their country's national and economic survival. Thus, the educatio-bureaucratic gaze has keenly focused on these socializing sites. Though Japanese schools may be considered as moral communities (each with its own, ideally at least, *kôfû* (school tradition or spirit)), in some respects they may be characterized as "total institutions" in which authority "is directed to a multitude of items of conduct – dress, deportment, manners – that constantly occur and constantly come up for judgment" (Goffman 1961: 41).

"Student regulations" no doubt help in creating feelings of unity (*rentaikan*) and solidarity (*danketsu*), and such rules may dictate rules about bodily management, uniforms, cleaning, eating habits, money usage, avoiding bad students, part-time jobs, returning home early and other daily activities.[3] At some schools, such rules are listed in small books that constitute a component of dress uniformity and must be carried by students. At other schools, in addition to being told to wear and not to wear certain clothing, students are prohibited from carrying on their persons toys, mirrors, cosmetics, accessories, cameras, comic books, magazines, cash and expensive items (cf. Sakamoto 1986: 17–32). There is a clear concern for hierarchization (teacher/student and junior (*kôhai*)/senior (*sempai*) students), categorization (into grades, classes, clubs, teams and other groups) and standardization (uniformity). Not surprisingly, "Japanese schools teach a buttoned-down sense of time and space not unlike what one finds in the military" (Rohlen 1983: 316).

Within a school, individuals are members not just of a moral community, but also of a unit whose mission is socialization and training for future roles as diligent workers and responsible parents. Each school is divided into subunits, such as homerooms, grades and classes (classes are further sub-divided into units called *han*). Such unitization, in addition to providing "scenes" in which agents (i.e. students) act, makes for easy management and oversight:

> When persons are moved in blocks, they can be supervised by personnel whose chief activity is not guidance or periodic inspection (as in many employer-employee relations) but rather surveillance – a seeing to it that everyone does what he has been clearly told is required of him, under conditions where one person's infraction is likely to stand out in relief against the visible, constantly examined compliance of the others (Goffman 1961: 6–7).

My Tokyo residence was situated a stone's throw from a middle school and, in the other direction, an elementary school. In the fall, I could hear students out in the sports field preparing for Sports Day. Day after day they would be put through the same training regime. A female teacher's voice boomed over the PA system, ordering the students to "stand there", "move there", "run here". The same orders were given over and over, as if aiming for perfection. Facing the sports field, I was confronted with uniformed squads of boys wearing blue gym shorts, white T-shirts and yellow caps, and girls were wearing the same, except that their shorts were very short and tight. These squads moved here and there, as if part of a miniature army on maneuvers. The point of the exercises seemed not to be to compete against each other nor to demonstrate their physical abilities, but rather to learn how to take orders, how to be mobilized and how to be moved in small units.

In addition to grades, homerooms and classes, students are usually required to belong to clubs which are regarded as a type of training in "human relations". In some clubs, rigid relations between junior and senior students are maintained (as in some sports teams). Note should also be made of student committees (*seito-kai*): "Every aspect of the students' lives – from the milk they drink to the clothes they wear – is supervised and managed by some committee or section", and "For each teacher section, there is usually a corresponding student committee, and students are assigned specific tasks, such as delivering the kerosene to the art room in winter." Lines of hierarchy add order to these committees, since "senior students are expected to instruct junior students in the correct way to carry out their tasks" (LeTendre 1994: 53), as do *rentai sekinin* (collective responsibility) and *rentai batsu* (collective punishment) (cf. Sakamoto 1989: 125).

Occasionally, there are special scenes and situations within the school, such as entrance ceremony, Sports Day, graduation and other school functions, in which spaces temporarily become stages on which students, more carefully uniformed than usual, present selves upon which the educatio-bureaucratic gaze is even more intensified. During such ceremonials, bodies are highly uniformed and ritualized: e.g. in auditoriums, students are lined up and are mobilized en masse. They are made to "stand!" (*kiritsu!*), "bow!" (*rei!*), "sit!" (*chakuseki!*) placed at attention by command and made to verbally respond on cue ("present!"; "thank you very much!"; school songs, Japan's national anthem).[4] But besides these key ceremonials, mention should also be made of the more quotidian but more numerous micro-rituals composed of daily acts of civility toward teachers and other students (especially one's seniors): introductions, greetings, bowings and other courtesies (*aisatsu*) (McVeigh, forthcoming):

> By using word ceremonial properly the individual can navigate without fear in a threatening social world. He can even ignore the true attitudes of others, as long as he can get by them with the proper ritual formulas of salutation, sustaining conversation, farewells, and so on. The actor has only to be sure of the face-saving ritual rules for interaction. Everyone is permitted the stolid self-assurance that comes with minute observation of unchallengeable rules – we can all become social bureaucrats (Becker 1990: 120).

Being Sociopsychologically Primed at Preschools

For most, the first exposure and experience with uniformed dress begins at the preschool level (nursery school, kindergartens or both). Here I examine uniformed dress and associated material culture at preschools.

Some preschool authorities say that uniforms are convenient because preschoolers come to school with clothes not suited to play or with expensive ordinary clothes (*shifuku*) that are not considered necessary and cause competition. Moreover, ordinary clothes are more difficult to wash and it is tiresome for a parent to put their child's name on so many different outfits. Some preschool authorities consider uniforms easier to move in when playing and to get in and out of. Other preschool officials note that uniformed preschoolers "look cute and like preschoolers" (*kawai-rashî kara enji rashî*); the color of uniforms is "cheerful" (*akarui*); and that "outside" uniforms act as "signs" (*mejirushi*) of the preschool (cf. Harada and Hasegawa 1996).

Preschools that do not stipulate the wearing of uniforms contend that with ordinary clothes (*shifuku*), they are "easy to run around in"; "students can dress according to the weather"; "they can wear the same clothes in school and at home"; "they're natural"; "individuality can be emphasized"; and if ordinary clothes get dirty "they can be quickly washed".

If a preschool does not have a uniform, it will almost certainly have requirements for other objects of material culture and dress. Typically, these might include: shoes (both indoor and outdoor); winter hat; summer hat; rain gear; play clothes (regular clothes, gym clothes, or a smock or apron-like outfit for keeping the uniform or regular clothes clean during lunch, playtime etc.); bathing suit; and towel (for pool). Other typical items are *randoseru* (knapsack); *kaban* (briefcase); drinking cup; handkerchiefs; play items (such as crayons, markers, pencils, paper, scissors, sketchbooks, notebooks, clay etc.); and bags for outdoor shoes when entering and exiting school. Wearing, carrying and caring for all these objects socialize preschoolers into a complex web of symbolic associations embedded in material culture: outside/inside (*soto/uchi*) distinctions, following instructions, lines of command, orderliness, cleanliness, punctuality, rhythms of daily activities at school, use of space and temporal distinctions. As for the latter matter, the politico-economic rationalization that Japanese society is famous for is apparent in a rather strict code: traditionally, on October 1, hot or cold, "rain or snow notwithstanding", summer clothes are put away. "Except for the occasional foreigner, all men will be wearing long shirts and long pants and no women will be wearing sandals or short sleeves. The transition is neat, orderly, organized and totally impervious to the natural elements" (Kiritani 1994). June 1 is the day of "changing clothes" (*koromogae*) when people wear lighter clothes (Japan's academic year beings in early April).

The aforementioned socialization primes preschoolers and is the first step in "management education" (*kanri kyôiku*); they are embodying certain *habiti* in preparation for the more complicated, demanding socialization and learning of elementary school. "School uniforms are supposed to stand for youth, diligence, cleanliness, truth, goodness and beauty" and have a "positive effect on students and help prevent them from behaving like poorly educated barbarians" (from a letter in "Readers' Forum: Can school uniforms effectively curb juvenile violence?" 1998).

But besides children, all this detailed attention to the child's personal collection of objects socializes parents – specifically and especially mothers – into the same complex web of symbolic associations as their children (though experienced from a different angle). Preschool authorities regularly send memos and instructions to parents about the preparation of material culture. Mothers are expected to ensure that their child is properly outfitted, to thoroughly wash all items, to write their child's name on all items, to sew name tags on all items of clothing and to carefully prepare box lunches (*bentô*) (Allison 1991). These preparations and practices are monitored and evaluated by the preschool authorities, ensuring that a woman is performing her role as a "good mother". Nomura reports a student who said that "When I would wear a sweater made by mother I was praised by my teacher who said she was a good mother" (1994: 246).

Harada and Hasegawa's (1996) investigation, though limited to 205 preschools, provides an idea of how widespread the practice of uniformed dress is at the preschool level (Table 3.2). Table 3.3 shows the type of regulation attire prescribed, Table 3.4 shows the time preschoolers spend wearing regulated dress.[5]

Table 3.2. *Regulation Attire at 61 Kindergartens and 144 Nursery Schools*

	Kindergarten	Nursery School
Has Uniforms	48	73
Has Play Clothes Different from Uniforms	30	18
Has Regulation Gym Clothes	30	23
Has Regulation Shoes	7	2
Has Regulation Bags	49	86
Has School Caps	46	99
No Regulation Clothing	3	22

Source; Harada and Hasegawa (1996: 23; modified).

Because of the nature of preschool activities, much thought is given to the type of attire best suited to "play time" (Table 3.5). Preschool authorities give various reasons why they have students change into play clothes: "if their clothes get dirty there's no need to worry and the students can play"; "they can run around"; they "can dress according to the weather"; play clothes are "easy to wash and cheap"; students "can have a sense of solidarity (*rentaikan*)"; students "can learn how to take their clothes off by themselves"; "they can become good at washing clothes"; "they can relax their minds and bodies"; and they can "modulate" (*merihari*) their daily life. Some preschool officials prefer to keep students in uniforms during play time and point out that "not changing into play clothes saves time and increases the time to play" and "when students are outside the school they are easy to recognize" (if in uniform). At some preschools children are allowed to play bare-chested, so students "can acquire resistance to colds" and "if they get dirty they can easily be washed".

Elementary, Middle and High School Uniforms

After graduating from preschool, the wearing, carrying and caring for uniforms and associated material culture continues into elementary school. In this section, I examine uniforms themselves. To introduce this section, note this description of elementary students on their way to school:

Table 3.3. *Type of Uniforms, Play Clothes and Gym Clothes at 61 Kindergartens and 144 Nursery Schools*

		Kindergarten	*Nursery School*
	Smock	19	64
	Blazer	24	5
	Blouse	16	4
	Polo Shirt	4	2
Uniform	T-Shirt	5	1
	Skirt	28	14
	Short Pants	32	19
	Long Pants	0	1
	Short Sweat Pants	1	1
	Other	9	6
	Smock	28	16
	Sweat Shirt	0	1
	Polo Shirt	0	1
Play Clothes	T-Shirt	3	1
	Short Pants	0	1
	Short Sweat Pants	9	1
	Long Sweat Pants	0	1
	Other	1	1
	Smock	0	1
	Sweat Shirt	7	2
	Polo Shirt	3	5
Gym Clothes	T-Shirt	15	14
	Short Pants	2	5
	Short Sweat Pants	20	15
	Long Sweat Pants	5	1
	Loose Pants	0	2

Source; Harada and Hasegawa (1996: 23; modified).

The smaller kids, the new first-graders, were practically bent over under the weight of their heavy loads. Besides their big schoolbags, which appeared to be full of enough books for a graduate research student, they had: bags for their exercise wear; bags for their chopsticks and napkins; and various other little bags hanging from the mother bag. Some were toting harmoniums and abacuses, swimming gear and calligraphy sets. And, oh yes, they wore their hard hats [to prevent head injuries while walking to and from school] (Anton 1992a).[6]

Table 3.4. *Time Preschoolers Spend Wearing Uniforms at 61 Kindergartens and 144 Nursery Schools*

	Smock		Besides Smock		Total By School Type		
	Kindergarten	Nursery School	Kindergarten	Nursery School	Kindergarten	Nursery School	Total
Commuting and While in School	11	13	7	2	18	15	33
Only When Commuting to and from School	5	25	18	7	23	32	55
Only While in School	1	1	1	0	2	1	3
Other	0	20	5	3	5	23	28
No Answer	0	2	0	0	0	2	2
Total	17	61	31	12	48	73	121

Source; Harada and Hasegawa (1996: 23; modified).

Table 3.5. *Type of Clothes Worn for Play Time at 61 Kindergartens and 144 Nursery Schools*

	Kindergarten	Nursery School	Total
Uniform	12	6	18
Change to Play Clothes	25	23	48
Sweats	3	2	5
Ordinary Clothes (*shifuku*)	11	104	115
Bare-Chested	1	1	2
Other	9	6	15
No Answer	0	2	2
Total	61	144	205

Source; Harada and Hasegawa (1996: 28).

For the sake of mapping some order on the different types of uniforms, I divide descriptions of uniforms into the most important sociopolitical category: gender. But before proceeding, a few words about the color symbolism of uniforms. Though there have been some recent changes, two points are conspicuous. The first point is the saliency of dark colors for both sexes – dark blue, black and grey – as the descriptions below demonstrate. Though there is a danger of reading too much into symbolism, it may not be too far-fetched to believe that dark colors carry (at least when uniforms were originally designed) meanings of seriousness, solemnity, orderliness – prerequisites for a stable schooling environment.[7] The second point concerns the role of white for both sexes (as the descriptions below demonstrate). Like dark colors, whiteness probably carries meanings about purity, sincerity and devotion (presumably in relation to one's academic endeavors and one's school).

Male Uniforms

Presently, the typical male student uniform might consist of the *gakuran*, a set of black or blue trousers and a jacket with a "stand-up collar" (*tsume-eri*) (Table 3.6). At some universities and high schools, male cheerleaders and martial arts clubs wear *gakuran*. This type of uniform, which has conservative connotations, is formal in appearance and reportedly not as comfortable as other uniforms consisting of a blazer and tie (Appendix A Table 1 provides some idea of the actual appearance of uniforms).

Table 3.6. *Type of Men's Uniforms at 535 Schools*

	Stand-Up Collar	Suit	Blazer	Other
Number of Schools	271	261	1	2
%	50.6	48.8	0.2	0.4

Source; Nomura (1993: 209).

Female Uniforms

The typical female student uniform, called a *sêra fuku* ("sailor uniform"), might consist of a navy blue pleated skirt and a middy blouse. If the *gakuran* and the stand-up collar (*tsume-eri*) typify and symbolize the male uniform, then the "sailor uniform" and its collar typify and symbolize the female uniform. In a "Sailor Uniform Chart" Mori lists thirty-nine schools, detailing how each school's uniform fits into the variables of: (1) color of collar; (2) color of line; (3) number and shape of lines; (4) type of bodice; (5) scarf/tie; (6) uniform color and characteristics; and (7) other (1985: 214). And in a "Catalog of Sailor Collars" Mori lists nine major types of collars (each with variations) and provides examples from specific schools: (1) white lines on navy blue; (2) white lines on navy blue and irregular corner; (3) white lines on navy blue with design; (4) white lines on navy blue with colored lines; (5) white lines on black; (6) white lines on grey; (7) white background with design; (8) white; and (9) lines on white (1985: 212–13). As part of the "sailor uniform" ensemble, skirts are also highly symbolically charged with gendered meanings.

Table 3.7 provides an idea of the color, design and type of female uniforms. Note should be made that more variety is permitted at women's schools (see also Appendix A Table 2).

Table 3.7. *Women's Summer Uniforms at 723 Private Middle and High Schools*

	"Sailor"	*Blouse and Skirt*	*One-Piece*
Number of Schools	142	576	5.0
%	19.6	79.7	0.7

Source; Nomura (1993: 212).

At schools that have them, uniforms are almost always worn (Nomura 1993: 213). Some schools have more than one type of uniform (probably to allow the phase out of older designs due to uniform changes) (Nomura 1993: 211).

An examination of an actual dress code provides a sense of how uniforms are utilized at a middle school. At the top of a document entitled "Clothing Regulations of Nakamura Middle School" (pseudonym) is the motto: "Clothes Express One's Heart, So Let's Obey the Clothing Regulations".

This document was compiled by the Nakamura Middle School PTA Off-campus Guidance Committee, the Nakamura Middle School PTA Parents' Committee and the Nakamura Middle School Life Guidance Committee. Under a heading called "Policy" it reads:

(1) clothing should be appropriate to middle school students; (2) clothes should be modest and clean; (3) clothes should conform to the standards determined by the school; (4) male and female student uniforms must be purchased at authorized stores determined by the school, and they must have the appropriate labels and conform to authorized item numbers [the document lists the names of stores that sell uniforms, socks, and other necessary accouterments and strongly advises students to patronize these stores].

Two diagrams of uniformed students, one male and the other female, have numbered comments indicating how to wear a uniform (Figure 3.1).[8]

For female students;

(1) Necktie should be nicely and evenly tied in a trapezoid shape;
(2) Hem of the skirt should be no more than 30 centimeters from the floor;
(3) Socks should be plain white (colors, designs and lace are prohibited).

For male students;

(4) The cap should have one white stripe with the school emblem;
(5) The shirt must have a collar, and the jacket collar must not be altered;
(6) High school jacket buttons should not be worn;
(7) The belt must be black, brown, or blue;
(8) Authorized uniforms must have the appropriate labels;
(9) Socks should be white and authorized.

For both females and male students;

(10) Shirts worn under the blouse or jacket should be thin, a light color and not be fancy;
(11) From October to March armbands must be worn at night;
(12) Straps on book bags should not be too long;
(13) Pants and skirts should be worn at the waist;
(14) Do not write or put stickers on book bags.

In addition to these rules, there are detailed instructions about the number of pleats a skirt should have (24 to 28); coats; rain shoes and snow boots (which should not be too expensive); shoes (indoor and outdoor) and the color of shoelaces; gym clothes and sports uniform (which have their own

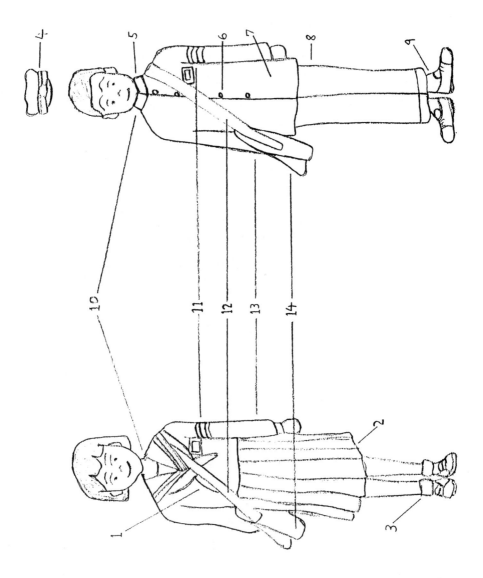

rules); school caps (with different instructions for hats worn commuting to school and sport activities); name tags (with school name, grade, group, student's name, guardian's name, blood type, address and telephone number); mufflers; what may be worn during club activities (either school uniforms or a special *unihômu* ("uniform") decided by the club), and windbreakers (navy blue), which may be worn by students riding to school on bikes.

The student role is incomplete without the accouterments of colorful pens, pencils, markers, erasers, rulers, pads and pencil cases, objects which are taken very seriously in Japan. Even in universities, where very few students take their studies seriously, students regard such accouterments as indispensable to playing the student role. I knew of two female university students who would place what can only be described as small buckets on their desks, filled with an assortment of pens and pencils.

Gaining and Maintaining "Institutional Face"

As moral communities, schools have a stake in how the outside world (*soto*) perceives them. Students, as it were, are the "face" of any school, and thus it is not surprising that school authorities show great concern for how they present themselves when commuting to and from school. If students from a particular school are seen with pierced ears, excessively long skirts or short skirts, etc., then students from other schools and parents may think that this school is "not high school-like" (*kôkô-rashikunai*) and regard it as a "school with problems" (*konnan kô*) (Aikawa 1994: 15). Such concerns are especially understandable given the decline in school-age children and the scramble for students. Thus, being "school-like" (*gakkô-rashî*) – along with the entire package of order, discipline and acceptance of official values – is the type of "institutional face" (i.e. *omote*), *imêji* ("image"), or *gaikan* ("external appearance" or "outside view") that many schools attempt to portray by utilizing the symbolism of uniformed students. But besides the students, school authorities have an interest in the actual appearance of and impression uniforms and "high school students-like" (*kôkôsei-rashî*) make on the outside world. This concern was often noted in the media throughout the 1980s and early 1990s (Tables 3.8 and 3.9), often justified by "adopting designs that respond to the change in times" (Isobe 1996: 95). Schools can be very sensitive to their perceived image: a public high school "recalled school festival posters depicting a young girl with hair dyed brown and wearing blue nail polish, claiming that such a portrayal would damage the school's reputation" ("Teachers nix brown hair, blue nail polish on poster", 1996; see below for discussion of "hair").

As for main changes: there was a switch from the "stand-up collar" (*tsume-eri*) of the male uniform to blazers as well as a change from black to navy blue (*nêbî burû*) or grey. For female uniforms, there was a change from "sailor uniforms" to blazers, and a move away from navy blue to more colors and checkered patterns (Isobe 1996: 106) which afforded the students a more "cheerful" (*akarui*) appearance.

Table 3.8. *Uniform Change Implementation at Private Women's Middle and High Schools by Year*

Year	'82	'83	'84	'85	'86	'87	'88	'89	'90	'91	Total
Number of Schools	8	15	11	17	21	19	36	57	56	62	302

Source; Nomura (1993: 214).

Table 3.9. *Uniform Change Implementation of Male Uniforms in Private Middle and High Schools by Year*

Year	'82	'83	'84	'85	'86	'87	'88	'89	'90	'91	Total
Number of Schools	7	10	14	14	14	14	29	50	36	46	234

Source; Nomura (1993: 215).

The most common reason for changing uniforms was "to improve the image of schools, start with uniforms" (Isobe 1996: 95). Some schools feel compelled to change their uniforms because their own uniform is too similar to other schools and they feel they might lose their institutional identity. For instance, two public high schools that reintroduced uniforms "hope the return of the uniforms will improve their image and bring about a sense of unity" ("Schools bring uniforms back to improve image", 1997). There are various other reasons for changing uniforms (Table 3.10).

Schools also implement uniform changes in order to improve institutional solidarity, unity and belongingness among students, values which presumably aid administrators in maintaining order on campus. At some schools, the opinions, concerns and ideas of students were taken into account when redesigning and adopting new uniforms (cf. Appendix A Tables 3, 4 and 5). Attention was given to the degree of comfort, whether students liked the

Table 3.10. *Why Private Middle and High Schools Decided to Change Their Uniforms*

Reason	Number of Schools
As a Part of Efforts to Improve the School's Image (*imêjiappu*) – Establish the School's Identity – As a Policy to Attract Students	168
Disordered Dress, Help in School Reorganization	86
We Wanted a New Design that Would Be Suited to the Times	57
An Increase in Schools with Uniforms Similar to Our Own	37
Too Much Guidance (*shidô*) to Correct Clothing Violations	34
Due to the Age of Internationalization, to Have Uniforms that Can Be Worn Even in Foreign Countries	29
Wishes of Students and Parents	25
Unpopularity of Stand-Up Collar (*tsume-eri*)	22
To Be Independent So that Students Will Be Proud of the School	22
Using School's Anniversary as an Opportunity	21
Other: To Standardize (*tôitsu suru*) Male and Female Uniforms in Coed Schools, to Meet Changes in Hair Regulations, etc.	–

Source; Nomura (1993: 216; modified).

color and design, whether uniforms were in tune with current fashion, whether they had a brand name, the degree of durability, whether or not they fade and price (Appendix A Table 6). Appendix A Tables 7 and 8 list the types of changes made as reported in Isobe's study (1996). According to school officials, there were effects and consequences after change in uniforms (Appendix A Tables 9 and 10).

Some schools have even discontinued uniforms and implemented the "privatization of clothing" (*shifuku-ka*) (Isobe 1996: 95) and allowed the wearing of *jiyû fuku* (literally, "free clothes"). Other schools permit students to wear whatever they want on designated days, allow students the choice of whether or not to wear uniforms, while others have adopted *junseifuku*, or "semi-uniforms" (Nomura 1993: 219). Though recently many have commented on a trend to do away with uniforms (or at least ease the regulations), at present this trend is not very noticeable (e.g. see Nomura's 1993 survey of 941 schools: Table 3.11; see also Uchino 1995).[9] Some teachers believe that to discontinue uniforms can lead to behavioral problems; thus it is said that uniforms place a "brake on [unacceptable] behavior" (*kôdô no burêki*) (Nomura 1993: 204).

Table 3.11. *"Does Your School Have Uniforms?"* *

	Women's Schools		Men's Schools		Coeducation		All Schools	
	Yes	No	Yes	No	Yes	No	Yes	No
Number of Schools	363	7	167	15	369	20	899	42
%	98.1	1.9	91.8	8.2	94.9	5.1	95.5	4.5

* 370 women's, 182 men's, 389 coed private middle schools (total of 941 schools)

Source; Nomura (1993: 207).

Not all schools have seen a need to change their uniforms. Nomura's research on 208 private middle and high schools lists various reasons for this: "We have a long history and want to treasure this tradition"; "Students, graduates, and parents say that the current uniform is good"; "The uniform has struck roots in the area"; "The students are proud and attached to the uniforms"; "What we have now is appropriate"; "Uniforms are not something that can be swayed by fashion and easily changed"; "The school will not be judged well by its appearance"; "There is no problem with the uniforms so change is not needed" (1993: 215). Isobe reports that some schools were not interested in changing uniforms because if they do change, the "school will lose its tradition" and "students are satisfied" with their uniforms (Isobe 1996: 105).

It should also be noted that not all schools require uniforms. Why? "Students should judge what to wear by themselves, according to age, individuality and place"; "To cultivate the power of independent judgment and a sense of beauty"; "To assert respect for freedom, self-government and individuality"; "Ordinary clothes (*shifuku*) are natural"; "To avoid standardization (*kakuitsuka*)"; "Freedom is a principle"; "We expect the students to be responsible and make themselves free" (Nomura 1993: 219).

Uniforming Teachers

Maintaining and gaining "institutional face" is not the sole responsibility of students. Teachers, of course, as school authority figures, are also expected to play their assigned roles. At some schools attempts at shaping subjectivity and how individuals present themselves via uniformed dress is not restricted to students. In Habikino, Osaka Prefecture, the local government proposed a plan to have teachers wear uniforms while on school grounds. The plan was met with stiff resistance: a 250-member teachers' union in Habikino launched a campaign demanding that the local government withdraw the proposal; primary and middle school teachers collected signatures from parents of students demanding that 10 million yen in appropriations for the uniforms from the municipal budget be deleted. But the most recent word was that both the local government and its board of education, however, are determined to go ahead with the plan on grounds that several teachers have been showing up at school sloppily dressed ("Osaka teachers begin anti-uniform fight", 1996).[10]

According to the local government the introduction of teacher uniforms is necessitated by three reasons: (1) more and more people are visiting schools as they open to the public and thus there is a need to distinguish visitors from teachers; (2) teachers' clothing is unkempt; and (3) children's attitudes are influenced by teachers (Kitamura 1996: 113; see also Wataguchi 1996: 24). The teachers have a different view: "It's a waste of tax money!" "The plumbing needs more attention!" "I'm surprised at how old the school's bathrooms are. Repair them!" (Kitamura 1996: 112). "Things are very busy at a school. There's garbage that needs to be thrown out, industrial arts class and physical education and serving food. It's a different world for *sararîman* who do work at a desk. We can't pay too much attention to style" (Wataguchi 1996: 26). For their part, the students say they like different clothes and would have a "bad feeling" if all the teachers dressed the same (Kitamura 1996: 113).

In the following section I explore how the educatio-bureaucratic gaze builds subjectivity among students.

Being Observed During the Uniformization Phase

In Chapter 2, I introduced four modes of command or what may be termed modes of "observation" that socialize individuals through monitoring/influencing/controlling. Here I illustrate these modes as they relate to practices associated with school uniforms in Japan.

(1) Other Observes Self ("me")

The "other-observes-self" mode is exemplified by school authorities, specifically teachers, principals and other educational personnel, observing students, who become the object of the official educatio-bureaucratic gaze. Hence, "other" does not only mean a single individual, but should be understood as usually in the plural or as an authoritative "generalized other". The self is passively positioned into a normative community (i.e. the school). More generally, this mode may be thought of as standing before others (*hitomae*), feeling the pressure of the eyes of others (*hitome*) or as *seken*, in which one experiences lines of vision converging on one's self. "One's appearance commands the gaze of the audience" (Stone 1990: 141).

Teachers instruct and monitor to what degree students observe dress codes and often record their findings (though this varies from school to school). Following rules, explicitly and implicitly, is responding to a teacher's gaze. At some schools, uniform regulations are meticulous and enforced with military-like "clothing inspections" (*fukusô kensa*) and "school gate guidance" (*kômon shidô*) as students enter the school gate in the morning. Teachers are on the lookout for dress code violations, such as "super long skirts" (*chô rongu sukâto*) and evidence of any other "strange clothes" (*isô*). If a problem is found, the students may be ordered to return home to rectify the violation. "Uniforms are regarded as one type of student guidance (*seito shidô*) which is an ordering of clothes in group living (*shûdan seikatsu*)" (Isobe 1993: 139). "Clothes guidance" (*fukusô shidô*) is an example of "educational guidance" (*kyôikuteki shidô*), which is part of a more inclusive "managed guidance" (*kanriteki shidô*) (cf. Hara 1996: 64–5) and the state's politico-economically "administrative guidance" (*gyôsei shidô*) (see Chapter 2) that produces statefulness. Faculty receive amazingly detailed diagrams and instructions on measurements of every part of the uniform, taken from several angles. These regulations are meticulous and among students, infamous. At some schools, teachers check students' underwear to ensure they are white; hair bands must be a certain color; and teachers measure the pants' hemline and how far above or below the knee the skirt falls. At other schools, the length of bangs are checked, nails are examined to see if they have been trimmed, and other items of personal care are inspected.

Hair, which may be regarded as part of a uniform and thus becomes susceptible to management, is often a sight of the educational system's bureaucratic gaze. Some schools stipulate the hairstyle known as *marugari* (close clipping) for males; sometimes teachers shave students' heads if they consider their hair too long; and stories abound about school authorities forcing students who do not have naturally straight, jet-black hair to dye their hair so as to look "more Japanese", or they must carry a note from that their parents that their hair is indeed naturally brown; sometimes their hair is checked against the sun to determine its natural, non-black color. Discourse about hair evokes strong sentiments:

> A certain famous pro-baseball manager . . . had this story to tell. 'If a team won the Koshien tournament [the National High School Baseball Tournament], it was given the privilege of visiting the U.S., but since the players would be thought to be convicts if they went there with close-cropped hair, we were allowed to grow our hair if we won the tournament. So during the game, we encouraged each other with shouts of 'America! America!' ("To hell with school uniforms!" 1997).

When the conflict between "personal freedom at school" and "educational authority" is discussed, hair is quite often the symbolic lightning rod. In one incident, a father "allegedly hit and injured a middle school principal and three teachers after a quarrel over the color of his daughter's hair" ("Father arrested in school row over daughter", 1996). Legal battles over hair length occasionally erupt. For instance, two brothers "endured years of bullying" because of their refusal to have their hair "closely cropped". Their high school conducted "greeting movements" at the school gate every morning in which a dozen or so members of the student council checked hairstyle, shoes, socks and other articles of clothing. Local authorities asked the school to desist its "greeting movements", though the school refused. The two brothers are preparing to sue the school ("Hairstyle rights", 1996). Note how in this aforementioned example, students – presumably under teacher guidance – do the morning inspections (see also "Pupil sues middle school over strict haircut regulations", 1993). At times the state can be strict and unforgiving. In 1988, a student was expelled from the school because she had permed her hair. Even though she apologized to the school, the school officials remained adamant that she leave. She sued the school, but the Tokyo High Court upheld Shutoku Gakuen High School's rule that prohibits students from having perms. "I couldn't believe it . . . I was an ordinary student. I want people to understand that my life plans for marriage and career have been ruined by the horrible treatment by the school and court in the past five years" ("Girl's school ouster due to perm upheld", 1992). The symbolic import of hair length was evident when at a news conference, Education Minister Akamatsu Ryôko stated that "she gets goose bumps when she sees male students with closely cropped hair". She later apologized because a politician explained that many students who participate in sports with short hair took offense at her comments ("Apology issued over haircut comment", 1993). That same year, the Japanese Trade Union Confederation (Japan's largest labor group) asked the Ministry of Education to review what it called "internationally strange school regulations, such as requiring male students to have closely cropped hair" ("Ax schools' hair rules, Rengo urges ministry", 1993). In another case that points to the disciplinary associations of hair, a teacher cut a third-grader's hair who had offended a gangster in order to appease him ("Student's hair cut to appease gangster", 1994).

Traditionally, jet-black hair was considered a defining feature of Japanese feminine beauty, and during the Edo period, there were methods to blacken hair. But the present-day discourse about hair and its meanings must be placed in the broader context of idealized perceptions of what "Japanese" *should* look like which are nation-statist in origin, and such perceptions are often legitimated by racial determinism, i.e. Japanese have a moral obligation (*normative*) to look a certain way because they were born (*biological*) a certain way. In letters to "Readers' Forum: What do you think of the recent trend in which people dye their hair brown in chapatsu [dyed-brown hair] fashion?" (1996), a Japanese man writes "brown [dyed] hair doesn't fit the yellow skin of Japanese people", and a Japanese woman believes that "As Japanese, our naturally black hair is something of which we should be proud".[11] Such sentiments are shared even by some non-Japanese:

> To dye the much-admired deep black hair of the Japanese is the worst of all offenses. Young people who have dyed their hair must be very shallow and have a low opinion of themselves to need to do such a thing to feel good about themselves . . . The Japanese were made with a perfect balance of skin, hair and eye color, but to upset the balance in any way, you make a great mistake. The end result is an all-round ugly person who reflects badly on this great country ("Readers' Forum: What do you think of the recent trend in which people dye their hair brown in chapatsu fashion?" 1996).

Some teachers, it should be stressed, take a more measured approach toward regulations: "We teachers want to let the students decide [the] dress code as much as possible. Ideally, a compromise should be reached between what the students desire and the image the school must foster in the community" (see letter to the editor "Dress to impress", 1997). Students quickly absorb the significance of being gazed at and of not being conspicuous (*medatsu*). A mother who marveled at all the items she was ordered to purchase for her daughter in middle school (although she already had many items, the school insisted that new ones be purchased) observed how

> Our daughter says she wants us to buy every one of the standard items because if she is in any way different from the others, she will surely be subjected to bullying. When I suggested that I should raise the question at the orientation meeting, she

nixed that right away, saying that just asking the question would draw the teachers' attention to her . . . Even before entering the school, our daughter is scared of an invisible force and is trying to protect herself from it by conforming to the standard. What actually awaits her when she gets to the school? ("Uniformity rules", 1997).

The concern with "fitting in" even extends to what should be worn on school excursions. The lathered discussions that preceded one school's excursion involved parents, who were requested to attend three meetings to discuss preparations: "Should the boys wear their usual (white) short pants or should they be permitted to wear long pants? Should they wear their own shirts and sweaters or should they wear their regular school shirt (white shirt with an orange collar, no joking) and school blazer (gray polyester)?" (Anton 1993).

Many teachers I have asked say they like uniforms, especially when on school excursions, since they make students easy to keep track of and mobilize. Table 3.12 lists how teachers view the pros and cons of student uniforms.

Table 3.12. *Arguments "For and Against" Uniforms from Teachers' Perspective*

For Uniforms	*Against Uniforms*
They have a long tradition and are student-like (*gakusei-rashi*)	They don't give respect to individuality. They deprive students of their student-like appearance
If students wear regular clothes their appearance may become gaudy (*hade*) and cause competition among pupils	At schools where uniforms are not worn, students do not appear gaudy (*hade*)
If there are uniforms students do not spend time trying to dress up	
Uniforms are economical	There are other clothes that are even more economical than uniforms
Uniforms prevent delinquency	Uniforms have no relation to delinquency

Source; Ôya (1995: 52–3; modified).

The official educatio-bureaucratic gaze is concretely illustrated in "confidential reports" (*naishinsho*), which are a teacher's record of academic performance, behavior and "character". These reports, which as a rule are not shown to students and their parents, are used by high schools for selecting students from middle schools and thus are especially important for a student's future. Another example of how the official gaze permeates school management through documentation is "education reports" (*kyôiku tsûshin*) which are used to evaluate students. The education report at one middle school has a section entitled "A Record of Behavior and Personality", under which are listed *kanten* ("viewpoints"; literally "observation points") that teachers are asked to evaluate: "Does the student lead a life in which his or her personal appearance is kept neat?" "Are the inside of the student's desk and locker kept in order?" "Does the student take care of things?" Such observation is not restricted to the school since teachers, especially for the lower grades, regularly send notifications home to parents about how students should ideally be presenting themselves (dress codes, accouterments, hygiene and health, bodily management, attire regulations for school ceremonies or an outing, etc.). Moreover, in addition to posting personnel at school gates to monitor dress-code compliance, some schools have teachers patrol local neighborhoods in search of students who are inappropriately presenting themselves or have put their bodies in the wrong places (movie theaters, game centers, karaoke centers, coffee shops, etc.). Spending time at such places is inimical to a student's academic progress, and also tempts a student with other "dangers" found outside the well-regulated, protective cocoon of the school campus. Teachers explain that such reconnaissance missions are meant to preclude students from misbehaving since "becoming bad students" might bring shame to the school, thereby causing a loss of "institutional face". One student I know was ordered by a teacher to remove his pants on a street because they did not meet regulations. But whatever the teachers' motivations, such scouting, as well as sending a continuous stream of notifications to parents, illustrate the degree to which the educatio-bureaucratic gaze radiates from schools to other spaces, such as the family, conventionally understood as outside the state's purview and possessing smaller dosages of statefulness. Indeed, besides teachers, store owners and clerks, as particular manifestations of *seken*, act as gatekeepers for the sale of alcohol or cigarettes, being able to distinguish if a certain individual should be allowed to purchase such things solely on the basis of school uniforms.

If constantly observed, monitored and regulated, one becomes passive, and though the comparison should not be pushed too far, students, like inmates in a "total institution", come to "treat self-presentation as an officially required task and, in comparison with individuals in noninstitutional settings, are not only unusually pragmatic performers but are also often overtly cynical ones" (Watson 1990: 196). Such cynicism "can be seen as a protest against the sorts of constraints that all of us face in more subtle forms" (Watson 1990: 196).

(2) Others Observe Other (as experienced by self)

The "others-observe-other" mode is *seken* in a very abstract sense, and means to be aware that people are constantly monitoring and judging the behavior of others. Whether or not one is the target of these lines of vision is beside the point, because simply observing and being aware of normative lines of vision can construct *seken*. Witnessing scenes of socialization, such as one's classmates being instructed or admonished by a teacher about proper self-presentation (in particular, modes that stress selves performed over selves expressed), can be just as instructive as having oneself observed. Observing the practices of constructing lines of authority between senior students (*sempai*) and junior students (*kôhai*) – in school clubs, circles or sports teams – also has socializing impact.

(3) Self Observes Other

When one observes another, something which we all do every day, one is constructing normative lines of vision through the mode of "self-observes-other". Of course, we may not intend to do so, nor are we necessarily aware that our facial expressions, demands, questions and ways of interacting are building lines of social vision, but nevertheless they are doing so. Because everyone participates as both an agent or a recipient of the official gaze, everyone supports the very social structures that constitute *seken*. In other words, everybody is complicit to some degree in the politics and socializing of normative visuality. Thus, when a student, as a "senior" (*sempai*), instructs, admonishes, or rewards a "junior" (*kôhai*) in a club or sports team, he or she is observing/integrating other students into lines of hierarchy, thereby acting as a link in the educatio-bureaucratic chain of socializing command and control.

Standing before the eyes of others in public is certainly an example of "other-observes-self" (in this context, "other" is better expressed plurally or as the "generalized other" which, in fact, resonates with *seken* in meaning). A uniform "allows the organization [school] to enlist the public's aid in enforcing controls upon its members since the norms and the deviations of uniform wearers are apparent to everyone" (Joseph 1986: 3). However, public spaces can also be described by the mode of "self-observes-others" (and for that matter, "other-observes-others"). The meaning of student uniforms in public spaces deserves mention for three reasons.

First, students use uniforms as totemic markers to judge what type of school an individual attends, and by extension, what type of student one is (i.e. amount of perseverance and intellect with which one is endowed). Many students are proud of their schools, especially if they are ranked academically high. At the same time, others are ashamed of their school's ranking and consider the uniform they must wear a type of stigma. Reportedly, some hide their uniforms with their coats. In public spaces (one student remarked that being on a train was like being in a "museum of school uniforms"), then, uniforms possess not just a supervisory use (teachers on patrol, shop owners, the gaze of the society's generalized other (i.e. *seken*)), but also a discriminatory function (Kataoka 1997: 124; Uchino 1995: 56) effected by academic competition, and ultimately driven by economic nation-statism.

Second, some students judge schools not for their academic standing but by the appearance of their uniform that they parade out in public before the eyes of others (*hitome*). This is why some public senior high schools in Tokyo, in order to attract students, "have resorted to introducing chic uniforms designed by top designers" ("Students judge schools by their uniforms", 1992) and adopting *burando no seifuku* ("brand-name uniforms").

> School uniforms are becoming more and more fashionable as an increasing number of schools adopt snappy outfits designed by notable talents such as Hanae Mori and Hiroko Koshino, in an attempt to attract freshmen despite the general decrease in the school-age population. An increasing number of uniform makers have begun marketing the high fashion-label uniforms under contract with top designers, purging the old image of plain and overly formal getups ("Designer uniform trend hits high schools", 1989).

Other designers recruited to design these uniforms, which are twice as expensive as ordinary uniforms, include Koji Watanabe and Sachiko Hanai.[12]

Third, uniforms grant students their own identity marker when out in public. Especially in the case of young women, uniforms afford a collective power vis-à-vis the establishment, specifically males and adults. Forms of self-presentation that were once considered rebellious and unfashionable – e.g. eyebrows plucked thin, pierced ears, brown-dyed hair, ultra-miniskirts (*chô minisukâto*), Burberry scarves, white "loose socks" (see below) – have become popular and standardized (Kataoka 1997: 122). As identity markers (again, specifically for young women), some students have invested uniforms with new meanings. "The uniform has become a symbol of young girls," according to a professor at Chiba University. "I often hear of girls who want to go to school with uniforms even if their parents suggest a school where they can wear plain clothes" ("Schools bring uniforms back to improve image", 1997). Rather than pieces of garments associated with being dependent, childlike and asexual, uniforms are transformed into attire laden with messages about being independent, adult and sexual. There is a movement from "though I'm sexy in spite of my uniform" to "precisely because of my uniform I'm sexy and cute" (*"seifuku dakara koso sekushî de kawaî"*) (Kataoka 1997: 123). In the words of an astute female university student, "a school uniform is not a tool to control or organize students, but is a symbol to identify students as cute girls. The category of *joshi kôsei* [female high school student] is, to some extent, created by the school uniform". Another young woman explained that students who attempt to make their uniforms "fashionable and cute" are "enjoying their limited time in their own world". Another university student said that such young women are "happiest when they're being cute", and according to another seventeen-year old female student, "nothing comes close to the power and aura of her school uniform. She is a junior in the famed Shibuya Joshikô (Shibuya Girls' High), renowned for its *cute* uniforms, *cute* girls and *cute* little schoolhouse located in the heart of town" (Shoji 1997; emphasis mine). This conversion of meaning for the most part occurs not within schools (where uniforms are tools of bodily control and associated with the self-performance of student roles), but out on the streets peopled with one's peers where "anonymous communication" (*tokumei no komyunikêshon*) (Kataoka 1997: 123) occurs via clothing that aids in impression management. In urban areas, not surprisingly, there are public spaces with higher concentrations of anonymous communication in which students, dressed up in their own versions of school uniforms, gaze and are gazed upon and engage in self-expression. In the case of Tokyo, the areas around Shibuya and Harajuku Stations are well known for their exchanges of anonymous communication and trafficking in glances of cuteness and sexuality.

It is worth noting that, at least according to some observers, the self-presentation styles of students differ depending on what type of school one attends. Mori also provides a description of the differences between local state and private schools (Table 3.13).

(4) Self ("I") Observes Self ("me")

An example of "self-observes-self" mode might be looking into a mirror to check one's self appearance. Actually, the "self-observes-self" mode designates the dynamic internalization of key social norms and expectations. Indeed, it is a highly complex sociopsychological behavior that usually transpires invisibly (i.e. "psychologically"), and here I should emphasize that the "I–me" relation is mutable, variable, inconstant and multifaceted depending on

Table 3.13. *"How [Tokyo] Metropolitan and Private Schools are Distinguished"*

Metropolitan Schools	Private Schools
Ponytail	Hair Tied Up or Hanging over
Some Other Badge Instead of	Shoulders
School Badge	More Original Jumper
Placement of the Badge Anywhere	Blouse with Initials
Cloth School Bags	Regulation School Bag
Long Skirts	Shoe Strings
Sandals	Permed Hair ("But Why Does
T-Shirts	Everybody Have the Same
Simple Jumper without Belt	Hairstyle?")
Deep Red Shoulder Bag with	Regulation Badge ("Students Like It
Various Badges Attached	Because It's Cute (*kawai*)")
Deck Shoes	Knee Socks ("A Trademark of Mission
Not Particularly Fussy about Hair	Schools")
Plaid Shirt	Black Loafers with Tassles
Skirt with Suspenders	Triple Braid
Lace Socks	Heart-Shaped School Badge
Sneakers	A School Bag Packed Just Like a
	Doctor's
	Socks Cuffed Three Times. Some
	Schools Have Initialed Socks
	Shoes with Straps

Source; Mori (1985: 198–9; modified).

the situation. For each individual, there are as many selves and "I–me" relations as there are social situations. Particularly, the distinction, as already discussed, between the expressed ("I" and "me" identified) and performed ("I" and "me" separated) modes of self-presentation should be noted. During the former, the self ("I") unmindfully observes itself ("me"), but in the latter mode, the self ("I") carefully observes itself ("me"). Though universal, these styles appear to be clearly distinguished in Japan due to the sociopolitical landscape delineated in Chapter 2.

Within the typical Japanese classroom, the "I-observes-me" mode is strongly encouraged through values such as "self-management" (*jiko kanri*), "self-control" (*jiko kisei*) and "perseverance" (*gaman*) (e.g. boys wear shorts in winter and long pants in the humid summer while girls wear skirts in winter). Such norms help with the "maintenance of discipline" (*chitsujo iji*). "An Osaka middle school bans scarves, earmuffs and sweaters while a Shizuoka school bans overcoats and mufflers" (Morikawa 1998). Uniforms, which, in Japan, aid in the internalization of these values, "have become common sense" (*jôshikika sareta*) and a "commonly accepted idea within society" (*shakai tsûnen*) (Ôya 1995: 53); or, it may be said, they assist in the reproduction of hegemonic values via the sociopsychological dynamic of self-("I")-observing-self-("me").

In Japan, the most commonly used term to describe an intense form of self-("I") observes-self-("me"), explicitly dictated by authorities usually after one has violated some social norm, is *hansei suru*, which means "self-examination", "critical self-reflection", or "introspection" of a decidedly moral nature. Often students are instructed to practice *hansei* as a group or to write *hanseisho* or *hanseibun* ("self-examination reports"). The writing of such continues after graduation since behavior or attitude problems are dealt with in a similar fashion at tertiary-level education and, significantly, at the workplace with *shimatsusho* (written explanation) to apologize for being late or some other minor mistake.

Uniforms as Objects that Socialize

As objects, how do school uniforms integrate the student into the socio-economic order and construct a rationalized subjectivity? Foucault is instructive here. In the most general terms, uniforms announce information about an individual's school, gender, grade, division (into which grades are subdivided) and name, "individualizing" the individual (1979: 192–4). The process of individualization is driven by and, in turn, eventually supports socioeconomic rationalization, eventually integrating each student into the workforce. Uniforms are part of an education system that "finely slices [students into layers] and is a human rights problem" (Uchino 1995: 56). More specifically, donning uniforms is intimately bound up with the principles of Foucaultian disciplinary practices. First, the minute control of activity teaches a general sense of discipline imposed by authority. Thus, there are detailed rules about how the uniform is donned. Second, repetitive exercises, such as donning the uniform on a daily basis, unconsciously build *habiti* that are demanded by the politico-economic order for productive purposes (cf. Bourdieu 1977). Third, students learn about the hierarchies ordering teachers/students relations and among students themselves, *sempai* (senior)/ *kôhai* (junior) relations (such distinctions are especially obvious in student clubs). Eventually, this knowledge of hierarchies is transferred to the workplace. Finally, through being taught to correctly wear uniforms, students are socialized to be aware of the normalizing gaze and its judgments (*seken*) (Foucault 1979: 141–56).

Uniforms effect rationalizing processes in three ways. First, they symbolize hierarchy: who must wear a uniform and who does not, who determines how a uniform must be worn, and what signs of rank on a uniform denote. According to one observer, the essence of uniforms is quite clear: to distinguish between "those who manage = teachers, and those who are managed = students" (Uchino 1995: 56–7).

Second, they symbolize social categorization: a uniform places one in a group, gender category, or age range. As categorizing objects, they have two functions. First, they are an emblem of membership for those inside an organization (school, company, occupation), hopefully instilling a sense of solidarity or identification. One observer finds "the beauty of unity in wearing uniforms" (from a letter in "Readers' Forum: Can school uniforms effectively curb juvenile violence?" 1998). A uniform is also a "certificate of legitimacy": "The uniform is a symbolic declaration that an individual will adhere to group norms and standardized roles and has mastered the relevant group skills," and besides revealing status position, a uniform may conceal status position (Joseph 1986: 66–7). Indeed, "The uniform suppresses individual idiosyncrasies of behavior, appearance, and sometimes physical attributes" (Joseph 1986: 68). This is why "The devices used by ordinary citizens to express their attitudes are denied to the uniform wearer – political buttons, religious insignia, and symbols of individual esthetic or ludic preferences" (Joseph 1986: 67). Second, uniforms act as a "group emblem"; they are for those outside the organization, who use them as a means of convenient classification, as a way of knowing who does what, of what role a person performs. "The uniform is not only an emblem but also a reminder of the behavior appropriate toward this emblem; it becomes a third factor in the interaction between wearer and other" (Joseph 1986: 66). A Japanese student who spent time in the United States explained to me that while the purpose of school uniforms in Japan is exclusionary (to emphasize who is not in "our group"), the purpose of school uniforms in the United States (for schools that have them) is inclusionary (to emphasize who is in "our group").

Finally, uniforms symbolize social standardization: regulated attire makes the individual more uniform ("one form"). This is useful for superiors who may utilize them as barometers of an individual's level of commitment. Thus, many schools in Japan enforce strict regulations concerning how a school uniform should be worn (though this point should not be exaggerated; many male students wear disheveled uniforms and earrings). Ritualizing one's dress (or having one's dress ritualized by an institution) is a way to express one's character, or at least one's level of commitment to the dictates and norms of the group. The body, then, is regarded as a meaning-laden, politicized icon, and its appearance becomes the visible expression of a moral system. Appearance is equated with character: "disheveled clothes mean a disordered life" (*fukusô no midare wa seikatsu no midare*) (Nomura 1993: 204) and students are warned about "behavior that disgraces the uniform" (*seifuku ni hajiru kôi*) and not to be "a student that is not suited to wearing a uniform" (Nomura 1993: 205).

Schools stipulate that students are not to remove their uniforms on their way home after school, and some mandate that even on days when there are club activities or school functions but no classes, uniforms must still be worn. As sites of socialization that produce statefulness, schools demand that students wear and carry the appropriate material culture, and regulations ensure that even outside the temporal and spatial boundaries of the school campus, individuals must announce and present their student selves/roles; playing the student role is a full-time job.

What Students Think of Uniforms

What do students themselves think of uniforms? In this section, based on discussions with university students who wore uniforms in middle and high school that I taught in Japan, I answer this question, while delineating the key themes that regularly made an appearance when uniforms were discussed: (1) unity, integration and solidarity; (2) social control and order; (3) lack of individuality; (4) "institutional face"; (5) being observed and monitored; (6) class distinctions and discrimination; and (7) Japanese ethnocultural and national identity. Other themes that occur frequently concern convenience, standardization and social roles. As we shall see, all these themes sometimes intersect and overlap in what individuals had to say about uniforms. We shall also see that, though organization and unit integration are ultimately inspired by statism, capitalism and simple administrative expediency, they are legitimated by a rhetoric of "solidarity", "comradeship", and by talk of immutable Japanese "tradition" or "history".

(1) Unity, Integration and Solidarity

The most common terms that came up in discussions about student uniforms were "integration" (*matomari*), "unit life" (*shûdan seikatsu*), "unit behavior" (*shûdan kôdô*), "affiliation", (*shozoku*), as well as "solidarity" (*ittaikan*) and "common consciousness" (*kyôtsû ishiki*). As one student explained it,

"Uniforms help students acquire unit consciousness (*shûdan ishiki*) when they're in units at school. By having everyone wear the same clothes, a feeling of unity (*tôitsukan*) develops. When a person is in a unit, a feeling of security (*anshinkan*) also arises." Another said that "Uniforms provide esprit de corps (*danketsushin*) for whatever school or company you belong to. Besides this, wearing uniforms makes people put their all into their work or study." After all,

> If you think about it, in Japan individuality (*kosei*) is kept in check, and harmony (*kyôchôsei*) is very important. I feel that with all the uniformity (*tôitsusei*) and integration (*matomari*) we're all doing military drills. I guess uniforms are important to build solidarity (*ittaikan*). After all, the unit is more important than the individual, so uniforms are important.

Speaking of the suits commonly worn by white-collar workers, one student noted that "As well as being a symbol of joining (*kamei*) some corporation, I think they also measure the uniformity of consciousness (*ishiki no tôitsuka*). Another said "Won't solidarity (*ittaikan*) arise if everybody wears uniforms? In a company, success and a sense of comradeship (*nakama ishiki*) are born." Some spoke of how uniforms are, within school culture, something "common-sensical", "proper", "right" (*atarimae*), and solidarity and unity are "born", "come into existence", or are "produced" (*umareru*) by donning uniforms. "Uniforms make students follow school rules. If everyone wears the same uniform, a sense of comradeship (*nakama ishiki*) is born and leadership (*tôsotsuryoku*) naturally (*shizen ni*) becomes stronger."

There is an aesthetic to uniforms that some admired. According to some students, ordinary clothes (*shifuku*) lack a "standardized look" (*tôitsukan*). "If everyone's appearance is uniformed (*tôitsu suru*), then their uniformity of consciousness (*ishiki no tôitsu*) can be measured":

> Student uniforms have a sharp look (*mitame*). I don't think its good for students to go to school wearing ordinary clothes (*shifuku*) that have a good look (*mitame*). Eventually they might start to wear dirty clothes. I think that, because of appearance (*gaiken*), differences between the rich and poor (*himpu no sa*) will appear. Because all students would hate this, I think uniforms are good.

Uniforms make students "cognizant of being a member" (*kôsei-in toshite no ninshiki*). Uniforms are associated with the "will to follow rules"; "school tradition" (*gakkô no dentô*); "school identity" (*gakkô no aidentîtî* or *sukûru aidentîtî*; written as "SI") and later in one's life, "corporate identity" (*kôporeito aidentîtî*; written as "CI") (Nomura 1993). Such sentiments seem to indicate an emphasis on the "self-performance" mode of self-presentation, in which one's "I" monitors one's "me" due to a strong awareness that others are carefully watching (see also the results of Uchino's 1995 surveys in Appendix B). Thus, whether with pride or with disgrace, donning a uniform possesses a theatrical aspect that one is obligated to perform, i.e. one acquires a "role" not just in the functional, social scientific sense, but also in its original, performative meaning.

(2) Social Control and Order

Notions of social control and order were evident in how some students explained that uniforms make it easy to identify one's social role and to which unit (*shûdan*) one is affiliated. "We have uniforms because they allow others to know with one glance (*hitome de*) what unit we belong to." Some liked uniforms because "they allow us to distinguish students from adults". After all, "These days, even primary school students want to be like adults, but by wearing uniforms everyone is the same and their student characteristics (*gakusei-rashisa*) can be expressed. Isn't this a good thing?"

Uniforms can teach students "discernment" (*kejime*) and "A certain amount of rules is necessary because the period of middle and high school is an emotional period. So, one's personal appearance (*minari*) should be determined [by rules]." Also, according to one student, "There are various school rules and wearing uniforms is one of them. People can learn how to follow regulations when they go out into society". Uniforms teach responsibility. They "make us have self-awareness" (*jikaku o motaseru*) and "One becomes aware of one's own status" (*jibun no mibun o jikaku suru*). Uniforms "make students aware of their identity as students". Some said uniforms make them feel "student-like" (*gakusei-rashî*). Indeed, it should be noted that students usually wear uniforms to university and college entrance examinations. While conducting entrance interviews at a college, I was told by one student that she wore her high school uniform so she could "do my best in acting like a student" (*akumade mo gakusei-rashiku suru*). Several students related uniforms to their school's tradition, or said that uniforms bring back good memories.[13]

Uniforms also provide the self-awareness that "if one individual does something wrong, then the reputation of a school or company will be hurt." Also, through uniforms people can "know their own social position (*jibun no shakaiteki ichi*)." Uniforms prevent juvenile delinquency: "If students wear uniforms, they play the role of preventing crime because someone can know immediately what school a student is from." Also, "If there were no uniforms, students would end up loitering around (*uro uro shite shimau*) on the streets."

"Wearing uniforms is different from ordinary clothes, and because of the eyes of those around (*mawari no me*), you could say that we are anxious (*kinchôkan*), and so we have a strong sense of responsibility. For example, uniforms prevent students from drinking, smoking, gambling, as well as discouraging adults from a loose (*darashinai*) lifestyle." Furthermore, "If there were no uniforms, it would have a bad influence on studying."

(3) Suppression of Individuality

On the negative side, a number of students tapped into the debate about how a dress code infringes upon their "human rights" and "freedom", denying them "expression of personality" (or roles in which they can "be themselves", i.e. self-expression). In Japan, there's a tendency to give more attention to the organization (*dantai*) rather than the individual (*kojin*). This is why our individuality (*kosei*) disappears a bit." Some students said uniforms are militaristic and reported that they have heard how non-Japanese think student uniforms look like military uniforms (cf. Taniguchi 1995: 109). Many stated that uniforms "suppress individuality" since the clothes that one chooses are "distinctively individual" (*jibun-rashî*; literally, self-like). After all, "Ordinary clothes (*shifuku*) allow one's self (*jibun*) to be expressed." Some students argued that while uniforms should be worn, the conservative *gakuran* with the stand-up collar were not desirable, since these give a bad impression, and in their minds are associated with the "army" or "funerals"; one student told me how he thought students wearing *gakuran* who stand in a line for ceremonies remind him of an army.

Some students, it needs to be stressed, believed that uniforms allow the expression of individuality (*kosei*): "I think that by having everyone wear the same clothes, the individuality of each person becomes clear." Another student explained that "Because everyone is wearing the same thing, any individuality (*kosei*) they have is easier to see."

(4) "Institutional Face"

Many students made a strong association between uniforms and frontage (*omote*) or a school's "image" (*imêji*). This indicates that, from the typical student's point of view, being a student means wearing the "institutional face" of a school – the primary *shûdan* for students – when outside (*soto*) or off campus. "In Japan, I think uniforms are also a face (*kao*). Uniforms categorize our status." Or "Uniforms are the symbols of schools and companies." As one student put it, "Because everyone can see which school I attend by my uniform, it makes me have a sense of responsibility. So I think we should have uniforms." Others explained that uniforms made them proud of their school and that "a uniform is the school's face": "When wearing a uniform, a person has the pride (*puraido*) of being a sign (*kanban*) for a company or school."

Commuting routes areas between school and home traverse the "streets" or "town" (*machi*) and constitute ambiguous, liminal areas. However, in addition to commuting routes, these areas also contain stores, coffee shops, cinemas, pachinko parlors, etc., which may, in the opinion of educational authorities, become sites of delinquent behavior. Thus, the street or town becomes a space of surveillance since it is in this "betwixt and between" zone where students, by wearing uniforms, "carry with them" their school's institutional face.

(5) Being Observed and Monitored

The impact of the official gaze is evident in how students linked uniforms to "eyes of those around" (*mawari no me*) and "the eyes of others" (*seken no me*), as well as what students had to say about how uniforms made them feel. They report that uniforms gave them a "consciousness of being under the control of [the school]" (*kisoku ishiki*) and very common comment about uniforms concerned how they allow teachers – as the official gaze made incarnate – "to keep an eye on" (*kanshi suru*) students who can thus be more easily monitored in public. "We can't go drinking, smoking, or to game centers, because while in uniform, it is easy for teachers to spot us." Some said that making them wear uniforms must mean that the school authorities do not trust students. Not a small number of students who were against uniforms idealized American schools by equating "casual clothes" with "individuality" and "freedom".

Linkages between one's appearance, organized group life and "Japanese characteristics" were often made: "I think Japan is a country where there's much unit life (*shûdan seikatsu*) and unit behavior (*shûdan kôdô*). I think that if there are uniforms in all these units integration (*matomari*) comes about. It seems that, more than uniforms, the look (*mitame*) of ordinary clothes (*shifuku*) lacks unity." Or in the opinion of another student, "I think that because Japan is a country where people are judged by their appearance (*gaiken*) uniforms are necessary. I don't like this, however, since it means that the thinking of present-day Japan is very rigid."

(6) Class Distinctions and Discrimination

Not a few students felt that uniforms hid class differences that might lead to jealousy and were important for instilling a sense of solidarity (especially during group activities). As one student put it, "wearing uniforms made us want to cooperate with each other, and they are able to foster people with character that do not discriminate or are not prejudiced". One student reported that "At primary schools there have been fights over the showiness of clothes (*fuku no kabi*). If some wear clothes such as dresses, there'll be many children with hand-me-downs (*osagari*). This causes discrimination." Thus, "There's a lot of emphasis on having everyone be the same so that everyone is equal" and "we consider cooperation important, and being 'average' (*hitonami*) is highly regarded. This is why everybody wears clothes that are the same."

When I entered middle school and started to wear a uniform, I was very happy, and thought that we should all wear them. But when I entered high school, I noticed that low- and high-ranked high schools all had their own uniforms, so people could tell right away what school one got into. If one were from a lower ranked school, people had a biased view of you. This is why I think high schools shouldn't have uniforms. "However, recently famous designers (*desainâ*) make uniforms which are cute (*kawaî*)."

Besides discouraging discrimination, uniforms possess another economical (*keizaiteki*) aspect: They are supposedly less expensive than ordinary clothes. I was impressed with the large number of students who said they liked uniforms and appreciated their economic sense and the convenience of not having to choose their clothes everyday. A phrase frequently heard was and "I never have to think about what to wear" and that uniforms make getting ready for school "easy" (*raku*). "Uniforms are so convenient (*benri*) because they save me the trouble (*tema*) of picking clothes every day." In addition, "Because young people don't have much money and can't always buy clothes, they can wear uniforms to funerals and weddings."

However, it should be mentioned here that many parents argue that uniforms are not necessarily less inexpensive than ordinary clothes. Some complain of price-fixing and about how uniforms must be purchased at "designated" shops that specialize in uniforms (except for shoes, most uniforms can be worn for three years). "It would be interesting to find out whether these appointed shop owners are related to the school officials who have created all these price-gouging mom and pop shops that are handed down from generation to generation" (see the letter to the editor "Bust the school uniform monopoly", 1997; see also the letter to the editor "Curb exorbitant uniform costs", 1997).

(7) Japanese Ethnocultural and National Identity

Some students linked uniforms to supposedly Japanese virtues and "tradition" (*dentô*). History was often invoked to account for why Japanese wore uniforms: "The uniform system (*seifuku seido*) we see today is connected to the wartime period. A sense of comradeship (*nakama ishiki*) and group consciousness (*gûrûpu ishiki*) was born from a national consciousness (*minzoku ishiki*)." Or as one student explained, "In Japan, since ancient times, it has been said that 'disheveled clothes, confused mind (*fukusô no midare wa kokoro no midare*)'. A person must be resolute and firm in front of others (*hitomae*) and do things right." Another student stated that "From ancient times, anything that did not fit in with the group (*wa*; literally circle) was considered bad. 'The nail that sticks out get hammered down.'" This is called life in a homogenous society (*dôshitsu shakai*)." According to another student,

> In Japan from ancient times, being the same (*dôitsusei*) has been highly thought of. Being the same as others was the correct way. This way of thinking has been handed down to us today. Presently, though the use of uniforms has decreased a bit, the actuality is that the eyes of others (*seken no me*) prefer to see people wearing uniforms rather than ordinary clothes (*shifuku*).

Certain national characteristics of the Japanese were associated with uniforms. For instance, "The consciousness of being affiliated (*shozoku suru*) with some place is very strong among Japanese", and "Uniforms make us work and study harder, so as for the spiritual aspect (*seishinmen*) of the Japanese, they perform an important role." Some pointed to the sense of security uniforms provide: "Japanese seek feelings of security (*anshinkan*) and solidarity (*ittaikan*), so if other people wear different clothes, it makes them feel extremely uneasy (*fuan*). Even though we are laughed at by people from other countries, wearing the same clothes makes us feel secure (*anshin suru*)." A special aesthetics of the Japanese also made an appearance: "Japan is a country that emphasizes the beauty of uniformity (*tôitsu no bi*)." Also, "Perhaps because Japanese prefer to visually (*shikakuteki ni*) and sensuously (*kankakuteki ni*) have things standardized (*tôitsu sareru*), many units (*shûdan*) use uniforms."

Japanese national traits – harmony, unity, politeness and personal appearance – were closely associated in the minds of many students. "Because uniforms have an image (*imêji*) of good manners (*reigi tadashiku*) and cleanliness (*seiketsu*), I think from now on they should be regarded as very useful (*chôhô*) in Japan." Discussing the outfit of the typical white-collar worker, one student observed that "First of all, Japan is a country where appearance (*gaiken*) and looks (*mitame*) are used to compete with others, and suits, as a type of uniform, look better than jeans or T-shirts. So, in order not to be rude to others, you must get others to like you" (though one student warned that "You can't determine one's personality just from appearance (*gaiken*)").

Japanese look very carefully at one's personal appearance (*gaiken no minari*). Even if one is just a bit disheveled, people will ordinarily have a bad impression of that person. For example, if a company employee wears a uniform well, people will see harmony (*kyôchôsei*) and cleanliness (*seiketsu*) and have a good impression of that person. In a company, uniforms have the job of giving customers a good impression. Uniforms are a method of gaining the trust of customers.

In Japan, comrades (*nakama*) and organization (*soshiki*) are important. Uniforms can be used as a sign of comradeship and strengthen unity (*kessoku-ryoku*). The appearance of uniforms increases the feeling that 'everyone is the same.' That's to say, when I see someone in ordinary clothes (*shifuku*) I think that person is an enemy. There's evidence that since ancient times Japanese wore uniforms. Even when people tried to get rid of them, they ended up wearing them. Because we are so managed, even if we stop wearing uniforms and suddenly became free, everybody would be puzzled.

Though it is very difficult to gauge to what degree uniforms construct ethnonational identity, it is worth at least noting the linkages. One student explained to me how wearing a uniform made her "proud of being Japanese" while another said "Uniforms protect the culture of Japan." Still another explained that "If my country becomes more free like America, we won't need uniforms. But I think it is better to protect Japanese culture." How non-Japanese view dress uniformity in Japan was an issue for some: "Having everybody wear the same clothes may seem odd (*iyô*) if viewed from other countries, but I think that wearing the same clothes as others becomes a type of status (*sutêtasu*)."

Besides the appearance or design of uniforms, their *kigokochi* or "comfort" was also an issue. Not a few students I asked complained that in the winter, uniforms were cold, and in the summer, hot. Isobe has investigated what university students think about middle and high school uniforms and asks: "Doesn't the will to learn and free thinking disappear when growing students wear uncomfortable things while taking classes? (1993: 137). Among forty-nine male middle and high school students, there were some complaints about "too few pockets", "long pants are hot" in the summer and the difficulty of wearing clothes over the uniforms. But a significant response is that "stand-up collars (*tsume-eri*) are restraining" (31.6 percent) and tops are "difficult to move in" (21.1 percent) (Isobe 1993: 139–40). When 117 female students were asked about tops, 23.9 percent of middle school students and 59.1 percent of high school students stated "I don't like it because the design is bad", while 21.6 percent of middle school students and 37.5 percent of high school students stated "I like it because the design is good" (Isobe 1993: 140).

Though it is very difficult to come up with definitive findings, my impression is that about one-third of students strongly support wearing uniforms, another third strongly opposes, while another third has mixed feelings, as expressed in the following quote:

> The image I have of uniforms is not bad. When I see one I get the image of standing up in a correct manner and becoming organized. People who wear uniforms are composed, and more than ordinary clothes (*shifuku*), uniforms lack a casual feel. However, they also have an image of constraint. There's no freedom and they make it feel like it's difficult to breathe. For the unit life (*shûdan seikatsu*) in places like schools, uniforms are one type of integration (*matomari*). The '*sei*' of uniforms (*seifuku*) means restriction (*seigen*), and so I feel like they can restrict. This is why I cannot totally agree with wearing uniforms.

Self-Presentation and Uniforms

Nomura's 1994 investigation of 1,977 students from 28 schools (8 men's, 9 women's and 11 coed schools) (959 male students from 19 schools and 1,018 female students from 20 schools) reveals the importance of the self-presentation mode of coupled roles. Among students of both sexes, "To Express My Self and Individuality" was the most chosen response to the question "When You Go Out, How Do You Decide What To Wear?" (Table 3.14). However, note that extremely few answered "To Be Conspicuous and Gaudy" and a large portion answered "To Be Appropriate to the Occasion (*ba*, which may be glossed as "situation" or "scene")", presumably indicating that self-expressions are displayed within a larger context in which the gaze of others (*seken, hitome, hitomae*) injects elements of self-performance and self-monitoring. Interestingly, it is women who are more concerned with presenting the proper self according to situation. Also, the response "To Be Clean" was relatively high among both men and women, evidence of the symbolic linkages between proper self-presentation and neatness, general order and avoiding "matter out of place."

Uniforms allow one "to look like a typical student" (*gakusei-rashiku mieru*); they "can organize" (*motomari ga dekiru*) student life; make one feel adult-like (*daijin-ppoi*); and are associated with "manners" (*reigi tadashî*) (with strong linkages, one imagines, to distal modes of self-presentation). Though such sentiments imply *kakuitsu-sei* ("standardization" or "uniformity") or distal roles ("I" observes "me"), they must be viewed within the context of other feelings; uniforms provide a "sense of camaraderie" (*nakama ishiki*), "equality" (*byôdô*) and "because everyone has the same clothes I can feel at ease" (*minna ga onaji fukusô de anshin dekiru*). "The uniform promotes

Table 3.14. *"When You Go Out, How Do Decide What To Wear? (choose 2)"*

	Among 959 Males (%)	Among 1,018 Females (%)
To Avoid Being Out of Fashion	153 (16.0)	171 (16.8)
To Express My Self (*jibun-rashiku*) and Individuality (*kosei*)	**468 (48.8)**	**519 (51.0)**
To Be Conspicuous (*medatsu*) and Gaudy (*hade*)	35 (3.6)	6 (0.6)
Not to Be Conspicuous and to Be Plain	88 (9.2)	35 (3.4)
To Be Appropriate to the Occasion (*ba*)	**439 (45.8)**	**710 (69.7)**
To Be Clean (*seiketsu*)	333 (34.7)	361 (35.5)
Listen to Others	17 (1.8)	4 (0.4)
Other	127 (13.2)	53 (5.2)

Source; Nomura (1994: 231; modified, emphasis mine).

democracy in civilian schools and military academies by eliminating the social class differences of the outer world" (Joseph 1986: 79).[14] On the negative side, uniforms "prevent one from self-assertion" (*jiko shuchô dekinai*) (Isobe 1993: 143) (or if phrased differently: my "I" observes my "me" too much).

Funada's study of 494 young men and women is interesting because it reveals differences in attitude between elementary and middle school students in their attitudes toward uniforms and for what it says about changes in self-perception and self-presentation after elementary school students become middle school students (note the change in Questions/Statements 4, 5, 6 and 7). The gender variable plays a role in these changes (Table 3.15). Funada reached several conclusions. First, the image that elementary and middle school students have of uniforms is formed from three factors: (1) an "emphasis on uniformity" (*tôitsu-sei jûshi*); (2) physical and psychological discomfort; and (3) the importance of "refinement" or "being polished" (*senren-sa*). She notes, however, that after entering middle school, the factor of "physical and psychological discomfort" becomes more salient. Second, the awareness of being an "individual uniform wearer" and the awareness of being a "uniform wearer as a member of a group" are deeply "intertwined" (which, of course, is the point of school socialization). Third, there is a difference between female and male students, with the former being more receptive and less resistant *in general* to the wearing of uniforms. However, we should not assume that this means female students wholeheartedly accept and advocate uniforms, since Funada's fourth conclusion is that there is a conspicuous change in female attitudes toward uniforms during the transition from elementary to middle school (Funada 1992: 60–1). Note that for Question/Statement 2 ("With Uniforms, Everyone Has the Same Clothes on So I Can Feel at Ease") 68 percent of female elementary school students answer "I think so" compared to 50 percent of female middle school students (for males, the change is from 55 percent to 47 percent). For Question/Statement 3 ("Uniforms Look Neat and Are Student-like *[gakusei-rashî]*") 77 percent of female elementary school students answer "I think so" compared to 55 percent for female middle school students (for males, the change is from 56 percent to 59 percent). For Question/Statement 4 ("Uniforms Are the Appropriate Clothes to Wear in School") 74 percent of female elementary school students answer "I think so" compared to 44 percent of female middle school students (for males, there is no change). For Question/Statement 5 ("By Wearing Uniforms Student Life Can Be Organized") 78 percent of female elementary school students answer "I think so" compared to 38 percent of female middle school students who answer 38 percent (for males, the change is from 49 percent to 37 percent). For Statement/Question 6 ("Detailed Rules for Uniforms Are Troublesome") 10 percent of female elementary school students answer "I think so", but female middle school students answer 62 percent (for males, the change is from 31 percent to 54 percent). For the Question/Statement 7 ("I Don't Like Wearing Uniforms But There's Nothing I Can Do About It") 10 percent of female elementary school students answer "I think so" compared to 32 percent of female middle school students (for males, the change is from 25 percent to 24 percent) (Table 3.15).

One can speculate that perhaps these changes in attitude among female students is due to a keener sense of fashion among young women who are accordingly more apt to notice how school regulations and culture limit feminine forms of self-expression.

Gender Differences

Many assume that male students are not as interested in appearance as female students, especially "young ladies" or *ojôsama*, a word which denotes fashionable but over-protected young ladies who have good breeding but are charmingly naive (literally, a polite term for "your daughter"). Female

Table 3.15. *Attitude of 494 Elementary and Middle School Students Toward Uniforms* *

Statement/Question		I Don't Think So	Either Way	I Think So
(1) Is Wearing Uniforms Proper (*tôzen*)?	**All**	12	34	54
	Elementary Female	10	31	59
	Elementary Male	13	36	52
	Middle School Female	16	38	46
	Middle School Male	9	32	59
(2) With Uniforms, Everyone Has the Same Clothes on So I Can Feel at Ease	**All**	11	35	54
	Elementary Female	6	26	68
	Elementary Male	13	32	55
	Middle School Female	12	38	50
	Middle School Male	11	42	47
(3) Uniforms Look Neat and Are Student-Like (*gakusei-rashî*)	**All**	10	23	61
	Elementary Female	4	19	77
	Elementary Male	14	31	56
	Middle School Female	9	36	55
	Middle School Male	11	31	59
(4) Uniforms Are the Appropriate Clothes to Wear in School	**All**	10	38	53
	Elementary Female	3	23	74
	Elementary Male	15	37	47
	Middle School Female	9	47	44
	Middle School Male	11	42	47
(5) By Wearing Uniforms Student Life Can Be Organized	**All**	13	37	50
	Elementary Female	4	17	78
	Elementary Male	14	36	49
	Middle School Female	17	45	38
	Middle School Male	15	47	37
(6) Detailed Rules for Uniforms Are Troublesome	**All**	25	35	40
	Elementary Female	44	46	10
	Elementary Male	29	41	31
	Middle School Female	14	24	62
	Middle School Male	15	31	54
(7) I Don't Like Wearing Uniforms But There's Nothing I Can Do About It	**All**	41	36	23
	Elementary Female	55	34	10
	Elementary Male	47	27	25
	Middle School Female	26	43	32
	Middle School Male	37	39	24

* In percentages
Source; Funada (1992: 59; modified, emphasis mine).

students are concerned with being "wrapped" in "brand name uniforms" that announce their schools; their concern is not with the educational quality of the school, but rather its image as portrayed by perception of the uniform. Such thinking must be understood within the context of Japan's highly gendered schooling system. Males and females are generally socialized to have different views of educational goals; though there are exceptions, the former view it as a means to long-term, steady employment, while the latter see it as a means to improve their chances in securing a marriage partner. Among female students, then, appearance and marriage prospects are closely linked, and displaying one's self as a woman who is interested in short-term employment as an "office lady" (see Chapter 4) followed by motherhood overrides more intellectual concerns (Sugiyama 1994).

Surveys reveal interesting gender differences. For example, there is evidence that females, more than males, choose which high school to attend based on its uniform (Nomura 1994: 233), and this probably explains the use of books such as Mori's among female students (1985, 1993). A survey by Nomura suggests that female students appear to like their uniforms more than male students, especially the traditional "sailor" type of uniform. Unlike young men, only 5.1 percent (for "sailor") and 12.4 percent (for blazer) of young women said that they "hate" their uniforms, while 23.3 percent (for stand-up collar) and 19.3 percent (blazer) of young men said they strongly dislike their uniforms (Tables 3.16 and 3.17) (see also Tables 3.18 and 3.19).

For female students who are proud of their uniforms common responses as to why included: "Because it is my school's uniform"; "It is cute (*kawai*)"; "It has tradition"; and "It feels clean (*seiketsu*)." For female students who are not proud of their uniforms common responses were: "I hate it because others (*seken no hito*) can know what school I attend"; "It is gloomy (*kurai*)"; and "The old design embarrasses me" (Nomura 1994: 238).

For male students who are proud of their uniforms, common responses as to why included: "Because it is the uniform of the school I wanted to attend"; "A uniform allows me to feel the tradition at my school which has an old history"; "Because of my love for my school (*aikôshin*)"; and "As a student it is appropriate clothing and I have no problems wearing it". For male students who are not proud of their uniforms common responses were: "Because it is the uniform of the school I didn't want to attend"; "Because I don't like the design and I'm embarrassed to wear it"; "Because it is old fashioned and I am embarrassed to wear it." Some said they thought uniforms were "strange looking" (Nomura 1994: 238).

What kinds of uniforms do students like? Male students seem to have a more conservative attitude. Female students appear to like the blazer type more than the traditional "sailor uniform" (though the latter is still popular)

Table 3.16. *"Do You Like Your Uniform?"*

	I Like It	I Don't Like It Too Much	I Hate It
Stand-Up Collar (490 Students)	131 (26.7%)	245 (50.0%)	114 (23.3%)
Blazer (409 Students)	117 (28.6%)	213 (52.1%)	79 (19.3%)

Source; Nomura (1994: 236).

Table 3.17. *"Do You Like Your Uniform?"*

	I Like It	I Don't Like It Too Much	I Hate It
Sailor Uniform (252 Students)	137 (54.4%)	102 (40.5%)	13 (5.1%)
Blazer (549 Students)	222 (40.4%)	259 (47.2%)	68 (12.4%)

Source; Nomura (1994: 239).

Table 3.18. *"Are You Proud of Your Uniform?"*

	Yes	Not Too Much	No
Among 796 Female Students	272 (**34.2%**)	412 (51.8%)	112 (**14.1%**)
Among 899 Male Students	167 (**18.6%**)	475 (52.8%)	257 (**28.6%**)

Source; Nomura (1994: 235, 237; modified; emphasis mine).

Table 3.19. *"Are You Proud of Your Uniform?"*

	Yes	Not Too Much	I Hate It
Among 899 Male Students	248 (**27.6%**)	458 (50.9%)	193 (21.5%)
Among 801 Female Students	359 (**44.8%**)	361 (45.1%)	81 (**10.1%**)

Source; Nomura (1994: 235, 237; modified; emphasis mine).

and a somewhat surprising number – about half – of male students liked uniforms with *tsume-eri* (stand-up collar), on particularly black uniforms, which in the words of one student "look good" (Tables 3.20 and 3.21). Preferences for certain colors also reveal interesting gender differences (though both sexes basically prefer the "traditionally" conservative colors of black and navy blue). Very few females like black, though a salient majority like navy blue (still a relatively traditional choice). Among male students, there is more variety, though about half have a preference for black (Table 3.22). Though many students (especially female) complain about lack of choice and diversity, it is interesting how, for the most part, they still (according to Nomura's 1994 survey), prefer colors usually associated with student uniforms.

Table 3.20. *"What Type of Uniform Do You Like?"*

	Sailor Uniform	Blazer	Jacket, Bolero	One-Piece	Other
803 Female Students	218 (27.2%)	**442 (55.0%)**	69 (8.6%)	20 (2.5%)	54 (6.7%)

Source; Nomura (1994: 243; modified, emphasis mine).

Table 3.21. *"Which Type of Uniform Do You Like?"*

	Stand-Up Collar (tsume-eri)	Blazer	Other
900 Male Students	449 (49.9%)	317 (35.2%)	134 (14.9%)

Source; Nomura (1994: 242).

Table 3.22. *"What Color Do You Like for a Uniform?"*

	Black	Navy Blue	Grey	Green	Other
900 Male Students	**475 (52.8%)**	**257 (28.5%)**	60 (6.7%)	23 (2.6%)	85 (9.4%)
803 Female Students	**50 (6.2%)**	**597 (74.3%)**	104 (13.0%)	16 (2.0%)	36 (4.5%)

Source; Nomura (1994: 243, 244; modified, emphasis mine).

Gender differences are also notable to some degree concerning regulations (i.e. school's official gaze). As Table 3.23 indicates, female students believe, more than male students, that school regulations are strict. As one young woman said, "If the rules are too strict I end up wanting to resist them. If they are too permissive, it seems that others think that our school has no education. There should be a compromise" (Nomura 1994: 241). According to one young man, "Each detail [of the regulations] is annoying. This type of education makes our individuality disappear. I want an education that can make us beautiful inside." The importance of self-expression is evident in what another male student said: "Because each person has a different face and personality, I think that even clothes should express our individuality" (Nomura 1994: 240).

Table 3.23. *"What Do You Think About School Uniform Regulations?"*

	Strict	*Can Agree With*	*Permissive*
900 Male Students	312 (34.7%)	442 (49.1%)	146 (16.2%)
803 Female Students	335 (41.7%)	403 (50.2%)	65 (8.1%)

Source; Nomura (1994: 239, 241; modified, emphasis mine).

Even in schools that do not have uniforms, young women seem to feel the pressure of the gaze more than young men (Table 3.24). Female students mentioned being warned about the length of their skirts, certain colors, blouses not buttoned high enough and wearing clothes that are too "gaudy" (*hade*) (Nomura 1994: 245). Female students also think about what to wear more than male students (Table 3.25) and believe that their parents would prefer that their school had uniforms (Nomura 1994: 246).

Table 3.24. *"Have You Ever Been Warned about Your Clothing?"*

	Yes	*No*
58 Male Students	0 (%)	58 (100%)
212 Female Students	37 (17.5%)	175 (82.5%)

Source; Nomura (1994: 245, modified, emphasis mine).

Table 3.25. *"Is Thinking about What You Will Wear Troublesome?"*

	Very Much So	Not a Big Problem	It's Enjoyable
59 Male Students	2 (3.4%)	54 (91.5%)	3 (5.1%)
211 Female Students	64 (30.3%)	126 (59.7%)	21 (10.0%)

Source; Nomura (1994: 244; modified, emphasis mine).

Should there be uniforms? In one survey, more females than males answered "yes" (Tables 3.26 and 3.27). If so, why or why not? Tables 3.28 and 3.29 reveal the opinions of students according to sex. Convenience appears to be a big concern (as revealed in responses to the question "Don't Have to Think about What I Will Wear Each Day") as is the economical side of uniforms (Table 3.28). As for reasons why there should not be uniforms, the issue of self-determination (see Table 3.29 "One Should Judge by Oneself What to Wear According to Age, Individuality and Place") carries significant weight, as does a dislike of over-standardization ("It Is Strange to Have Everyone Wearing the Same Clothes") and too much control ("It Always Feels as if One Is Being Managed (i.e. Clothing Violations)").

Table 3.26. *"Should Your School Have Uniforms?"*

	Yes	No
957 Male Students	637 (66.6)	320 (33.4)
1,016 Female Students	788 (77.6)	228 (22.4)

Source; Nomura (1994: 248; emphasis mine).

Table 3.27. *"Should Your School Have Uniforms?"*

	Yes	No
59 Male Students	8 (13.6)	51 (86.4)
214 Female Students	58 (27.1)	156 (72.9)

Source; Nomura (1994: 248; emphasis mine).

Table 3.28. *Reasons There Should Be Uniforms (may choose two reasons)*

Reason	637 Male Students (%)	788 Female Students (%)
They Foster a Sense of Camaraderie (*nakama ishiki*)	83 (13.0)	54 (6.9)
Maintain a Sense of Fairness. By Wearing Them Problems of Discrimination Do Not Arise	**121 (19.0)**	**194 (24.6)**
Don't Have to Think about What I Will Wear Each Day	**495 (77.7)**	**702 (89.1)**
Dignified Tradition Can Be Felt and Handed Down from Senior to Junior Students	32 (5.0)	23 (2.9)
They Are Appropriate to School Life	96 (17.9)	124 (15.7)
Even Off Campus the Comradeship of Students and Teachers Is Easy to See	67 (10.5)	46 (5.8)
Provide Uniformed (*tôitsu sareta*) Beauty of the Group	88 (13.8)	135 (17.1)
They Are Economical	**194 (30.5)**	**298 (37.8)**

Source; Nomura (1994: 247–9; modified, emphasis mine).

Resisting the Gaze

The politico-economic elites behind the official ideology hope to transform distal roles (e.g. "acting like a good student") into coupled roles (e.g. "being a good student") in which one acts enthusiastically and unquestioningly in support of official projects. But in spite of the best efforts of the state and its economic allies, individual subjectivities are imperfectly reproduced. There is no such thing as total socialization, no matter how totalizing and hegemonic a system may be. Subjectivity, which always involves a "subject" (i.e. agent), is too elaborate and complex a process to be a mere microcosm of socio-political operations, and it is in practices of "resistance consumption" where the "expression" side of self-presentation and the agentiveness of social actors clearly manifests themselves. In Chapter 6 I discuss resistance consumption and how students subvert school regulations, but here a few examples will suffice.

Table 3.29. *Reasons There Should Not Be Uniforms*

Reason	320 Male Students (%)	456 Female Students (%)
One Should Judge Individually What to Wear According to Age, Individuality and Place	**153 (47.8)**	**158 (69.3)**
Not Everyone Looks Good in a Uniform	23 (7.2)	18 (7.9)
It Is Strange to Have Everyone Wearing the Same Clothes	**98 (30.6)**	77 (33.8)
It Is Unpleasant to Have the Same Clothes as Others	33 (10.3)	18 (7.9)
One's [Fashion] Sense Is Not Fostered if Clothes Are Always Regulated	37 (11.6)	26 (11.4)
It Always Feels as if One Is Being Managed (i.e. Clothing Violations)	**154 (48.1)**	88 (38.6)
It Is Not Clean to Wear the Same Thing Everyday	46 (14.4)	51 (22.3)
It Is Economical Because One Can Wear the Same Clothes at Home	45 (14.1)	20 (8.8)

Source; Nomura (1994: 247–50; modified, emphasis mine).

By far the most common example (and from the number of individuals who do it, the most acceptable) of resisting the official gaze is *rûzu sokusu* (loose socks), which started out as a subversion of the standard white socks that most female students wear. Many female students claim that the baggy, loose socks (which are sometimes glued to the legs) make their legs look thinner (though a few say it makes them look like they have "elephant legs").[15] Another obvious object/agency of individualistic self-expression among both male and female students is hair dyeing. Light brown hair (*chapatsu*) is very popular, though rust, blond, orange, red, green and blue can also be seen. Some students claim that "black hair is boring", or that different colored hair matches clothes better. One young woman in high school describes dyed hair as "cute (*kawaii*) and colorful".

Sometimes acts of resistance are minor. As one student told me, "School-children often crush down the backs of their shoes as a mild form of rebellion against authority." One teacher was forced to apologize to her students after she put pins in their shoes to prevent them from flattening the backs of their shoes ("Teachers put pins in students' shoes to stop the rebelling", 1998). However, some acts of resistance are not minor. A disturbing "fashion accessory" adopted by students as a challenge to authority is knives (Otake 1998a). In some areas, recent stabbings prompted teachers to inspect children's belongings at schools ("Children's belongings to be checked", 1998).

Some students, even though in uniform, adopt an "untidy fashion" (*darashinai fuasshon*) as a way to resist, and I have been surprised at the number of uniformed students with disheveled uniforms, earrings, body piercing and hair dyed yellow, orange and green (leading one to wonder what actually does go on at their schools). Indeed, it should be pointed out that some schools are remarkably lax in their interpretation of how students may present themselves while in uniform, as if aware of just how hard it is to enforce regulations. Sometimes authorities give in to fashion pressures; four public schools "will officially allow girls to wear uniform skirts as short as five centimeters above the knees", saying "freedom of choice" is important, but according to one official, "in the end, schools couldn't prevail over fashion" ("Chiba schools OK short skirts in concession to fashion trend", 1997).

It is very difficult to judge just how widespread resistance to school regulations are, especially since the media, in a society focused on rules, regulations and ritualized forms of self-presentation, jumps on any phenomenon considered a violation of convention. Perhaps this is why we should keep in mind that

> The media may project an image of today's teens as brown-haired girls offering companionship for cash (*enjo kôsai*) [see Chapter 6] and teenage boys with knives in their pockets, but it is also a reality that far greater numbers of teenagers attend schools that regulate even the color of their underpants (Morikawa 1998).

Notes

1. Besides the grander ideological forces driving the donning of uniforms, there are other more purely commercial interests that propagate the usage of regulated clothing. This fact is illustrated in the numerous industry associations that represent and organize clothes manufacturers. For example, the *Zenkoku gakkô fuku rengôkai* (National School Clothing Federation), established in 1955, has an annual *fuasshonshô* ("fashion show") at which school uniforms display their products. The slogan of their 1994 meeting was "Building a bright (*akarui*) school spirit begins with the proper wearing of uniforms" (Nomura 1994: 251). There is also the Japan

Uniform Manufacturers Association (more literally, the Japan Federation of Clothing Manufacturing Associations) (*Nihon hifuku kôgyô kumiai rengôkai*; abbreviated to *Nichihiren*) which publishes detailed codes on what constitutes the "Standard Type of Student Uniform". Founded in November 1959, it is officially linked to the Ministry of International Trade and Industry. It has five branches (which are listed as associations) and is linked to nine other industrial associations. The official purpose of this organization is the "planning for the rationalization and stability of management of members and association members and carrying out business necessary for planning the development and improvement of small- and middle-sized manufacturers of clothing for domestic demand". Mention might also be made of the Japan Apparel Federation (*Nihon iryô hôseihin kyôkai*; abbreviated to *Nichihôkyô*), which was established in December 1973, and is also linked to the Ministry of International Trade and Industry. The official purpose of this organization, which is an incorporated association (*shadan hôjin*), states that "through the rationalization and comprehensive improvement of the apparel manufacturing industry, [this organization] aims for the production, distribution, trade, consumption and healthy development of apparel. It contributes to the maintenance of the rich clothing habits of the nation" (*Zenkoku kakushu dantai meikan* (National Directory of Organizations) 1993: 751–2). See also Nomura on the role of the "uniform industry" (*seifuku gyôkai*) (1994).

2. For a treatment of uniforms during the early Meiji period, see Ishizuki (1992: 196–239). For a brief discussion of the history of female students, see Nomura (1993: 199–204).

3. Cf. Sakamoto (1986: 163–75; 176–81).

4. Due to Japan's undigested wartime past and resistance, the national flag (Hinomaru) and anthem (Kimigayo) did not become "official" until 1999.

5. See Harada and Hasegawa (1996: 27) for price ranges of preschooler uniforms.

6. Centralized education systems seem to produce similar scenes, cf. a scene in France: "Every schoolday morning and evening, the streets of Paris are filled with children and teenagers staggering under the weight of big, hard-sided backpacks, groaning with textbooks." Sixth-graders "carry more than a quarter of their average body weight – a burden whose adult equivalent would be over 40 pounds. But for a 70-pound third grader, a 15-pound backpack is heavy no matter how you weigh it" (Trueheart 1998).

7. Perhaps the meaning of dark colors resonates with the aesthetic of *jimi*, which may be interpreted as plain, sober or quiet.

8. See also White for description of regulations and uniforms (1994: 223–5).

9. However, Hara reports that among ninety local state ("public") schools in Nagano Prefecture, 47 percent do not have uniforms and are "liberalized schools" (*jiyûka kô*) and 53 percent have uniforms (1996: 64–5).

10. One commentator notes: "The way a teacher dresses can affect students. If a teacher is neatly dressed, the students might imagine that the teacher will attend a meeting or have a date with someone later. If a teacher's hair is disheveled, students may think he overslept that morning" (Kawachi 1996). See also Nakamura (1996) and "City to make teachers don uniforms" (1996).

11. However, another Japanese woman has a different opinion and believes that people should not judge by appearances: "I think it is a big problem because it is connected with racial discrimination" (from a letter to "Readers' Forum: What do you think of the recent trend in which people dye their hair brown in chapatsu fashion?" 1996).

12. See also "Students judge schools by their uniform" (1992).

13. For an example of how memories are built around school uniforms, see Hirosawa (1995).

14. See also Coser (1962: 44); Gillis (1981: 169–70); Musgrove (1965: 159–60); and Young and Willmott (1962: 175–7).

15. A stir was created when the High School Baseball Association of Kagawa Prefecture prohibited female managers from wearing loose socks in dugouts ("Females told to keep their loose socks out of dugouts", 1998).

4

Patterns and Practices of Dress Uniformity

In this chapter, I continue the analysis started in the previous chapter by discussing the last two phases of the three-phase life-cycle ("de-uniformization" and "re-uniformization"). Then, in order to demonstrate the effects of the massive politico-economic forces in the construction of subjectivity, I provide examples of patterns and practices of dress uniformity by placing them on a "continuum of uniformity". Specifically, I examine patterns of dress uniformity among "office ladies" and public transportation workers.

Second Phase: De-uniformizing

Regardless of what many may think, time spent at a university or college in Japan is rarely for studying. Indeed, Japan's institutions of higher education do not, for the most part, accomplish their proclaimed aims (though from the perspective of statist and corporatist interests, they are useful as selection devices and storage centers for labor). They are, in fact, institutional tokens, meant to stand for what are called universities and colleges outside Japan. Their actual purpose – regardless of their promising and inspiring pledges found in glossy and colorful brochures – is quite different from what one would ordinarily believe. The lack of interest in university education, of course, is not true for all students and schools, and there are some exceptions, especially in the science and engineering programs which, supposedly, are of better quality than social science and humanities curricula. But for the most part, Japan's universities and colleges are severely criticized domestically and internationally as being nothing more than "leisure lands", "playgrounds", and "play lands".

Why the lack of interest and effort at the tertiary level of education? It is often said that in Japan, university and college students neglect their studies because the tertiary "educational" experience is a period of well-deserved rest and relaxation between their high-pressure high school days and the drudgery of work. University life is regarded as time off for good behavior (i.e. studying hard to pass the examinations to enter university) from the heavy demands of a hyper-rationalized society. Indeed, it is easy to make the argument that the de-uniformizing period is possible because the gaze of the politico-economic powers is not as focused on students during their time spent at university. This is because, from the view of the politico-economic elite, students have already been socialized and received basic skills, and higher education functions as the final screening device and as a labor repository until the economy is ready for them (Refsing 1992). This is why after students have been admitted to a university, there is no need to study.

The de-uniformizing period is "betwixt and between" childhood and adulthood, socialization and employment, training and production and studying and working.

The de-uniformizing period is liminal, and at least in comparison to what went before and what will come after, is astructural or even anti-structural in the Turnerian sense (1969).[1] This de-uniformization and its antistructural features are relative since there are always social conventions that shape uniformity in dress to some degree. In any case, while in university or college (and, one imagines, at vocational schools), students taste freedom, express their individuality (*kosei*), socialize, experiment, mature and learn what types of self-presentation will *not* be acceptable after entering the world of work with all its responsibilities. It must be stressed that these students are not yet considered adults, or *shakaijin* ("member of society"; literally, "social person").

Concretely, de-uniformizing has its own anti-structural code which takes on a great variety of permutations. For males and females, this code prescribes jeans, sneakers (both associated with leisure), untucked plaid shirts and long hair (males), though many students would certainly pass as clean-cut. Some students, however, have what may charitably be called in these politically correct times, an earthy sense of humor. In one class I taught, a male student wore a T-shirt with a picture of a penis wearing a tie, captioned with the words "You can dress him up, but you can't take him out". Another student wore a T-shirt with a picture of two cartoon dogs in sunglasses copulating under the words: "Bury the bone". I do not know if any of the students had their sensibilities offended by such clothes. Recently, the unisex and 1960s styles have seen a revival among the young. Some female students experiment with flashier (as of this writing in 1999, black platform boots are in vogue), even provocative styles (e.g. short, tight leather skirts).

How Gender Restrains De-Uniformizing[2]

In this section I examine the dress code of Takasu International College (pseudonym) in order to show how the variable of gender constrains de-uniformizing practices. The purpose of this section is to illustrate how women's dress – associated with daily practices, acts and microrituals – is more regulated than men's even during a period of general de-uniformizing. At least at the tertiary educational level, there are sites where women are expected to accept more doses of discipline than men.[3] Creating docile female bodies is more socially acceptable. At Takasu, students are expected to present themselves as good *Takasusei-rashî* (typical Takasu students). This role, however, does not only have significance for the stage/scene known as Takasu International College. Playing the student role at Takasu is actually a rehearsal for other future performances and sets the foundations for other roles, such as mother, wife, worker (specifically "office lady") and a good "Japaneseness". As I have explained elsewhere (McVeigh 1996b, 1997b, 1997d), all of these roles and their concomitant values are interlinked. In particular, "Japaneseness" is built through an ironic, complex discourse centered on incessant talk about "internationalization" (i.e. nationalization). Here it should be noted that the literal name Takasu International College in Japanese is Takasu Women's Junior College, but when rendered into English school authorities use "International" to present a more cosmopolitan "institutional face". In terms of clothing, it is the kimono, worn at school events and special activities in displays of self-performance, that exhibits important messages about the wearer's identity as a "Japanese woman". Here a few words about the kimono are in order. In terms of clothing, national identity is expressed by both sexes by donning the kimono. Individuals usually seen in kimonos or "traditional Japanese dress" are *sumô* wrestlers (when not wrestling), traditional comic storytellers (*rakugoka*), Buddhist priests (*obôsan*), waitresses (*nakai*) in traditional restaurants and hotels (called *ryotei* or *ryokan*) and traditional artisans. However, as repositories of the "national spirit", women are closely associated with this "traditional" clothing, so that kimonos tightly link Japanese femininity with national identity. Indeed, kimonos might be described as a type of national identity uniform, particularly for women. Women's kimonos actually implicate an entire range of behavioral and bodily prescriptions, proper manners, and national identity. Putting on a kimono is actually a rather long and complicated affair (there are *kitsuke* or "dressing" schools for kimono), and traditionally a kimono comes in a "kimono kit", a *komono*, which, besides the kimono itself, includes ten items, such as special underwear, belt (*obi*), neck bands, waistbands, *tabi* socks, *zôri* (for summer) or *geta* (for winter) sandals and handbag.[4] The colorful versions are usually worn for important rites of passages (e.g. graduations, weddings, funerals, etc.), events considered heavy with "Japaneseness" (tea ceremony, neighborhood festivals (*matsuri*), certain holidays), New Years, welcome ceremonies at companies, other formal festivities and, of course, weddings. This national costume speaks "kimonoese" (Dalby 1993), a language that announces the wearer's age, the season and personal taste.[5] Reportedly, due to expense, few opportunities to wear them and the difficulty associated with donning them, kimonos are in decline (Tatsuta 1997; Mizui 1998a). However, *yukata* appear to be more popular (Mizui 1998b).

Like many women's junior colleges in Japan, Takasu produces future "office ladies" (relatively low-paid secretaries who work as short-term labor) who are expected to be feminine in appearance and attitude. Though Takasu does not require students to wear an actual uniform, it does request that they observe school regulations about dress. Takasu has its own "semi-uniform" whose code is spelled out in a student guidebook. Though students may wear their own clothes, this dress code prescribes feminine clothes and prohibits jeans and other "unladylike" attire (faculty and administrative personnel are also prohibited from wearing jeans). Students must also purchase white pumps that are only worn in the main building. Make-up and other accessories complete the costume that students don while performing as "ladylike" students on campus. The dislike of women wearing jeans is not limited to Takasu. In the "Do's and Don'ts column section of the business section of a newspaper, it was related how, after a customer complained of seeing a female bank employee wearing jeans to work (female workers often change into company uniforms after they arrive at work), the bank forbade female workers to wear the offending clothing even while commuting to and from the office ("Japanese Business", 1994).

Jeans are probably the most student-like (*gakusei-rashi*) piece of clothing, and like students anywhere, Takasu students stated that they symbolize casualness, comfort, recreation, sociability and youth. In fact, old jeans (as well as sneakers), symbolize American culture and are in high-demand in some circles. For serious collectors, jeans can range in price from ¥100,000 to ¥230,000 (about US $910 to $2,090 in 1999) (Kageyama 1997). However, the Takasu administration has a different point of view, and associates the same garment with negative meanings: anti-establishment sentiments, protesting students, a lack of discipline, leisure and most importantly, unladylike behavior. As the most popular type of garment the world has ever seen, jeans have become a *tabula rasa* garment since the 1960s, upon which has been written a rich range of meanings about gender, sexual relations, political orientation, status and leisure (Davis 1992: 58–76, Friedmann 1987). Students wearing jeans are simply not allowed into the main Takasu building, and both the administration and students take this rule seriously. I heard that a student who had no classes in the main building phoned a Takasu professor who was waiting for her report, and asked that she hand it to him somewhere far from the main building, since she had worn jeans that day (she was visiting Takasu's affiliated coed university which does not prohibit jeans).

Students at Takasu are very aware of the reason for the dress code. As one student wrote in a report, "If we make our appearance disorderly (*darashinaku*), then our interior (the way we feel) becomes disorderly (*darashinaku*) ... jeans are not acceptable to society (*shakai*), or in other words, to companies (*kaisha*)" (to the student, there was a connection between "society" and "company" since she pointed out how they are written with the same characters, though inverted). Students were also quick to notice that even when permitted to wear what they wanted, codes were in operation. One student, commenting on the college's annual Christmas party in which students are expected to wear their best as a type of ladylike training, stated that "Even though everyone's individuality was clearly expressed, everyone was in a type of uniform." This same student (rather sarcastically) critiqued, compared and rated what other students wore.

A look at training manuals, written by and primarily for flight attendants, but used by Takasu students training to be OLs ("office ladies"), is in order. In Japan, flight attendants exemplify femininity: "Stewardesses meet the most beautiful ideal of womanhood: intelligent, beautiful and gentle," according to the editor of *Stewardess Magazine*, Kumi Kaseya (cited in Landers 1996). In the words of one aspiring flight attendant, "A stewardess doesn't show her inner self [her "I" carefully monitors her "me"], but there's a strength inside." Airlines have strict rules about self-presentation. "All Nippon Airways, for instance, forbids earrings more than one-tenth of an inch in diameter, hair below the shoulders or more than one ring ... The airlines rule out women with birthmarks on their wrist, as passengers might be discomfited by their sight." As for fashion, because flight attendants are considered an "elite, trend-setting club", many "Japanese women snap up any designer shoe or cosmetic cream that news reports say is favored by flight attendants" (Landers 1996).

As if pre-empting the complaints about company uniforms that most OLs must wear, students are told by the flight attendant training manuals that though uniforms do not express one's individuality, they are important for "making everyone equal and *tôitsu-bi*" (literally, the "beauty of uniformity") (*JAL suchuwâdesu 9 nin no taiken sekkyakujutsu* 1988: 28). Also, clothes, shoes, make-up, jewelry, accessories and hair style (though some companies, students are reminded, forbid make-up or jewelry) should all receive proper attention, with the aim of giving those around one *kôkan* (good feeling). Tips for how not to be showy are given, since the ideal OL is "clean, elegant and moderate" (*JAL suchuwâdesu no iki iki manâ kôza* 1989: 50). Students are asked to refer to a diagram detailing the proper way one's hair, blouse, accessories, bag, skirt, shoes, stockings, uniform, hands and make-up should be. They are to give themselves points for each item. After all, one is a "walking billboard" for the company (*JAL suchuwâdesu no iki iki manâ kôza* 1989: 112), or for one's school. Not only is bodily dress and adornment important, but so are personal possessions, since how one treats their possessions indicates one's personality. Lockers, work areas and one's immediate work space should be kept neat since "Your desk is a mirror that reflects your character" (*JAL suchuwâdesu no iki iki manâ kôza* 1989: 165).

Training to become an "office lady" can be better appreciated if the role of "microrituals" is understood (this is true for other socializing projects as well). These micropractices are put to use by those in authority at an educational site in order to imbue participants with cherished norms in Japanese society about being "ladylike" and "Japanese" (McVeigh, forthcoming). Obeying rules about bodily dress and adornment, following sociolinguistic conventions and complying with other daily patterned behaviors, prepare the ground for major ceremonies which, in turn, verify the messages of these small actions. The result is a hermeneutic circle, in which the meanings of micropractices and large-scale events reinforce each other. Wearing "ladylike" clothes, white pumps and make-up, and speaking and managing bodily movement in a formalized manner may not appear very significant in themselves. However, if these techniques of self-presentation are carried out daily, an extremely powerful symbolic charge accumulates unawares. Mundane routines that ritualize the body modify belief and shape behavior. These behavioral staples are, in a certain sense, just as important as the more clearly marked events, though the social significance of minor behaviors often goes unnoticed since they are often executed without much conscious effort. But the accumulative weight of incessantly repeated actions and words carry implicit cultural codes that are undoubtedly registered nonconsciously, thereby shaping thought patterns.

Third Phase: Re-uniformizing

The final phase sees students being integrated into the socio-economic order. After graduation and assuming they have secured employment, they are now expected to act like *shakaijin* ("members of society"). Not long after, they should hopefully complete the picture of being a true member of society by marrying and having children. Actually, part way through their tertiary education career (when they turn twenty), many students will participate in the Japanese rite de passage called Adult Day (*Seijin no hi*), held on January 15. This ceremony, held in public halls where young people meet classmates and old friends and according to some, "listen to boring speeches" by local officials, is the first sign that students are being re-uniformized, apparent in how men sport suits or *hakama* (formal pleated skirt) and women (usually) wear kimonos.

For university and college students, probably the most important rite of re-uniformizing is the graduation ceremony, when males don suits and females wear special graduation gowns over stylish dresses. But about one year before graduation, a sign that students are being re-uniformized is their interest in how to manage their self-presentation for job interviews. Bookstores sell manuals on such matters, and students begin shopping for conservatively cut "recruit suits":

> The suits for these students [who are looking for jobs] may appear identical, but the designs are slightly different to match the images of specific careers, such as those in finance, manufacturing, and even the media. For example, students looking for a career in banking are told: "We recommend traditional suits with a center vent and without a tailored waist. Coordinate with a regimental tie. This will help emphasize a clean and sincere character." A navy blue suit with an even striped tie in black and gray is one of the department store's recommendations for would-be bankers. A navy blue suit with a maroon tie with thin green stripes is recommended for the manufacturing sector. It represents a "clean and subdued image", the store says (Hani 1994).

After graduation, students become workers who must be re-uniformized and integrated into the socio-economic order. For many women who become "office ladies" (who are regarded as cheap and expendable labor at many companies), re-uniformizing is expected to increase their docility (though whether it does or not and in what way is problematic; this issue deserves another article). Thus, the wearing of company uniforms is inevitably associated with "office-lady" work.

Make-up and Self-Presentation

For men, symbols of re-uniformization are suits, ties and briefcases. For women, probably the most powerful symbol of re-uniformization is make-up, and unlike other types of bodily adornment, make-up carries special meaning since it symbolizes the dividing line between pre-adult and adult

(as mentioned in Chapter 3 schools typically forbid cosmetics and the wearing of make-up though many students do so anyway). One female university student explained that make-up is part of *jiko hyôgen* (self-expression) and *jiko* PR (self-public relations). Here I will not attempt to answer the old debate of whether wearing make-up is used by patriarchal power structures to control and oppress women, or whether practices associated with make-up are tactics women use to assert their independence, individuality and sexuality (cf. Turner 1974). As usual, the truth lies somewhere between, but I want to view make-up as a key agency in feminine (and to a lesser degree, masculine) self-presentation linked to consumption, commercialization and capital accumulation. Make-up is serious business in Japan. Indeed, Japan

has the second biggest cosmetics market in the world. Recently, two companies have developed computer systems that "customers can use to try on
virtual makeup without worrying about mistakes". From a menu, the user
chooses either "features" or "complexion". In the latter, the computer assesses
the user's face (e.g. "feminine and glamorous"), based on categories of "cute",
"mature", "sharp" and "soft". In the case of "complexion", the computer
judges the user's face to be either "pink" or "yellowish". Based on these
assessments, the computer advises what type of make-up the individual should
use ("Shiseido, Kao offer virtual makeup", 1998).

The use of cosmetics is spreading to younger groups, apparently encouraged
by commercial interests. Using slogans such as "you will be a lady starting
today", "toy manufacturers are fiercely competing in the sales of cosmetics
for girls 12 and younger . . . The manufacturers dispatch make-up consultants
to the toy corners of department stores to teach young girls how to use"
cosmetics. Takara sells a package that includes a heart-shaped bag, two
lipsticks, two bottles of water-soluble fingernail polish, a compact, a bracelet
and a comb ("Toymakers give fresh face to cosmetics mart", 1995). There
are even fashion wigs for children marketed under the name Doki Doki, the
Japanese phrase for "the sound of the heartbeat of someone excited" ("Tops
for tots", 1992; see also "Adults find kids' lotions softer on their skin",
1993).[6]

Recently, in response to the "small face boom", beauty products, special
kits and massage regimens have been introduced that supposedly "shrink"
faces ("Small is big", 1997). One imagines that engaging in such make-up
practices resonate with the aesthetic of cuteness (see Chapters 5 and 6). Such
practices are not just for women. Indeed, the use of cosmetics is also spreading
among men and there are make-up kits just for men. "They dye their hair
brown, they pierce their ear lobes, they trim their eyebrows and they take
loving care of their skin" ("Beautiful boys", 1998), apply "a daily regimen
of lotions and liquids" to their hair (Lazarus 1994a) and follow fashion
magazines as religiously as women do. "Male teens buy facial packs and
may wear foundation makeup for ordinary occasions" (White 1994: 129;
Naito 1998).[7]

Related to cosmetics, of course, is hair care.[8] Though many individuals
do relatively unconventional things to their hair during the de-uniformizing
stage, once they enter corporate culture, they must re-uniformize their hair
care practices that are more in line with what they were taught during the
uniformization phase of their lives. In an article called "Most companies see
black hair as beautiful" it was reported that a survey revealed that 11 percent
of corporate workers in their 20s dye their hair. But according to one company
spokesperson, "We may hire people with brown hair, but we tell them to

stop dyeing their hair after they begin work. We don't want to offend our customers" (1996). The attention that corporate culture gives to hair resonates with school culture. An employee who had dyed his hair brown sued and won a court case against his employer that had fired him because he did not completely dye his hair back to black as ordered by the company. For its part, the company claimed that "he disrupted the harmony of the company" ("Driver wins right to color his hair", 1997).

Regardless of the more conservative side of corporate culture that have a preference for "traditional Japanese" hair color, many individuals, especially women, do dye their hair. Some women like to dye their hair different shades of brown because it allows them to express their individuality, and many say they like light brown because they say their own black hair seems "heavy", "hard" and "stern", but light brown looks "girlish and soft". According to one female university student, "they don't want to be strong like a woman, but want to be pretty, sexy, lovely and weaker than boys. Western women want to be called tough and mature. But a Japanese would get angry if you said that to them" (such sentiments resonate with the aesthetic of "cuteness"; see Chapters 5 and 6).

Continuum of Uniformity

At this point, I want to introduce some order into the discussion by conceptually coordinating degrees of uniformity with forms of self-presentation and the rationalized politico-economic order. Such conceptual coordination can be further elaborated by viewing the positional meanings of the symbolism of uniforms and dress uniformity on a continuum which has a "highly uniform" and an "anti-uniform" end of a continuum (cf. Joseph 1986: 13, 18–19, 200). This scheme is not specific to Japanese society and has universal relevance. Depending on the mix of different variables – age, gender, occupation, place, etc. – the hegemonic structures vary the intensity of their normalizing gaze (*seken*), so that a person regulates his or her attire according to what may be called a "continuum of uniformity" (Table 4.1). The contours of this continuum resonate with styles of self-presentation.

Though the normalizing gaze is always present to some degree, certain social spaces – classrooms, workplaces and arenas for rites of passage and ceremonies – draw its attention and increase its intensity. Social actors are expected to wear uniforms where state projects are being taught, exhibited, or fulfilled. The continuum of uniformity ranges from (1) the extreme of military uniforms to (4) styles that violate social conventions such as being *seken-nami* (average, ordinary standard of *seken*). In between these two poles

Table 4.1. *Continuum of Uniformity and the Correspondence between Dress Uniformity and Self-Presentation*

Highly Uniform ◄——— *Non-Uniform* ———► *Anti-Uniform*			
Distal Role/Performed Self		Coupled Role/Expressed Self	
Integrated into Rationalized Politico-Economic Order		*Not Integrated into Rationalized Politico-Economic Order*	
(1)	(2)	(3)	(4)
Highly Ordered	**Ordered**	**Relatively Ordered**	**Disordered**
Highly Standardized	Standardized	Non-Standardized	Anti-Standardized
Clearly Categorized	Categorized	Uncategorized	Anti-Categorized
Group-Dominated	Group-Oriented	Shows Individuality	Overly Individualistic

are (2) less strictly enforced clothing ensembles (e.g. school uniforms). Also between the poles of (1) and (4) are (3) ordinary or casual clothes (*shifuku*), which more literally means "private" or "personal" clothes" and avoid being too *seken-banare* (different from *seken*, "eccentric", "strange") or *medatsu* ("conspicuous"). How nudity fits into this continuum is admittedly problematic (cf. Joseph 1986: 185–9). In any case, nudity may be intimately bound up with self-presentation, commercialization and commodification, with pornography being a good example of such trends (but see "platform girls" in Chapter 6). Below I elaborate on these different categories and provide examples.

(1) Highly Ordered

As symbols, highly ordered clothing ensembles usually evoke associations of order, control and authority. They also strongly suggest something serious, important and distinct from ordinary activities, and are contrasted with ordinary, casual or plain clothes (*shifuku*; literally "private" or "personal" clothes). As material culture connected to the act of donning, attire differs depending on what type of garments one clothes oneself in: one gets into and wears a uniform, but one puts on and sports casual clothes. More specifically, highly ordered clothing ensembles are related to formalized actions, standardized responses, disciplined bodies and restrained movements in the service of some collective goal. They are linked to group identification and affiliation, unity of purpose, missions pursued, solidarity, fixed social roles, clarification of duties and commitment to tasks. As ensembles of material culture, military uniforms exemplify such values, with police and security uniforms being somewhat less ordered, next in line in terms of degree of typification. Such uniforms, in fact, are laden with the symbolism of statefulness and are clearly linked to the state core (Chapter 2). However, it is important to point out that:

> The uniform is an artificial construct insofar as one of its characteristics, uniformity, is a matter of definition and learned perception rather than immediately apparent fact. We are taught to look for uniformity in the clothing of a group such as the military and police and to overlook differences; homogeneity is relative and may occur only in the eyes of the beholder (Joseph 1986: 115).

However, state authorities are always keen on softening their image of uniform symbolism. For instance, the National Police Agency was apparently concerned about its institutional appearance and had new uniforms designed: "The new uniforms are more fashionable and are designed to emphasize power and vitality with a smarter look," according to a spokesperson ("New police uniforms show designer touch", 1992). And during the 1998 Nagano Winter Olympics, the international community was presented with "a softer look" when the 6,000 or so police deployed around Nagano donned blue-and-yellow ski parkas instead of their usual riot gear; and shields and helmets were left inside buses ("As world watches Nagano, city endures culture conflict", 1998).

(2) Ordered

Though not as full of statefulness as highly ordered and somewhat removed from the state core, ordered clothing ensembles still stand for and prompt relatively high degrees of standardization, categorization and group orientation. Included in this category are "quasi uniform for occupational dress" (cf. Joseph 1986: 143–66), e.g. nurses,[9] lab technicians, beauticians, waitresses, waiters and other service personnel. "Quasi uniforms are associated with nongovernmental organizations, usually private bureaucracies, including hospitals, airlines, merchant ships, railroads, and religious orders" (Joseph 1986: 149–50). Regulations covering such uniforms are enforced by "private bureaucracies" and are not as strict as "public bureaucracies" (i.e. the military) (Joseph 1986: 150–1).

Also in this category are company uniforms and factory wear, which in Japan are called "work clothes" (*sagyô-i* or *sagyôfuku*). Traditional workmen's outfits that date from the Edo period (1603–1867) are still seen: "There is the clean-looking, all white dress of the sushi boys with their *hachimaki* (headband) and geta [wooden sandals], and the carpenters and gardeners with their *haramaki* (belly-band), baggy breeches, and *jikatabi* (workman's footwear), and sometimes full body tattoos, a kind of permanent uniform" (Lapenta 1983: 114). Sometimes an occupation's "uniform" is highly specialized: 526 new company recruits for a swim-wear maker were sworn in wearing swimming suits in a ceremony at an indoor water resort ("Firms welcome 1.1 million recruits", 1993).

Even many young workers, who are usually regarded as people who eschew conventional forms of appearance, prefer "performance" work, "meaning wearing flashy uniforms and seeing the workplace as a sort of 'stage.'" Such work includes gas stations (attendants often wear smart, colorful uniforms), ski resorts, video rental stores, bookstores, amusement parks and fast-food restaurants (where workers wear head-phones for speedy transmission of orders). In line with this view is another commentator's opinion that young job applicants are only interested in finding "glamour" or "prestige" positions ("It's tight times for part-time workers", 1994), presumably because such jobs offer opportunities for self-performance.

Many uniforms, then, being closely linked to work, labor and production, symbolically condense a range of associations that stand for rationalization, i.e. sociopolitical processes of hierarchization, categorization and standard-ization that, while found in many places, appear particularly salient in Japan (McVeigh 1998a, 1998c). Most school uniforms (already treated in Chapter 3), which are linked to labor since they are worn by individuals training and being primed for the work force and future social roles, probably fall somewhere around the ordered area. However, considering the latitude some schools grant students, not a few fall in the relatively ordered area, while at schools where enforcement of regulations is strict and daily inspections are routine, the highly ordered area may be more appropriate.

The aforementioned semantic associations (or the conceptual–ideological pole of a symbol) are defined and reinforced by the visuality (or the perceptual–sensory pole of a symbol) of uniforms via their aestheticization. As discussed below, many Japanese companies pay particular attention to what is called *tôitsusei* (uniformity, standardization) and *tôitsu-bi* – the "beauty of uniformity" or "uniformed beauty" – and regularly link the introduction of new uniforms with *imêjiappu* (improving the image; from "image up") and with "a strategy for [improving] image and employee management" (*imêji senryaku ya koyô kanri*) (Watanabe 1994: 18).[10] There is, in fact, a lucrative "corporate identity" (CI) business to help corporations "image up". This industry has generated "personal identity" (PI) businesses that specialize in improving an individual's skills at impression management. One such PI business, called Impression Inc., uses its own textbook that explains, among other things, how important first impressions are and how suit designs should compliment the wearer's face and physique, and offers advice on suit materials and necktie patterns. Instruction on the proper combination of shoes, wristwatches, spectacles and other accessories is also given, and specific hairdressers and clothing stores are introduced upon request ("Personal image business is starting to take off", 1990).

Some organizations, it should to be noted, attempt a balance between the "beauty of uniformity" and more distinct forms of attractiveness. For example some airlines in Japan have eliminated hats and gloves because they "convey an image of regimentation and militarism" and without them flight attendants "can express their individual personalities"; "Hats often limit the hairstyle of flight attendants.[11] With hats, they had to wear their hair tied back or bundled up. That can convey an image of tidiness and propriety, but our company would rather promote friendliness by having our flight attendants wear different hairstyles" ("Air Nippon attendants set to lose hats, gloves", 1998).

The aestheticization of company wear is apparent in the view that the uniforms of "office ladies" (see below) in particular should emit "cheerfulness" (*akarusa*) and a "sense of cleanliness" (*seiketsukan*). It must be noted that "being cheerful" is something that many Japanese companies admonish employees (particularly female ones) to be, and some even have special exercises to learn how to embody this attitude. Another example of the aestheticization of work clothes involves a company whose construction workers' uniforms were light green, the same color of their cranes and earth movers, and on Air Nippon, flight attendant uniforms are charcoal gray, which match the interior of the airline's aircraft ("Air Nippon attendants set to lose hats, gloves", 1998).

Thus, uniforms are utilized as symbols, which indicate their multivocal and ambiguous properties. This is apparent in their various usages: impressing clients ("cheerful" and "clean" "office ladies"); convince clients (sharply dressed men in pressed white-collars); advertising (scantily dressed women in identical outfits hawking products in front of stores); "traditional" uniforms (kimonos for ceremonials, special clothes for rites of passage, ceremonial dress for religious purposes); sexualized (women wearing high school uniforms in pornographic magazines).

In the world of sports, uniforms play an obvious role. However, their function is not limited to sports players since fans and "fan clubs" (*ôendan*) identify with their favorite teams and players via donning special attire and carrying material culture. Kelly relates a scene from a baseball game among the fans of the Hanshin Tigers: "Tiger paraphernalia and motifs are everywhere. It is a throbbing sea of yellow and black face paint, of Tiger happi coats [traditional livery coats], Tiger uniform shirts and jerseys and head-bands. It seems as if everyone is wearing a Hanshin baseball cap and beating together a pair of miniature plastic baseball bats to accompany their lusty chants" (1997: 67).

The censure of perceived violations of ordered dress codes are well known in Japanese schools and companies, but castigation occurs in other places. For instance, during the 1998 Winter Olympics, the Japan Olympic Committee was "flooded with calls complaining that free-style skiing gold medalist Tae Satoya did not remove her cap during the medal awards ceremony". For her part, Satoya explained that she did not remove her cap "because my hair was a mess". Soon after the incident, the JOC issued a directive to other Japanese athletes, presumably to maintain Japan's "national face", "to mind their manners at the medals award ceremonies" ("JOC critical of medalist's manners", 1998).

(3) Relatively Ordered

Acts, practices and forms of self-presentation in the relatively ordered area are considerably removed from the state core and have low degrees of statefulness, i.e. the official gaze (*seken*) is not as focused. However, the official gaze still exerts its normalizing influence. If highly ordered and ordered areas on the continuum concern uniforms per se, then the relatively ordered area concern uniformity of dress. In other words, uniforms as conventionally understood are not the only examples of material culture that suggest the saliency of regulated dress in everyday Japan. The relatively ordered category includes what may be called "standardized clothing", which "differs from quasi uniforms in that the former denotes membership in a diffuse, unorganized group and the latter in a specific organization" (Joseph 1986: 144). But the relatively ordered category also includes "leisure wear" (cf. Joseph 1986: 167–81), though what may be worn as leisure may also be, depending on one's occupation, worn for work (Joseph 1986: 167).

Consider the typical attire of the *sararîman* ("salary men", i.e. white-collar workers who receive a salary): standard white shirt, tie,[12] dark suit (almost always blue, grey or black) and dress shoes constitute the typical outfit. Some workers might wear a company pin (*shashô*). In order to appear more "uniform", some young men, concerned with presenting the appropriate "businessman" self, might even carry an empty briefcase. Though if viewed en masse the *sararîman* seems uniformed, compared to the dress of "office ladies" they are actually given more latitude to express themselves (color, tie, cut, style, shoes, shirt, etc.). Recently, there has been talk of Japanese firms relaxing their dress codes, as long as employees abide by the three principles of cleanliness, refinement and modesty, and wear a tie, which seems to remain the "indispensable item for businessmen even in the hot weather" ("Color shirts are 'in,' but no-tie casual look is still 'out'" 1994).[13] However, according to a "Do's and Don'ts in Japanese Business" newspaper column, "There is a need to maintain uniforms because they make employees aware of their responsibilities" ("Uniforms are symbol of professionals", 1994). Even fields that are considered as less "conservative" in regards to appearance, such as journalism, may have strict rules. A worker who was asked to screen applicants for a major newspaper was told to deduct points "from the scores of those who didn't wear suits. And those who didn't even bother to wear a dress shirt would be immediately disqualified because 'they know no manners'" ("Pussycat attack", 1998).

Here mention should be made of the domestic counterpart of *sararîman* – housewives. Though less uniformed than their "corporate warrior" (*kigyô bushi*) husbands, they can often be seen in slippers, aprons and make-up, walking with their young children, lugging groceries home and running errands in the neighborhood. In the summer, some carry parasols and wear hats (and occasionally gloves) to protect their "white skin" from the sun.

Now consider the typical day of a *sararîman* and how his self, material cultural objects and others all interact. Donning his clothes may be conceived as one's person dressing his body. But at another level, it may be said that he is carrying out a coupled role in which his "I" is directing his "me" (i.e. one's person/body). Facing a mirror, he looks at his reflection. However, a more informative description would explain how his "I" observes and judges his "me" (image). Walking to work, he unexpectedly bumps into a close colleague and presenting a coupled role, expresses a relaxed self as he chats about plans for an upcoming vacation. Then, upon entering the office building, he sees his company's president coming out the door and performs a distal role by unthinkingly straightening his tie, wiping the breezy grin off his face and delivering a snappy "good morning". At his office desk, a coupled role emerges as he takes off his suit jacket and sips a cup of tea. Gathering his thoughts before his work day begins in earnest, his mind wonders. He imagines his own self sunbathing on a beach with his wife, his "I" and "me" calmly joined. Then his "mindscape" changes to a conference room – it is his 9:00 presentation in which he must address several important clients. As he wonders whether he can pull his talk off successfully, a distal role emerges as he imagines the clients assailing him with questions he cannot answer. As his anxieties increase, he visualizes himself embarrassed with his "I" losing control of his "me".

Though material culture associated with the relatively ordered area may at first glance not seem as symbolically laden as what one would find at the other end of the continuum (highly ordered and ordered), items and objects categorized in the relatively ordered area can nevertheless be highly charged with meaning. For example, Buruma notes that "No Japanese cook worth his salt would want to be seen without his tall white hat; 'interis' (intellectuals) sport berets and sunglasses, like 1920s exiles on the Left Bank of Paris" (1983: 70). Or note how even "homeless people" must be clearly categorized:

> A shop owner's association near JR Kawasaki Station on Wednesday began a campaign to rid the streets of discarded chewing gum by employing homeless people to clean up the mess. But the requirement that the workers wear numbered identifications on their backs, each bearing the word "homeless," may create a stir . . . All of the homeless people in the cleanup operation are required to wear a cloth identification on their backs, reading "Cleanup Operation Member-Homeless No. 6," for example ("Homeless employed in cleanup, but required to wear emblem", 1994).

A good example of how the official powers can be disturbed by a perceived breech of the dress code is illustrated by a local assembly member in Misawa in Aomori Prefecture. Yuki Ito was suspended for five days after he refused to follow the assembly's dress code, apparently established because Ito attended meetings in casual clothes, which required "male members to wear a tie and females to dress 'moderately'". The assembly became Japan's first and only municipal assembly with such a code. Ito eventually gave in to the assembly's demands, but he noted that the assembly is "keen on the externals because they lack substance . . . They say the way I dressed undermined the assembly's dignity. But I wonder which is more degrading: not wearing a tie, or reporting a fictitious business trip?" ("Maverick assemblyman fights dress code, graft", 1997).

It is worth pointing out that even when the authorities themselves loosen rules about dress, there is resistance. For example, a new policy of the Tokyo Metropolitan government to have officials dress down (i.e. no jacket or tie) during the summer in order to cut energy costs met with mixed results. "Despite room temperatures of 28–C, most officials appeared more uncomfortable about shedding their ties" ("Cool as a cucumber", 1998). One official said that "Wearing no jackets may be okay, but Tokyo residents might think we look too casual and slovenly without ties". Another official said he would not dare enter the governor's office without a tie, even though it was the governor himself who pushed the new policy. But according to the governor, the policy has other benefits besides helping the environment: "The no-tie policy is also important because the new casual style will lead us to be more frank in our discussions" ("No jacket (or tie) required, as metropolitan government goes summery", 1998).

Another example of the symbolism of material culture: certain pieces of clothing associated with socioeconomic class distinctions can make one "feel" affiliated with one class or another. Noguchi comments about a train worker who, though "he wore a white shirt with his uniform, he thought of himself as a blue-collar worker and not a salary-man" (1990: 137–8). Also,

> One worker remarked that he wears a uniform while carrying out his duties in the station. Part of this uniform is a tie and white-collared shirt. He felt that wearing a tie and white shirt meant that he should not be doing blue-collar-type work. At times, especially during cleaning duty, he felt that he was not a white-collar worker at all (Noguchi 1990: 72).

The bureaucratic ethos of hierarchization, categorization and standardization have even permeated spheres of social existence that are usually regarded as relatively free from the official gaze of education and employment. For example, the official dictates of sociopolitical categorization influence casual and leisure wear, so that even acts of "non-uniformed" clothing signal who is "in" and who is "out" (*uchi/soto*). Thus, besides having twins or young siblings dress the same, sometimes a mother and her young daughter wear identical clothes (such sets are sold in stores) and somewhat less rarely, dating couples can be seen wearing the same clothing, or at least wearing a piece of clothing, such as a T-shirt, that is the same. The power of statist and corporatist ordering, then, is visible in an entire range of activities, whether understood as leisure of labor, so that regulated dress resonates with bureaucratic ethos (see Chapter 6). After all, "Clothes are an enclosure that confirm 'one's own' existence" (Washida 1996: 26):

> In Japan there are fairly clear-cut roles and expectations for work and play. Not only are there right times and places for these activities, but there are also appropriate dress and behavior – looking and acting the part is important. Appropriate uniforms – including the standard salaryman's suit as well as special outfits for golf, tennis, hiking – all help people get into their roles. Whatever the activity, it is expected that one will be wholeheartedly engaged and do his or her best (Miyatake and Norton 1994).

Thus in Japan, attire and personal accouterments are given attention not just for highly ordered and ordered self-expressions, but even for leisure pursuits. Such attention to detail and appropriate appearance can be seen in individuals outfitted for fishing, hikers, golfers, skiers and other sports and hobbies. They are not just equipped with what they need; rather, they are bedecked and adorned with garb and items that announce their role and pursuit.

(4) Disordered

The last area on the "Uniformity/Non-Uniformity" continuum is that of the disordered area. Far removed from the state core, here one finds the lowest expressions of statefulness. However, one's practices still contain a particular degree of statefulness because, regardless of any acts and practices conventionally understood as anti-standardized, anti-categorized and overly individualistic, one is still participating in the hegemonic order (i.e. substructure; see Chapter 2). In other words, though ostensibly not directly integrated into the rationalized politico-economic order in terms of production, such practices are intimately bound up with the rationalized politico-economic order in terms of consumption – which, of course, is absolutely vital to any productivist regime – or what may be termed "resistance consumption", a topic I treat in Chapter 6.

"Office Ladies" And Uniformed Femininity

Among all the different types of occupational women's uniforms, it is the "office lady" uniform that is most strongly associated with female workers.[14] As relatively low-salaried secretaries who are expected to work for several years and then quit to become "good wives and wise mothers" (i.e. devote themselves to housework and raising children), "office ladies" are regarded as temporary and supplementary to the permanent and core male workforce. They are, in short, expected to assist – not fully participate in – Japan's patriarchal corporate culture. Not surprisingly, then, the uniforms of "office ladies" – of whom, according to one estimate, 90 percent wear uniforms (Watanabe 1994: 18) – evidence the notion that uniformed individuals are those who occupy the lower ranks of an organization (or nationwide economic system) in terms of status and power; indeed, Watanabe notes that "uniforms = auxiliary posts" (1994: 23) and Uchino writes that uniforms are "sexually discriminatory and a tool of management" (1995: 56). The prescribed dress codes of "office ladies" and their mandated styles of self-presentation illustrate the relation between labor, capital, femininity and male dominance of the workforce. Some regard the uniformization of female office workers tantamount to treating women as children who cannot make judgments for themselves and lack self-determination (Watanabe 1994: 23). Many women ask why "only women workers have to wear uniforms in the office?" Men counter by saying that a suit is a type of uniform. However, men are able (or more accurately, allowed) to choose the color and cut, and they are not forced to wear certain types of clothing (Watanabe 1994: 23).

Some male workers like uniforms because if women wear ordinary clothes, "I end up calling them by their names". But uniforms allow men to address all the women in the office, and if women wear ordinary clothes, they end up competing and wear gaudy clothes, which leads to a tension-filled workplace. Moreover, by wearing uniforms, women can don the "symbolic colors" (*shinboru karâ*) of the company and are "mobile advertising poles" (*ugoku kôkokutô*) (of an office) (Watanabe 1994: 18–19). One government official argued that wearing uniforms gives rise, among members of an office, to a sense of pride and the "consciousness of being under the jurisdiction" (*kizoku ishiki*) of an office (Watanabe 1994: 20). Indeed, uniforms can be used as a "barometer of respect" (*sonchô no baromêtâ*) of women (Watanabe 1994: 18). If women are not required to wear company uniforms, they are still expected to wear "ordinary clothes (*shifuku*) that don't give a bad feeling to the customers" (Watanabe 1994: 18–19).[15] Thus, from management's point of view, women's uniforms are key to running a good company:

> The uniform is the company symbol. It represents the company's esprit de corps and gives customers a feeling of cleanliness and trust. If employees dress according to each individual's preference, their lack of uniformity will give visitors an unpleasant impression. In the case of women, if the choice of apparel is left to individual tastes, it is likely to become too showy which will not only be detrimental to the atmosphere of the workplace but also distract attention to clothing ("Japan's civilian army proud of its duds", 1992).

Regardless of the female workers who do not like uniforms, some do and others are even eager to don them. This is especially true if the uniform represents a prestigious corporation. "One example is a dark blue outfit worn by beauty consultants at Shiseido Co. Many women reportedly have sought entry into the firm just to wear the elegant two-piece ensemble." In the words of one employee who used to commute to work wearing her uniform, "I took special care to remove stains and wrinkles from my uniform so I would not hurt the company image . . . I think I gave more attention to that uniform than I did to my own clothes" ("Uniforms are symbol of professionals", 1994). According to a housewife,

> While I was still working, I wore a uniform like all my female colleagues. It was lovely, and I liked it very much. If it weren't for the uniform, I would have been troubled by choosing the right dress that suits the workplace, represents good sense and is functional. When all female workers wear the same type of clothing, everybody feels at ease because you are not rated according to what you wear. Living alone in Tokyo, I would have been hard-pressed by the expense of buying proper outfits. In addition, the uniform reinforces one's awareness as a company employee ("Japan's civilian army proud of its duds", 1992).

In order to illustrate the use of women's uniforms, below I present survey data collected at commercial firms, textile companies, banks and bus companies. Though it is not always clear from the surveys, most of these uniforms are probably designed for "office ladies". Note that women who wear uniforms in bus companies are most likely "bus conductress" (not drivers, but women who sit near the almost always male conductor and act as a guide).

Purpose.   Why do companies adopt uniforms for women? According to five surveys, "uniformity and uniformed beauty" and "improving the company's image" were the most common reasons (Tables 4.2, 4.3, and 4.4, 4.5 and 4.6).

Table 4.2. *Purpose of Adopting Women's Uniforms at 31 Commercial Firms (multiple answers)*

Item	Number of Commercial Firms	%
Uniformity and Uniformed Beauty	27	87.1
Improve the Company's Image	18	58.1
Functional for Each Type of Work	12	38.7
Distinguish Customers from Employees	10	32.3
Control Gaudiness	4	12.9
Other	4	12.9

Source: Uno and Nogami (1993: 98).

Table 4.3. *Purpose of Adopting Women's Uniform and Work Clothes at 116 Textile-Related Companies (multiple answers)*

Item	Number of Companies	%
Uniformity and Uniformed Beauty	98	84.5
Improve the Company's Image	58	50.0
Functional for Each Type of Work	41	35.3
Distinguish Customers from Employees	22	19.0
Control Gaudiness	15	13.0
Other	7	6.0

Source: Uno and Nogami (1992: 137).

Table 4.4. *Purpose of Choosing Women's Uniform and Work Clothes at 116 Textile-Related Companies (multiple answers)*

Item	Number of Companies	%
Uniformity and Uniformed Beauty	98	84.5
Improve the Company's Image	58	50.0
Functional for Each Type of Work	41	35.3
Distinguish Customers from Employees	22	19.0
Control Gaudiness	15	13.0
Other	7	6.0

Source: Uno and Nogami (1992: 137).

Table 4.5. *Purpose of Adopting Women's Uniform at 34 Banks (multiple answers)*

Item	Number of Banks	%
Improve the Company's Image	24	70.6
Uniformity and Uniformed Beauty	19	55.9
To Impress Customers	16	47.1
To Improve Work Efficiency (Functionality)	1	32.4
Other	1	2.9

Source: Uno and Nogami (1990: 95).

Table 4.6. *Purpose of Adopting Women's Uniforms at 41 Bus Companies (multiple answers)*

Item	Number of Companies	%
Uniformity and Uniformed Beauty	38	92.7
Improve the Company's Image	28	68.3
Functionality	11	26.8
To Clarify Types of Work	9	22.0
Other	5	12.2

Source: Uno and Nogami (1994: 117).

Considerations When Adopting Women's Uniform. What considerations are taken into account when adopting uniforms for women? "Design" (such as "cheerfulness" or *akarusa*) ranked highest in five surveys, as does "functionality" (which ranked highest in banks) (Tables 4.7, 4.8, 4.9, 4.10 and 4.11).

Table 4.7. *Important Considerations When Adopting Women's Uniform and Work Clothes at 116 Textile-Related Companies (multiple answers)*

Item	Number of Companies	%
Design (Color, Cheerfulness, Sense of Cleanliness, etc.)	94	81.0
Functionality	74	63.8
Economical (Durability, Price, etc.)	57	49.1
Suitable to the Mood of the Workplace	29	25.0
Other	5	4.3

Source: Uno and Nogami (1992: 137).

Table 4.8. *Important Considerations When Adopting Women's Uniform at 31 Commercial Firms (multiple answers)*

Item	Number of Commercial Firms	%
Design (Color, Cheerfulness, Sense of Cleanliness, etc.)	31	100.0
Functionality	22	71.0
Economical (Durability, Price, etc.)	15	48.4
Suitable to the Mood of the Workplace	6	19.4

Source: Uno and Nogami (1993: 98).

Table 4.9. *Important Considerations When Adopting Women's Uniform and Work Clothes at 116 Textile-Related Companies (multiple answers)*

Item	Number of Companies	%
Design (Color, Cheerfulness, Sense of Cleanliness, etc.)	94	81.0
Functionality	74	63.8
Economical (Durability, Price, etc.)	57	49.1
Suitable to the Mood of the Workplace	29	25.0
Other	5	4.3

Source: Uno and Nogami (1992: 137).

Table 4.10. *Important Considerations When Adopting Women's Uniforms at 34 Banks (multiple answers)*

Item	Number of Banks	%
Functionality	21	61.8
To Improve the Image of the Bank	19	55.9
Design and Fashionableness	9	26.5
Other	1	2.9

Source: Uno and Nogami (1990: 95).

Table 4.11. *Important Considerations When Adopting Women's Uniforms at 41 Bus Companies (multiple answers)*

Item	Number of Companies	%
Design (Color, Cheerfulness, Sense of Cleanliness, etc.)	40	97.6
Functionality	27	65.9
Economical (Durability, Price, etc.)	13	31.7
Other	5	12.2

Source: Uno and Nogami (1994: 117).

Methods of Determining Uniforms. What methods of determining which uniforms are to be worn are used? How are final selections of uniforms made? Entrusting the decision to workers, checking fashion magazines or catalogues and relying on designers were all very common (Uno and Nogami 1990: 96–7; Uno and Nogami 1992: 138; Uno and Nogami 1993: 99; Uno and Nogami 1994: 117–18).

Adapting to Current Fashion. To what degree are attempts made to conform to current fashion trends? (Tables 4.12, 4.13, 4.14 and 4.15). "Adapting partially" and "not be too concerned with fashion" were common responses.

Table 4.12. *Method of Adapting to (Women's) Fashion at 30 Commercial Firms*

Item	Number of Commercial Firms	%
Adapt Partially	16	53.3
Not Be Too Concerned with Fashion	12	40.0
Other	2	6.7

Source: Uno and Nogami (1993: 100).

Table 4.13. *Method of Adapting to (Women's) Fashion at 112 Textiles-Related Companies*

Item	Number of Companies	%
Adapt Partially	57	50.7
Not Be Too Concerned with Fashion	43	38.4
Adapt to the Newest Fashion	9	8.0
Other	3	3.9

Source: Uno and Nogami (1992: 139).

Table 4.14. *Method of Adapting to (Women's) Fashion at 33 Banks (multiple answers)*

Item	Number of Banks	%
Adapt Partially	22	66.7
Not Be Too Concerned with Fashion	7	21.2
Adapt to the Newest Fashion	3	9.1
Other	1	33.0

Source: Uno and Nogami (1990: 96).

Table 4.15. *Method of Adapting to (Women's) Fashion at 40 Bus Companies*

Method of Adapting	Number of Companies	%
Adapt Partially	28	70.0
Not Be Too Concerned with Fashion	10	25.0
Adapt to the Newest Fashion	2	5.0

Source: Uno and Nogami (1994: 118).

Most firms surveyed did not use a designer, though the number that did was not insignificant (Uno and Nogami 1990: 96, 100). The number of uniforms that were proposed when adopting a new design varied (Uno and Nogami 1993: 99; Uno and Nogami 1992: 138; Uno and Nogami 1994: 117) (see Appendix A Tables 11, 12, 13, 14 and 15 for description of typical women's uniform ensembles).

Uniform Accessories.   Different kinds of accessories that supplement the ensemble of women's uniforms. Name tags and company badges seem to be key components of the identity kits of women's uniforms. Belts, hats, shoes, ribbons, neckties, occupation title tags, brooches, gloves, scarves, bandannas, tie tacks, handkerchief, stockings, whistles, parasols, rain boots, pouches and travel bags (Uno and Nogami 1992: 144; Uno and Nogami 1990: 100; Uno and Nogami 1993: 105; Uno and Nogami 1994: 123).

As for how long women's uniforms are used until they are changed, there is great variation (on average from two to six years) with many companies having no set policy (Uno and Nogami 1992: 139; Uno and Nogami 1994: 119; Uno and Nogami 1992: 139; Uno and Nogami 1993: 100; Uno and Nogami 1990: 97). The price of uniform ensembles can range from 10,000 yen to 70,000 yen depending on type, season and the number of itmes included in the outfit (Uno and Nogami 1993: 101; Uno and Nogami 1992: 143; Uno and Nogami 1994: 121–2; Uno and Nogami 1990: 100).[16]

Public Transportation Workers

If uniformed students are ubiquitous in Japan's public spaces, so are public transportation workers who ride the mass transit systems and populate the countless train, subway and bus stations. Some public transportation workers wear uniforms that, while not as "militarized" as security personnel attire, are nevertheless "quasi-militarized".[17]

A brief outline of uniforms worn by Tokyo's *Teito kôsokudo kôtsû eidan* (Teito Rapid Transit Authority; subway system) since its founding offers an idea of how public transportation employees have presented themselves. Originally, conductors wore an "Italian blue" (*itarian burû*) uniform, with brass and gold buttons and gold collar badges. The train crew wore navy blue uniforms. From 1950 to 1972, uniforms were navy blue with gold buttons stamped with an "S". When promoted, employees would wear collar badges. Different types of neckties were worn. From 1972 to 1984, gray "suit-type" uniforms were adopted, with three buttons and a cochineal-colored necktie that went well with the uniform's color. During this period, an image of a "cheerful (*akarui*) subway that will be liked" was presented. From 1984 to 1991, the "suit-type" uniform was maintained. This outfit had three buttons that matched the navy blue color of the uniform and a cochineal-colored necktie was worn. Beginning in 1991, consultations were held with designers Mori Takahira and Ishizu Kensuke, and a color scheme of olive green that reflected the environment of the subway was adopted. This ensemble provides a slightly softer image and allows for easy movement. The necktie matches the color scheme of the jacket, which has three brass, gold-bronze buttons. The hat is an original "De Gaulle" (*dogôru*) style.[18]

Though there is variation depending on the system or company, public transportation personnel are commonly seen in hats and occasionally wear white gloves (in contrast to taxi drivers who always wear them). Some have epaulettes and gold braid on jackets and hats. As for rules about railway uniform regulations, Noguchi comments that

Whereas in the past the manner of dress was strictly enforced, in the 1980s several of the former restrictions had been relaxed. The new practices allowed for longer hair and even for working bare-headed. I can recall during the first fieldwork an occasion on which a young worker had been reprimanded before his peers because he was not in full uniform and was told to run and get his hat. This supervisor had even been concerned about the proper angle of an employee's hand when saluting his superiors. Some younger workers had replaced the shiny black shoes of the official uniform with blue-and-white jogging shoes (1990: 77).

Public transportation personnel occupy an interesting place in the socio-economic class system. "It is somewhat difficult to place the railroad worker into a white- or blue-collar category. The employee wears a white collar and is salaried, but he also on occasion wears a blue shirt under his uniform and is generally a member of a union" (Noguchi 1990: 72). For example, Noguchi points out that "Kokutetsu [Japanese National Railways] employees wear blue uniforms, white shirts, and dark ties. However, most of the workers did not perceive themselves to be among the class of white-collar 'salary-man'" (1990: 162). At one particular train station, "employees admitted that they wore the visible symbols of the white-collar work environment". However, "some were quick to add they did engage in such unenviable (and not white-collar) tasks as cleaning the rails (*senro sôji*) and mopping the public latrines (*benjo sôji*)" (Noguchi 1990: 162).

Surveys that investigated men's uniforms resonate with the findings of investigations into women's uniforms. A look at Table 4.16 shows that "improving the company's image" and "uniformity and uniformed beauty" are key concerns for adopting uniforms (as they are for women's uniforms) (though one survey has somewhat different results; see Table 4.17). As for the purpose of adopting (Table 4.16), the method of determining male uniforms (Uno, Nogami and Sakurai 1991: 152), and the method of adapting (Table 4.18), there are no significant differences with women's uniforms (Appendix A Table 16 illustrates male uniform ensembles).

Table 4.16. *Purpose of Adopting Men's Uniforms in 23 Railroad Companies (multiple answers)*

Purpose	Number of Companies	%
Improve the Company's Image	18	78.3
To Impress Customers	17	73.9
Distinguish Customers from Employees	16	69.9
Uniformity and Uniformed Beauty	14	60.9
To Improve Work Efficiency (Functionality)	14	60.9
To Clarify Types of Work	11	47.8
Other	2	8.7

Source: Uno, Nogami and Sakurai (1991: 151).

Table 4.17. *Important Considerations When Adopting Men's Uniforms at 23 Railroad Companies (multiple answers)*

Important Considerations	Number of Companies	%
Improve the Company's Image	12	52.2
To Impress Customers	8	34.8
Distinguish Customers from Employees	7	30.4
To Improve Work Efficiency (Functionality)	5	21.7
Uniformity and Uniformed Beauty	3	13.0
To Clarify the Type of Work	1	4.3
Other	2	8.7

Source: Uno, Nogami and Sakurai (1991: 151).

Table 4.18. *Method of Adapting to (Men's) Fashion at 23 Railroad Companies*

Method of Adapting	Number of Companies	%
Adapt Partially	12	52.2
Not Be Too Concerned with Fashion	10	43.5
Adapt to the Newest Fashion	1	4.3

Source: Uno, Nogami and Sakurai (1991: 152).

Notes

1. This three-phase cycle follows Turner's ritual analysis in only the most general way. It is the second phase in which Turner's (1969) notion of liminality is most evident.

2. Some data in this section appears in McVeigh (1997b check). See also McVeigh (1995b).

3. There are, of course, instances in which women, compared to men, are not expected to undergo rigorous discipline (e.g. military and sports).

4. Purists complain of seeing young ladies wearing shoes and boots in snow while dressed in kimono.

5. Kimono can be expensive: an entire package might cost ¥1,000,000, though there are now versions sold for a much more reasonable price.

6. Of course, make-up use by non-adults is certainly not limited to Japan: in the United States in 1997, teenage girls spent about $4.2 billion, while girls under 12 spent $109 million ("Kiddy cosmetics", 1998).

7. Also like women, some men remove body hair, a very common practice in Japan.

8. Hair care starts early for some. There is a special barber that caters to children, from six months to twelve-year-olds (Sawaguchi 1997).

9. The Japan Red Cross, in order to improve the image of its nurses, created the Tokushi Nursing Association in 1887 with its own special nursing uniforms (Ishi and Ôami 1995).

10. The internal unit of a company that decides on uniform style, regulations, changes, etc. varies by company. In their study on uniforms, Uno and Nogami note the responsible unit may be a general affairs division (in a general affairs department); personnel division (in a personnel department); labor division (in a management department); welfare division (in a personnel or general affairs department) or others (1992: 136).

11. Gloves seem to carry a range of symbolic meanings that have to do with signaling one's diligence and sincerity. White gloves are worn by taxi drivers and politicians while giving campaign speeches. Performers often wear them, though they prefer more flashy colors, and members of the Imperial family are often seen clutching them. Ironically, despite the great concern with cleanliness in Japan, many dentists and health professionals do not wear or change their gloves. A Japanese nurse explained that she does not wear gloves because "patients would be insulted", feeling that "the nurse was suggesting their blood might be dangerous or not clean" (cited in Kiritani 1996).

12. Ties can carry heavy symbolism. Sayle notes that when corrupt state officials are arrested, their neckties are removed: "sign of a criminal" (1998: 6).

13. However, since the late 1970s and early 1980s some companies have instructed workers to not wear jackets or ties and to don short-sleeve shirts during the summer in order to cut energy costs.

14. The "office lady" uniform is associated with a wide range of meanings, such as friendly assistance, femininity and erotic images. For two weeks a man repeatedly called a Tokyo bank and asked if the female workers would sell their uniforms to him for ¥60,000. No one ever discovered who he was or what his motives were ("Mad for uniforms", 1998).

15. But at some companies, women who are so bold as to wear ordinary clothes (*shifuku*) due to pregnancy are harassed because office workers believe that since they are about to give birth, they should quit work (cf. Yamada 1993).

16. Uniforms for flight attendants are relatively expensive; Air Nippon uniforms are ¥98,000 (winter) and ¥65,000 (summer) ("Air Nippon attendants set to lose hats, gloves", 1998).

17. Noguchi relates a train worker who liked life in the army and strongly associated his uniform with Japan's military forces: "The uniform of a platform worker, he claimed, was no match for that of a soldier in the Ground Self-Defense Force. For him, the uniform in the entire Kokutetsu [Japanese National Railways] organization that comes the closest in appearance to the GSDF uniform is that worn by conductors on the high-speed trains. The uniforms of the conductors on the Shinkansen bullet train are beige in color and contrast markedly with the dark blue uniform worn by the regular workers in Kokutetsu" (1990: 136–7).

18. From the *"Metoro Q & A"* column in number 17 of the *Metoro natsu matsuri gaido* (Metro Summer Festival Guide, 1 July, 1998: 25).

5

Wearing Ideology and the "Cult of Cuteness"

Introduction

Cute objects are encountered everywhere in Japan. Whether in advertising, company logos, greeting cards, pornography or in the posters of state-sponsored public safety campaigns, brightly-colored balloons, baby faces, smiling children, tiny bunnies and beaming bears are used to inform, warn, advise, admonish and shape opinion. Cuteness as a human sentiment is so potent because it communicates power relations and power plays, effectively combining weakness, submissiveness and humility with influence, domination and control. It merges meekness, admiration and attachment with benevolence, tenderness and sympathy. In short, affection is associated with authority, harmony with hierarchy. Living in Japan, one simply cannot escape from this candied, cartoon and comic-book atmosphere. It is difficult to convey in written text the visceral impact and buoyant feel of things made cute, just as it is not possible to fully describe what seems to be the audio counterpart of cuteness; the high-pitched, very feminized, falsetto voices of polite female sales clerks, TV announcers and other women who deal with the public. As we shall see below, there is baby cuteness; very young cuteness; young cuteness;[1] maternal cuteness; teen cuteness;[2] adult cuteness; sexy cuteness; pornography cuteness; child pornography cuteness; authority cuteness; and corporate cuteness. Not a few commentators on this chapter have pointed out that "cuteness" is not unique to Japan and can be found quite readily in North America (or any other society for that matter).[3] This is true enough, but I would argue that it is all relative: in Japan, cuteness is a much more powerful theme than in North America, permeating numerous spheres of Japanese daily life. Indeed, here I should emphasize that cuteness is not just a fad in the fashion cycle of Japanese pop culture; it is more of a "standard" aesthetic of everyday life.

Why is cuteness so prevalent in Japan? As I suggested in Chapter 1, the consumption of cuteness is a form of "resistance," a daily aesthetic that counters the dominant "male" productivist ideology of standardization, order, control, rationality, impersonality and labor. Indeed, cute images are usually associated with women and leisure (cf. Cowherd's "'Cute' usage defies understanding by men", 1989), and thus I pay much attention to the gendered aspect of cute things in Japan: why they are usually associated with women and how they communicate messages about being the "ideal" woman. After dealing with the methodological and theoretical issues concerning my analysis of cuteness, I discuss the meanings and cultural values that, embedded in all the varied images of cuteness, constitute a socionormative commentary about how women should behave, especially vis-à-vis men, and though to a lesser degree, how men should behave vis-à-vis women. Indeed, though very strongly associated with young females, the use and appreciation of cuteness is not necessarily restricted to this group. Young men are occasionally spotted wearing something cute. Or some – in contrast to their apparent attempts at affecting a hip image by wearing sunglasses and driving (usually white) sports cars – have furry, brightly-colored animals dangling from the rear-view mirror or peering out the rear window at the cars behind. Nor is it very unusual to see truck drivers with their own collection of stuffed animals, carefully positioned on the dashboards of their huge trucks. And "Cute boys in Japan deliberately look goofy and sweet and make what one American teen calls 'Bambi-eyes' at girls, begging for indulgence like puppies, not meaning any harm, evoking nurturant responses rather than sexual ones" (White 1994: 129). That both genders use cuteness indicates its ambiguous and multivocal nature.

Before proceeding any further, a caveat is in order. It must be emphasized that *not all* Japanese women like cute things. Indeed, some are vocal in their negative attitude toward cuteness. Though young women seem to have the highest interest in what is cute, we should not assume that they lack a critical, ironic sense about this sentiment that runs in and out of so much of their lives. Some have a qualified view of cuteness: "I like cute things, so I buy cute stationery, but I would never want to be seen in cute clothes because people would think that I was childish." Not a small number of women have commented negatively on being cute. Some used words such as "childish" (*yôchi or osanai*). Others used stronger language: "It's *baka*" (foolish) or "*tarinai*" (stupid). As one woman in her twenties explained it, "cute" is a word used by young girls who have a limited vocabulary and do not know any other expressions. Indeed, the list of what is cute seems almost limitless, and many constantly use "*kawaî!*" in their conversation. According to one young woman, "It's very useful to neutralize the atmosphere. For example, when a girlfriend of mine tries some new fashion or jewelry on, I can just say 'it's cute,' whether I like it or not". Regardless of women who are critical of cuteness and its uses, in this chapter, I focus on the views of those women who positively valorize cuteness.[4]

Capturing Meaning: Cute Things as Symbols

Cuteness is a concept of great cultural ubiquity and is often used to characterize objects (toys, small things), persons (children, young girls, women), behavior (certain words, facial expressions), an attitude (one's feelings toward a thing or person) and even handwriting and slang (Kinsella 1995: 222–5).[5] Recently, some young people have begun to describe things and people as *chô-kawaî* (super cute). Consequently, attempts at defining it for methodological purposes are problematic. However, I will start with the premise that as a conceptual entity, cuteness is symbolic in social operation. Thus, for my present purposes, I argue that cuteness is best thought of as a key symbol in Japanese society in the same manner that uniforms are. Exactly what it symbolizes is addressed below.

In my attempt to analyze cuteness, I employ Turner's (1967) four properties of symbols throughout this chapter (as introduced in Chapter 1): multi-vocality; condensation; ambiguity; an interacting, reinforcing movement between conceptual (ideological) and perceptual (sensory) aspects. Below I frame and discuss different examples of cuteness in three sections. These sections correspond to three aspects or ways of interpreting symbols (Turner 1967: 50–2, 292–6). The first aspect ("The Indigenous Interpretation of Cuteness: Towards a Definition") concerns the exegesis of a symbol: how the people who use a symbol explain its meaning (to themselves and researchers). The second aspect ("The Positional Meaning of Cuteness") concerns how a symbol derives meaning from its relationship to other symbols in a complex of meanings. The third aspect ("The Operational Meaning of Cuteness") concerns how people use a symbol in everyday action to do things. Or, more to the point, how people use a symbol to make other people do, think or feel certain things. This is the operational, practical and sociopolitical aspect of a symbol. These three types of interpretation overlap to some degree, but if applied to a body of data they can be distinguished for practical purposes.

The Indigenous Interpretation of Cute Things: Towards a Definition

Why the apparent obsession with things cute among many Japanese women? The most common responses to this query were "It's comforting", "soothing", "relaxing", "makes one feel warm inside", "adds a feeling of security", or cute things are simply "nice". If asked why they admire cute things so much, the typical response might consist of a polite giggle, a shrug of the shoulders and then a "Doesn't-everyone-like-them?" sort of answer. Asking Japanese about cuteness was similar to inquiring about beauty or love. It's just something one knows and knows about. Asked to define or analyze it, and one is met with a puzzled response, followed by a knowing smile, and then perhaps something along the lines of "Cuteness is something one can't talk about. It's something one can only feel, in one's heart. Besides, what's so serious about cuteness?" For many women, discussions of cuteness were approached in a rather matter-of-fact manner: there was nothing terribly silly or cloying about it. Bringing it up as a topic did not always result in the ironic reactions one would expect, say, in North America. Cuteness, after all, was something everyone knows about and somehow experiences. It only becomes problematic if it is consciously thought about for too long. But even then, talk of cuteness usually ended with the conclusion that "it's just one of those things".

In a more analytical vein, there were those who explained that cuteness is a form of escape from the real world, or at least from the high-pressure social world of Japan. Cuteness is a type of "fantasy", stated one young woman, "it's a way of forgetting about the unpleasant things we all have to put up with everyday". Another said "cuteness in Japan shows that Japanese women feel great pressures on them and they become childish so they can forget about the real world". If the everyday tempo and concerns of living in Japan are considered, it is hard to deny that there may be some truth to this. Certainly, anyone making their way through Japanese society deserves an occasional dose of fantasy, especially one sweetened with bright colors, playful images and youthful vigor. It is a society in which the powerful bureaucratizing forces of statism and corporate culture are difficult to ignore. Thus, one is socialized to be constantly aware of the many obligations one has accrued, in which a strictly regulated, controlled and highly competitive educational system decides one's fate to a remarkable degree; where passing through life is a continuous series of exam preparations, exams and more exams; where *karôshi* (death from overwork) is reportedly on the rise; and where the most insignificant social interaction can quickly escalate into a carefully choreographed ritual. Cuteness sweetens social relations, making what is otherwise a ritualized, serious, formalized social existence more spontaneous, lighthearted and intimate.

However true the above explanations are, they lack explanatory power. What, then, does "cuteness" mean? Part of the argument of this section is that because cuteness is so semantically rich (multivocal and ambiguous) it cannot be readily defined. However, some conceptual starting points can be suggested. White notes that "cute" characterizes anything or anyone that is "sweet, happy, and upbeat – and vulnerable, something to be taken care of and cuddled" (1994: 126). Typical Japanese dictionaries define it as anything or anyone that is "lovely" or "charming". More authoritative and detailed definitions can be found in reference sources such as the *Daijirin* (Great Dictionary), which provides two basic definitions:

> (1) something or someone that is young or small which makes one want to take care of this thing or person; (a) something or someone that is charming, attractive. Mainly used for young women and children (A cute child. A cute girl); (b) something childlike that is smile-provoking [*hohoemashî*] (A cute appliqué apron) [*sic*]; (c) something small and smile-provoking (A cute boat that looks like a toy); (2) something that arouses pity, compassion. To feel sorry for someone (1988: 528).

According to one young woman, cuteness can be defined four ways: (1) something that moves you out of pity or compassion (*aware*); (2) to have your heart moved by a person or animal so that you want to take care of it; (3) to think that a child's face or shape is lovely; and (4) any small object that causes you to have "feelings that make you want to treat it nicely".

What makes something or someone cute? Note what a certain Dr Takasu has to say, who has some definite ideas on the archetypical image of cuteness. In his *The Magnetism of the Heart – Becoming A Cute Woman: Mesmer Explains the 5 Rules for Becoming a Good Woman*, he writes that cuteness has three basic principles. The first is having features of an infant, such as a wide forehead, small chin, big eyes, low nose, small lips and white skin. Here it might be added that the portrayal of girls and women in *manga* (comics) is notable because often they have excessively large, round eyes with bright expressions that *kira kira suru* (glitter). One observer notes how there is a trend to reshape people "to conform to the cuter, cuddlier specifications of cartoon characters" in order to make them appear in print media as figures in *manga*. "The most blatant such example is a trend of chopping off the heads of prominent celebrities and then superimposing them in much larger size, thus creating the same basic anatomical dimensions as a typical comic-book creation" (Lazarus 1994b). The second is an ability to arouse the protective instinct in others. The third is the desire of a cute person to want to be liked. This, according to Dr Takasa, is accomplished by expressing weakness (1988: 35–6). Dr Takasu's opinion on these matters presents us with evidence that thinking about being cute is not an issue of insignificant concern for some, and his description of an infant's face is exactly the same as the baby-faced images of cuteness. I introduce his thinking on this subject because the theme of infantilization will reappear later.

A common and important element in cute images is animals. Babies and small children are often dressed in animal costumes, as are things; I once spotted a huge crane in Tokyo painted as a giraffe. Even in situations that would be considered dangerous, introducing animals seems to make circumstances less menacing. I once came across a newspaper picture of zoo officials drilling to deal with an animal escape. Uniformed and wearing helmets, they are brandishing staffs and shields as they attempt to corral a colleague dressed in a cartoonish gorilla costume with an oversized smiling face ("Going ape", 1993). Another picture shows marchers in Kyoto donning animal and Japanese cartoon character costumes to show support for UN meetings on climate change ("EU ready to yield on cuts", 1997). According to one twelve-year old girl the following are all cute: dogs, cats, stuffed animals, goldfish, babies, accessories, horses, a small purse, penguins, rabbits, giraffes, pumpkins, frogs, earthworms, hamsters, mice, chicks, lambs, cows, goats, dolphins, dolls, gloves, carrots, small girls and small boys (*"Kawaî tte nanda tsuke"*, 1990). As a young woman once told me, "anything and everything" may be called cute. Why the use of animals in the cultural discourse on cuteness? For one thing, they seem to require loving attention from people. As one young girl once told me, they need to be "protected, cuddled and held". Also, as living, breathing, active things, they exist somewhere in between being human but not quite human, controllable but not too controllable, allowing us to project our own selves onto them. But another young woman explained that, at least in the case of bears (which are extremely popular as cute images), there is a lack of gender markers, thereby making them free from any sexual implications or tensions.

In Japan, the 1980s saw something commonly described as the "pet boom" in Japan. And along with this, a drastic increase with pet shops that specialize in everything from shampoos, snacks, toys, beds, miniature outfits for dogs to sanitary napkins for cats. An example of the extremes to which economic interests cater to the pet boom can be seen in some of the products made for animals. Everything from special food to hotel accommodations, pet sitting and photo services are provided for pets. Sanwa Bank has introduced a "deposit service for home pets" ("Pet pampering proves popular productive pastime", 1993). Small pets, particularly hamsters, which have become very popular among children and young women, do not impose a burden on owners. According to Shinji Miyadai, an expert in youth culture, "That is why it is easier to reflect the owners' subjectivity. Similar to role playing and pretense, caring for the pets enables people to act out roles they would not have in real life" ("Stores finding big bucks in little pets", 1998). Japan's leading manufacturer of bathroom fixtures, Toto Ltd., has designed a toilet for use by both people and cats: "The fixture is large and yellow, and consists of a single tank and two seats, one standard-sized and the other a bit smaller. Attached to the flush handle in the middle is a plastic ring shaped like a fish. The idea is that you and your cat can sit side by side during this particularly intimate moment, and either one of you can flush afterward." One of the designers visited pet shops and asked if they had cats that could flush a toilet. He was told no. However, since a video called *Professor Rocky's Toilet Training* provides instruction in persuading one's cat to use a toilet is available, he believes it's possible (Lazarus 1992). A downside to the pet boom is that, in the words of a female university student, "people throw away their pets once they grow up just because they are not cute anymore. They become too big."

While perhaps a useful starting point, the indigenous interpretations just provided fail to account for the semantic tentacles of cuteness which afford it such communicative power in Japanese society. Thus, an examination of how cute objects are situated in a wider web of meanings is necessary.

The Positional Meaning of Cuteness

The concept of cuteness can be better appreciated by positioning it in a complex of meanings from which it derives its significance in relation to other concepts. Below I list meanings usually associated with cuteness on the left and on the right, their opposites (Table 5.1). It must be stressed that these concepts are not necessarily associated or mobilized *in toto* within an individual's mind; some concepts may be used for particular purposes while others may be excluded. If condensed (as explained above), these various meanings can all be boiled down to two key concepts: power and powerless (or controllable/controlled and controlling/controller). This dichotomy is a sociopolitical axis around which the other concepts revolve. At the unconscious level, the different ideas that make up a symbol may associate and interact with other ideas:

Cute images, as images, exist for the most part on the margins of awareness, part of the everyday embellishments that form a pervasive background of mundane existence. Images derive their staying power from their half-idea, half-feeling vagueness, a sort of mental dimness where ambiguity allows for a multiplicity of interpretations (multivocality). Being marginalized from the center of conscious reflection, however, only adds to the power of images, since it is what we do not explicitly ponder that often shapes our subjectivity.

How does the sentiment of cuteness actually build a normative framework? Being socialized into a certain world of values occurs through exposure to pieces, parts and incomplete definitions of a worldview. There is rarely

Table 5.1. *Themes of Cuteness and Their Opposites*

Powerless: controllable/controlled	*Power: controlling/controller*
females	males
weakness	strength
femininity	masculinity
cheerful	gloomy
bright colors	dark colors
infants, children	adults
youth	maturity
light-hearted	serious
outgoing	taciturn
small	large

anything systematic about socialization. Much of what is communicated to us about the social world is done so in such a subtle, insidious manner such that the dynamics of socialization are sometimes difficult to pinpoint. Images that we are repeatedly exposed to and that exist on the margins of our awareness eventually reach the point of becoming automatic and instinctive sentiments. It is the repetitive, ubiquitous nature of seemingly insignificant small pieces of information in our environment which makes images effective mechanisms for belief-building. Speaking of the new sociopolitical norms that the late nineteenth century Swedes were expected to internalize, Frykman and Löfgren write that "The important cultural codes were transmitted more effectively through trivial everyday routines than through cultural preaching" (1987: 271). The same could be said for how cute images communicate important cultural assumptions about gender relations. And embedded in the unthinkingly and incessantly used objects of everyday life, this sentiment is rarely questioned, but always perceived.

Here it might be noted that the ideological and sensory aspects of cuteness are also associated and forged unconsciously, so that the abstract and concrete reinforce each other. The abstractness of cuteness allows it to be generalized across different situations and semantic domains, e.g. infants –> young girls –> women. Examples of conceptual, normative associations (ideological pole) of cute things include: powerlessness, controllable, controlled, weakness, femininity, cheerfulness and youthfulness. Examples of perceptual, concrete associations (sensory pole) of cuteness include: females, bright colors (especially pink), infants, children, small size and toys.

The Operational Meaning of Cute Objects

In this section I examine how cute objects are used by people to do things and used by people to make (i.e. via socialization) others do things. This is the sociopolitical aspect of material culture. I will examine the sociopolitical uses of this material culture from three angles which illustrate its elastic, multipurposeful nature. In the first subsection, I relate cuteness to some fundamental norms of Japanese society which *appear* to keep some women economically, politically and sexually subservient. The reality is far more nuanced, complicated and dynamic, since women can use cuteness to their own advantage. This is why I examine in the next section how cuteness is used by women in feminine self-presentation. Next, I explore what I call "authority cuteness". I save the discussion of the economic, commodified and commercialized uses of cuteness (which ensure that its icons are widely traded and exchanged, effecting its communicative reach and potency) for the next chapter.

The Social Logic of Cute Objects

Cuteness is a multi-use concept, and in examining its social logic we should pay close attention to its political aspects: (1) who is attracted to cute things; (2) who wants to be cute; and (3) who wants others to be cute. Cuteness is an expression of a sociopolitical theory visible in the commodities of everyday life and touches upon the relations between the powerful and the less powerful: family structure, the ubiquitous hierarchical junior/senior relations and, in particular, male/female relations. Being cute toward those above is often a way of obtaining favors and attention, while displaying cuteness to one's subordinates is a method of appearing non-threatening, thereby gaining their confidence, and perhaps more cynically, control over them.

Below I outline what I take to be three main normative themes underlying this aesthetic of everyday life: (1) hierarchy; (2) obedience; and (3) empathy. These themes are part and parcel of the repertoire of values found in Japanese society at large, and though they are expected from both males and females, women in particular are admonished at home, school and the workplace to espouse these values.

Hierarchy. In Japanese society vertical relations, such as *kôhai/sempai* (junior/senior) and *seito/sensei* (student/master), are extremely important, forming the basic social structural constituents from which Japanese build their social world (cf. Nakane 1970). The sentiment of cuteness, I believe, is used to *soften* these superior/inferior relations. However, by "softening" I do not mean that the vertical lines of control are weakened; on the contrary, the lines of power are reinforced since they become emotionally charged with positive feelings of loyalty and commitment. In Japan, social relations based on hierarchy strongly imply gratitude: those on the top receive favors and attention from those below. This is an extremely basic value in Japan, expressed in the words *kansha* (gratitude) and *arigatai* (thankful). Moreover, cuteness sometimes softens these lines of control to the point of disguising them. Or, in the words of one young woman, through cuteness, "smooth communication" (*enkatsu na komyunikêshon*) among people is formed, and according to another young woman, "I pretend to be cute at the office where I work part-time. This is because I do not want to be bothered with complicated human relationships. You could say I abuse cuteness."

Cuteness is used to symbolize, reinforce and communicate norms which privileges males over females and is the ideal sentiment for strengthening lines of authority, since on the surface it is, according to one young woman, *atarisawari ga nai* (inoffensive, harmless). However, another female student explained to me that usually men do not like to be referred to as cute, because *kawaî* "is used for someone we regard as weaker than us". This apparently innocent feeling is not neutral, since "power is tolerable only on condition that it masks a substantial part of itself. Its success is proportional to its ability to hide its own mechanism" (Foucault 1980: 86). Thus, "cute culture has a built-in method of deflecting criticism, simply by nature of its silliness. How angry can you be at plastic barrettes and ankle socks? How seriously can you take a subculture that is, by definition, profoundly inane?" (Schomer and Chang 1995). Those at the bottom of the hierarchy can express their cuteness by being *akarui* (bright, cheerful) and by not being *kurai* (dark, gloomy). *Akarui* is in fact a word frequently heard in discussions of cuteness, connoting sunshine, happiness, smiles and a general state of positiveness (a sunny disposition is especially expected of women). *Yôki* (cheerful, light-hearted) is another similar term often encountered. These concepts indicate a positive attitude, strongly encouraged by authority figures in schools, the company and other social groups in order to effect smooth and efficient operations.

One approach to the sociopolitical dynamics of inferior/superior relations is to examine *amaeru* and *amayakasu*, which capture the sugary emotional bonding between superiors and inferiors. Complementary in meaning, the former means "to solicit the indulgence of another", and the latter, "to indulge, spoil or pamper". These terms are usually used to describe a child's attitude toward his or her parents (particularly the mother) and conversely, the parents' attitude toward the child. Though in itself *amae* (the noun form of the verb *amaeru*) is basically positive, it can sometimes carry a negative evaluation, as expressed in the term *amaekko*, "a young child who is overly indulged". Describing *amaeru* as a sugary sentiment is appropriate since it is related to *amai*, meaning "sweet". This term is often used to refer to someone who is irresponsible, too naive and consequently unprepared for the realities of life. But for present purposes, it is pertinent to note that the desire to look cute is "a typical expression of *amae*" (Doi 1986: 163).[6]

Amaeru and *amayakasu*, as complementary concepts, form a mutually reinforcing emotional dynamic: the powerless is the supplicant and the powerful is the nurturant. The child displays his or her needs, and within the parent – usually the mother – the need to indulge is triggered. However, *amaeru–amayakasu* relations are not limited to the world of the child. This ethnomorality of human emotional bonding is extended to the adult world: a subordinate expresses his or her wants to a social superior and the wish to grant a favor is aroused: "it is clear that the *amaeru–amayakasu* interaction is immensely desirable or useful to most Japanese" (Lebra 1976: 55). But what is notable about *amaeru–amayakasu* relations is their very gendered dimension: this form of passive dependency and its counterpart binds girlfriends to boyfriends, wives to husbands, and in general, women to men, with females ideally soliciting the indulgence of males (though sometimes these roles are reversed).[7] And cuteness, embedded in material objects, does not merely reflect the social world; rather, via communicative acts of self-presentation, it constructs gendered relations.

Obedience. Being "obedient" (*sunao*) is another important cultural desirable in Japan. *Sunao*, which is used toward children as well as adults, actually carries a heavier semantic load, denoting submissiveness, gentleness, meekness, receptiveness, compliance or co-operativeness. White states that, in an educational setting, it is used to describe the "good child" and has many nuances: open-minded, nonresistant, truthful, naive, natural, simple and mild (1987: 28). It also strongly implies positive acceptance of what one is told, and "to not be cute" (*kawaikunai*) can sometimes mean "to be disobedient". Being obedient, of course, reinforces one's position in any hierarchy, whether it is in the family, a school, the workplace or any other social setting. But it is women, more than men, who are expected to be obedient. By being cute, women are able to occupy their "proper place".

Empathy. One cannot be cute unless another recognizes one's charm. Or one's helplessness. The word *kawaî* (cute) is related to *kawaisô* (pitiful, touching) and *kawaigaru* (to love, make a pet of, take loving care of). To be cute triggers a sympathetic response in another, leading to an emotional involvement and perhaps an attachment. A focus on powerlessness – whether seen in infants, small animals or pretty but defenseless females – leads to empathy. Lebra writes that in Japan, empathy (*omoiyari*) "ranks high among the virtues considered indispensable for one to be truly human, morally mature, and deserving of respect. I am even tempted to call Japanese culture an *'omoiyari'* culture" (1976: 38). One learns to become empathetic by avoiding its commonly heard opposite, *wagamama* (selfish).

Empathy also relates to the concern superiors should feel toward juniors. Being in a position of power and privilege, a superior is expected to look out for the welfare of those below. Conversely, juniors should worry about the well-being of those above, usually indicated by feelings of loyalty and devotion. But regardless of which way empathetic concern travels – from superiors to juniors or vice versa – it is assumed that the direction follows a vertical path of either up or down (hierarchy).

However, like obedience, women are expected to invest more of their emotional capital in being empathetic. Children, husbands and male colleagues expect sympathetic treatment from their female counterparts. Thus, in training manuals for OLs, a key term is *omoiyari*. Female workers are expected to demonstrate concern for clients, customers and colleagues.

Personal relations, of course, are important in any society. In Japan, they are stressed to the degree that impersonal, generalized and what may be called rationalized relations (though an inevitable part of social intercourse) imply the undesirable opposite of a caring (*omoiyari*) social life. Japanese regard particularistic and sentimentalized personal relationships as indispensable for one's existence. But the important point is that women, more than men, are expected to internalize this value, or perhaps more accurately, at least display selves that are more oriented toward the personal.

Presenting Oneself as Cute: Femininity and Sexuality

The sentiment of cuteness is most readily associated with young women, and apparently it is this social category of persons that is attracted to cuteness. However, it is not uncommon to see women in their twenties and even older concerning themselves with what is cute (adult cuteness) by dressing in cute clothes and admiring cute styles. Indeed, cuteness is often linked to sexuality (sexy cuteness), sometimes by combining it with more sophisticated styles, in attempts, at what are for some, an attractive form of self-presentation vis-à-vis men.

Though it is quite easy to see how authority figures and powerful instit-utions use images of weakness and cuteness for their own benefit, the social dynamics of everyday aesthetics are complex since those in positions of inferiority can also strategically employ cuteness for their own ends. In this context issues of gender take center stage and from the standpoint of females, young and not so young, being cute is a vital ingredient of feminine self-presentation. This should not be surprising, since the strong association of the characteristics of children with women indicates a symbolic attempt on the part of men to place females in a controllable social position. This is most clearly seen in the portrayal of women in commercials, *manga* (comic books; read by all ages in Japan) and pornography (pornography cuteness). Somehow childlike women are less threatening to men. Since cuteness is part and parcel of the discourse surrounding gender definitions, it is not surprising to find cuteness so much a part of pornography, including child pornography. When portrayed as sexually charged images, women are, to a remarkable degree, presented as very youthful, innocent and naive.[8]

This was suggested to me by a group of young Japanese men who explained that they usually feel more comfortable with cute rather than beautiful women. The latter possessed a certain *sang-froid* which they found unappealing. They also made a distinction between cute women and *burikko* (or a related word, *kawaiko-chan*; "cutie"), a term of relatively recent origin literally meaning a "pretending child". The word is formed from *furi* (to pretend, affect, pose as) plus *ko* (child). Cute women are "really cute" since they are sincere and their attractiveness is natural and unforced. But the term *burikko* has basically negative associations, since females so described are "too cute" and manipulative, and their attempts at being attractive are affected and forced, i.e. an individual's activation of her gendered distal role – of her "I" self-consciously directing her "me" – is not appreciated. Describing OLs, Lo writes that "Consistent with the *burikko* act, women cluttered their desks with toys and pins of Disney characters" (1990: 43). Not all women like the *burikko* act. According to a female university student:

> I hate this word [*burikko*]. Girls in Japan tend to be different when they are with girls or with boys. Their voice changes. I have seen my sister, so I know. When the telephone rings, they clear their throats, and I don't know where this voice comes from, but a cute little voice comes out from somewhere. I hate this moment. They are lying to the people they are talking to. This might be said to be normal for a girl. But when it comes to Seiko Matsuda [famous star] they seem to hate her. *Burriko* women are hated by most women and liked by only a few men. I just want them to stop pretending.

Other young women have described both "cute" women and *burikko* as "good at being coquettish". One woman said that "I often see 'cute' girls chattering with boys while they act vulgar, squatting on the floor. I guess they try to attract others by their 'cute image' and they think that just because they are cute enough their rude behavior can be excused."

Talk shows, women's journals, magazines and books offer tips on how to become cute, and there is a definite awareness of how cuteness can be strategically used to a woman's advantage, one writer describing it as a "weapon" (Takasu 1988: 36–8). A good example of how cuteness can be used as a tactic in self-presentation is Satô Ayako's *A Clever Women Lives in a Cute Manner*, in which methods for using cuteness are explicitly dealt with in an almost Goffmanesque discourse. In the beginning of her book she writes, "I'll say it frankly. This book is for those who keep locked away in their heart a complete plot of their own life, but want to express their attractive self as a cute woman" (1988: 3).

It wasn't until I had a class of female college students draw pictures of themselves and their families as an exercise in an English workbook that I realized that not a small number of Japanese women regard themselves as basically cute and many surrounded themselves with cute things. This was seen in another assignment that netted pictures of their rooms in which not a few drew assorted stuffed animals, teddy bears, dolls and according to one student's written description, "teddy cats". One student told me that "girls want to be like a baby, innocent and pure". Or at least they would like to be regarded as such. Of the thirty or so pictures I received, all could easily be described as cute, with a definite tendency toward infantilizing: big heads, large eyes (usually round), cheerful smiles and dispositions and extremely youthful parents. Here it might be noted that feminist Andrea Dworkin takes a very dim view of the infantilization of women, since it is a way of keeping women "inferior, weaker, smaller and dumber" . . . "It would be a lie to think that is about adult women. It's about children, about having a sexual interest and obsession with children" (Schomer and Chang 1995).

After they reach their late twenties or early thirties (or after they get married, since this rite of passage is the most important temporal marker of adulthood for a Japanese female), the interest in the material culture of cuteness diminishes somewhat. "Somewhat" is relative, because although they put away their stuffed animals and throw away their brightly colored outfits embroidered with chicks and penguins, cute creatures and the like can be seen populating the surfaces of the daily conveniences of middle-class life: a cheerful mouse on an apron, a grinning piglet on a vacuum cleaner, or perhaps a pink elephant beaming from the corner of a refrigerator door. Some mothers and their daughters can be seen wearing matching clothes. The polysemic and ambiguous nature of cuteness has allowed its images to move to the margins of daily utensils, dress and adornment. But they have not been totally banished. Far from it. Indeed, it may easily be argued that rather than diminishing, the power of cuteness increases for a married woman since it exerts its pervasive pull on their heart strings in a more subtle, indirect and implicit manner. In an example of adult cuteness, married women should still be cute, but not publicly rejoice in it. However, some women do make a fashion statement about being cute by buying certain objects:[9]

> Young working women and female college students, the nation's foremost fad followers, are buying toiletry for babies and kids. The selling points of soaps, shampoos, creams and toothbrushes made for toddlers are their mildness and cute designs and packaging . . . The never-ending quest for cuteness also explains why young women buy mild perfumes made for children ("From the cradle to the toiletry market: young women go gaga for baby products", 1995).

A female Japanese acquaintance of mine is in the habit of drawing pictures of herself next to the text in her letters to me. Not unlike the images found in comics, her cartoon-like images supplement the written word by expressing emotions and are accompanied by the appropriate onomatopoeia. And of course, she portrays herself in these self-portraits as very young, cheerful and lovable.

Significantly, the new wife will soon acquire another social role that will have her buying, using and more or less devoting herself to all types of cute things and images with a passion: she will become a mother. It will be in this capacity that she treats her offspring with doses of affection and authority, creating in the child's mind the paradoxical relation between softness and firmness, sweetness and sanction and, of course, mothers will dress their charges in cute outfits (baby and very young cuteness). Indeed, cuteness points to an association between "baby-ishness" and motherhood (maternal cuteness). More concretely, cute objects are attractive to women because they link an affinity for babies and being a good mother to children (and by extension, a good husband).

Even as mothers become older, cuteness is not left behind, since there is "a growing number of elderly people obsessed with the idea of being 'cute'". The best examples of "elderly cuteness" are the media phenomena Kin-san and Gin-san (their names mean "gold" and "silver" respectively), twin sisters who, as of 1998, are 106 years old and frequently appear on TV. One survey reported that 70 percent of women and 24 percent of men between 60 and 74 said they wanted to be seen as cute. One fashion designer who makes "cute" dresses for the elderly said: "Nobody will approach a horrible-looking elderly woman. Expressing cuteness is a key to smooth communication with younger generations and avoids their resistance." However, not all elderly people like cuteness. The essayist Haru Ataka says that "Something is wrong in society if they [the elderly] have to behave 'cute' because they fear that they will be hated if they behave as they want" ("'Cute' grandma syndrome redefining societal norms", 1996).

Authority Cuteness

There is another side to the softening of hierarchical relations, *the display of weakness by authority figures or centers of power*. Such softening can be called authority cuteness, and concerns those who use images of weakness and subordination. We should be aware of how centers of authority (state agencies, educators, large companies, etc.) attempt to associate themselves with smiling babies, innocent children, talking animals, pretty colors, innocent funny creatures and *akarui* (cheerful) things. If those in positions of power can convince those below them that they are in fact not intimidating, the task of persuading, influencing and controlling them becomes easier.[10] In advertising, powerful people and institutions make themselves appear weak by employing images of women (to stress female vulnerability, often with tearful faces). Banks and companies place stuffed animals here and there inside their offices. Often they have specially made dolls representing clerks and workers placed on desks with their names written on them. Like cuteness, attractive young women also "soften" authority and are apparently a necessary accompaniment of many candidates. Dressed in bright colors and wearing white gloves, they can be seen waving from candidates' vans or platforms during campaigns, smiling and shouting to pedestrians: "Hello! Please give us your support!" For example, there was the political candidate who "took to Tokyo Bay in a motorboat filled to the gunwales with stuffed bears, balloons and pretty young girls" (untitled photo, DY 5 February 1990: 3). The Liberal Democratic Party distributed "cute" dolls designed in the likeness of Prime Minister Hashimoto Ryûtarô before a general election ("LDP courts voters with 'ryu' doll", 1996).

The use of cuteness to persuade, warn and admonish is quite conspicuous. From the warning signs of construction sites, public service announcements, to materials put out by the government on health-related matters, warnings from authorities are softened and made more acceptable to the general public. Japan Railways uses posters with a picture of the Rika doll (the less sexualized Japanese sister to the Barbie doll) to campaign for better etiquette on trains and in train stations. In one poster, Rika is portrayed holding a cellular phone that is as big as she is, thereby making her look cuter. It is not uncommon to see danger signs posted near lakes and ponds with colorful cartoon figures thrashing about in the water, or posters with comic book characters being knocked down by speeding cars. If it were not for their serious subject matter these warning signs would come off appearing remarkably silly. Five workers' unions have launched a campaign in an attempt to cut back on energy consumption. The campaign character is a cute bear called "Coco-chan".

A good example of authority cuteness is how the Self-Defense Forces exploit cuteness in a recruiting ad: in the foreground the smiling face of a young girl with military personnel in the background. But the best instance of authority's use of cuteness is notable for its incongruity – its use by police.[11] This is a good example of the ambiguity and polysemic aspect usually associated with a key concept. I saw an example of this when a large number of officers were stationed at the Meiji Jingu Shrine one New Year's Eve for purposes of crowd control. Sporting crisply pressed blue uniforms, wearing no-nonsense faces and armed with all the necessary equipment, their stern appearance was contrasted with bright yellow armbands displaying smiling suns. Some police officers, in order to direct the flow of the crowd, held up huge signs with a picture of "Pipo-kun", a cheerful mouse-like creature used in public safety campaigns. Pipo-kun, together with the smaller Pipo-chan, act as PR figures for the police. They can be seen on signs warning impatient drivers of the dangers of speeding and next to scowling mug shots of the most-wanted criminals in Japan, gleefully asking for public assistance in tracking them down. Beaming Pipo-kun and Pipo-chan can be seen observing pedestrians and traffic from some police boxes (*kôban*) – the official gaze rendered less threatening by being made cute and cartoon-like. The names come from the sound a siren makes in Japanese: *pipo pipo*. *Kun* and *chan* are diminutives added onto names. My local police box in Tokyo had Pipo-chan standing on the window sill, smiling at passing pedestrians. I once stopped by to inquire as to where I could purchase a member of the Pipo family. Without the slightest trace of irony, a police officer seriously but politely explained to me that I could not buy Pipo-kun or Pipo-chan in any department store. They were specially made for the police.

In a more international vein, the Japanese Foreign Ministry published a half-page ad in Russia's largest daily, *Trud*, welcoming Yeltsin to Japan. The robotic cat cartoon character, Doraemon, who is popular with children, appeared in the ad, saying "I heard that Mr Yeltsin is coming to Japan on Monday. Please make a lot of friends in Japan". According to an official of the Ministry, it was hoped that the ad would win over Russian public opinion, helping in the sensitive negotiations over the return of the northern territories to Japan: "If the Russian people feel more friendly toward Japanese (as a result of the ad), it will be easier for Yeltsin to decide to return the islands" ("Doraemon ad in Russian welcomes Yeltsin's visit", 1992). At times the contrast between serious matters and the cute images used to address them become noticeably incongruous, at least according to a visitor to the Earthquake Science Hall in Tokyo: "My only criticism of the Science Hall is that it fails to engender a similar feeling of horror in its static displays. Candy-box cartoons running around over cracked pavements and homely, cartoon mothers smiling and giving sweet advice hardly reflects the feelings of having to survive in the teeth of disaster" (Hadfield 1989).

One very common manner in which authority cuteness expresses itself is by making uniformed figures – security personnel, train station employees, construction site workers – cute. For example, signs warning pedestrians of the dangers at work sites have what may be called "infantilized" workmen with large heads and wide eyes. Often bowing and surrounded by wavy lines indicating the trembling of apprehension, they politely warn those passing by to be careful or offer apologies for inconveniencing pedestrians. In an apparent bow to "internationalization", some signs display blonde, blue-eyed women cheerfully warning pedestrians. Another example: not far from my Tokyo residence is a small factory with a sign on the fence near the entrance. The sign has a uniformed and infantilized figure, diagramming "protective helmet", "chin strap", "cuffs", "safety boots", "cuffed pants", "safety belt", Written above him are the words: "Verify correct dress and protective gear." Next to this representation is a mirror so workers can check themselves against the diagram.

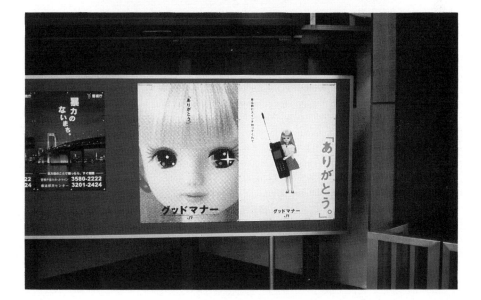

Table 5.2. *Types of Cuteness*

Innocence

• Baby Cuteness	• Authority Cuteness
• Very Young Cuteness	• Corporate Cuteness
• Young Cuteness	• Maternal Cuteness
	• Adult Cuteness
	• Elderly Cuteness
	• Teen Cuteness

Infantile   **Mature**

	• Sexy Cuteness
• Child Pornography Cuteness	
	• Pornography Cuteness

Eroticism

Conclusion

To sum up what I have contended about just how pervasive and elastic cuteness is as a concept in Japan, I map some conceptual order onto cuteness in Table 5.2. Note that this Table illustrates types of cuteness which are given off during self-presentation and perhaps used as an interpersonal strategy by a social actor (or as the case may be, institutions) *and/or* are attributed to an individual or group of people by others. The most obvious expressions of cuteness are plotted, though there are undoubtedly others.

In the next chapter, I provide examples of how cuteness, as something that is encountered everywhere, is a sentiment that has been objectified, commodified and commercialized, affording it not only communicative potency among social actors but also transforming it into a form of consumption that suggests resistance – though diffused, incidental and random – to the dominant official world view of production for production's sake.

Notes

1. Note White's observation that "the *kawaii* culture spans several age groups" (1994: 127).
2. See "*Kawaii* Culture: Cuteness Is All" (White 1994: 126–7).
3. E.g. Schomer and Chang's "The Cult of Cuteness" (1995).
4. See Kinsella's discussion of "anti-cute people" (1995: 246–50).
5. Traditional aesthetics in Japan have frequently emphasized the miniature (personal communication, Kathe Geist).
6. The concept of *amae* was made famous by Doi Takeo, a psychiatrist who claimed that to *amaeru* was a strong need among his Japanese patients. Basing his theorizing on Freudian psychoanalytic theory, he argues that the influence of *amae* can be seen in a wide range of social institutions and cultural phenomena in Japan. His tendency to overgeneralize the importance of *amae* and reduce complex social phenomena to this one concept weaken his work. Interestingly enough, as Lebra points out, Doi did not take the counterpart of *amayakasu*, into consideration in his explanation of *amae* (1976).
7. Goffman notes that, at least in the West, some draw on parent-child relations to interpret adult interaction, particularly male-female relations in which super-ordinates exercise "benign control" over subordinates: "whenever a male has dealings with a female or a subordinate male (especially a younger one), some mitigation of potential distance, coercion, and hostility is quite likely to be induced by application of the parent-child complex" (1979: 5). I am grateful to Daniel Miller for alerting me to Goffman's observation.
8. Cuteness in pornography also seems to play another role: that of making sex less threatening, somehow more safe, even comical. Some pornographic magazines

have cartoon figures of anthropomorphized sexual organs, both male and female, talking, walking and often giving advice about effective sexual techniques. In a more pedagogical vein, sex and cuteness come together in *Sekusu no ehon* (A Picture Book of Sex), a sex education video for children (ages 2–10) in which male and female genitalia are anthropomorphized. A manual on sexual technique in the form of a comic book (*For Beginners, sei,* (Sex)) uses cartoon figures in its explanations. Even a guide on AIDS (*For Beginners, eizu: sei, ai, byôki,* (AIDS: Sex, Love, and Illness)) employs cute images to get its dire points across about the need for safe sex. And an AIDS-awareness exhibition by Akiyama Takashi displayed posters and paintings with smiling anthropomorphized condoms ("AIDS awareness with art", 1992). One observer notes that while flipping through a pamphlet on AIDS, he noticed how the HIV virus "was depicted as a snaggle toothed critter with antennae and a pointy tail" (Brasor 1995).

9. Recently, there has been a trend for young women to buy soaps, shampoos, toothbrushes and mild perfumes especially made for children ("From the cradle to the toiletry market", 1995). I am grateful to Meg Miller for pointing out the association between "baby-ishness" and motherhood and for providing me with the *Nikkei Weekly* article.

10. It is worth noting that such convincing and persuasion has its counterpart in language. Concerning the proper sociolinguistic forms which should be used by the powerful in Japanese, Mizutani and Mizutani make the following point: "The underlying idea is that influential persons should act so as to conceal their power and put their weaker associates at ease. It is generally regarded as good and even considerate for influential persons to occasionally show weakness. Needless to say, such weakness should not be vital ones, but it is better to have some weaknesses than to be perfectly strong and consequently powerful or intimidating" (1987: 44).

11. Japan, of course, is not the only society in which authority is sweetened with cute images. A newspaper article mentioned how new tax forms in Hungary "bear cheerful cartoons explaining how they should be filled in" (LeCallier 1988).

6

Countering the Official Code by "Consuming Cuteness"

Resistance Consumption

There are numerous reasons why people consume, but in this chapter I explore what I term "resistance consumption", i.e. acts of consumption (implicated in purchasing, wearing, admiring, displaying, giving, trading, exchanging, adopting a certain style) that counter the dominant, official world view. The adoption of a certain style "offends the majority, challenges the principle of unity and cohesion, and contradicts the myth of consensus" (Hebdige 1979: 18).

There are any number of styles, of course, through which the act of resistance consumption is manifested. Below I focus on and offer instances of cuteness as an example of resistance consumption for three reasons. First, its thorough permeation of popular culture characterizes it as central to any understanding of self-presentation (especially the mode of expressed selves, though elements of stylized and performed selves are also important) in Japan. Second, as a ubiquitous daily aesthetic, cuteness and its associated themes mirror the official ideology of statist and capitalist production, i.e. cuteness/leisure is the antithesis of seriousness/labor. In the same way that "Sullenness, muttering, irony, joking, and sarcasm may allow one to show that something of oneself lies outside the constraints of the moment and outside the role within whose jurisdiction the moment occurs" (Goffman 1990: 107), adorning or associating oneself with cuteness positions one, if only temporarily, outside the demands of the highly ordered regimes of labor, and gives rise to displays of *jibun-rashisa* ("self-likeness"). Third, in spite of the fact that cuteness appears to oppose (at least at the aesthetic level) Japan's productivist capitalist order, at a deeper level cuteness exemplifies the inherent connections between productivist capitalism and consumptivist capitalism. Ultimately, production and consumption, work and play and labor and leisure cannot be divided, since they all feed off each other. Put simply, presenting oneself as cute requires money, and this in turn requires participation in corporate structures.

By "resistance consumption" I do not mean a conscious, organized and systematic insurrection against the statist and capitalist order. Resistance consumption does not forcibly question, it raises some doubts; it does not directly challenge, it playfully provokes; it does not deride, it humorously mocks; it does not threaten, it ignores; it does not attempt an overthrow, it briefly displaces; it is not insurgent, it is carnivalesque; it does not subvert, it diverts attention (if only temporarily) from the dominant structures; it does not attempt to stage a political revolution, it encourages participation in hedonistic agitation. Practices associated with the consumption of cuteness are not antistate or anticorporate in any organized, explicit or obvious sense; they are not self-conscious "political statements". Resistance consumption, then, does not directly target power structures; indeed, resistance consumption is more often than not inherently ironic, since the same individuals who so desire to consume devote themselves to the officially condoned productivist lifestyle in order to accumulate capital so they can consume. Resistance consumption is where productivist and consumptivist ideologies come together and indeed, mutually reinforce each other, and I contend that it is through the consumption of "cuteness" that these two ideologies most obviously meet. Though there are undoubtedly prewar antecedents of these processes, it was during the postwar period, particularly during the period of the high economic growth of the 1960s, that the engines of lathered production and heated desire went into full drive:

> Once "democratization" was replaced by economic development as the overriding objective, most Japanese had little choice but to become socialized to corporate and national goals. As time passed, such regimentation was sweetened by the material rewards of prosperity and hardened by nationalistic appeals. The emergence of a mass consumer society created an ethos of "middle-class" homogeneity and contributed immeasurably to depoliticization (or preoccupation with personal and local matters) (Dower 1993: 31).

In Japan's bureaucratized landscape, communications lines should be hierarchical; institutional affiliation (school, workplace, company, nationality) should be clearly categorized; presentations of selves should be performed and displayed in a standardized fashion ("I"-observes-"me"); and individual qualities should not be personalized but modular (the reality, of course, is far more complicated and nuanced). But with so much pressure to accept these imperatives of rationalization, it is no wonder that the official values of the state (especially as seen in school educatio-socialization) and capital (corporations) discourage one from being *seken-banare* (different from *seken*, eccentric, strange), *seken-shirazu* (unaware of *seken* rules, naive), or "standing out" (*medatsu*). Though there is much rhetoric about the importance of expressing one's individuality (*kosei*), in the actual daily practices of schooling and labor such expressions are often muted, especially since one is warned about the trap of adopting the individualism (*kojin shugi*) of "foreign" (read non-Japanese) ways; one's "I" should carefully monitor one's "me".

However, despite the best efforts of official power structures – whether manifested through teachers, parents and managers – total socialization, or the complete shaping of the subjective substructures is impossible. Indeed, individuals may absorb ideological imperatives but appropriate these same imperatives for purposes that counter elite goals. Furthermore, different individuals may pursue the same goals but use dissimilar tactics (or vice versa). In any case, there are times, places and situations in which "being conspicuous" and "showing off" are encouraged, and it is through the acts and practices of resistance consumption that such "showing off" is implemented. According to one young woman, "fashion is no longer about looking nice to please other people ['I' monitors/manages 'me']. I dress for myself ['I' & 'me' equated/identified] . . . I dress to feel good, and to get my picture out there . . . and then I'll get a lot of respect from my friends" (quoted in Shoji 1998).

Recently, the media has made much of the appearance of young junior and high school females who dye their hair light brown (*chapatsu*), wear miniskirts and wear make-up so as to have a pale complexion but contrast it with dark lipstick. Young women who adopt these styles are often associated with juvenile delinquency, *enjo kôsai* (young women paid to date men, sometimes for prostitution) and *oyagi gari* (young women hunting middle-aged men for money), though such associations seem to indicate hyped-up, voyeuristic journalism rather than objective reporting. In any case, it was reported that currently, female high school students make up only 4 percent of Japan's population, "but these young women in particular command a disproportionate share of the media and marketing spotlight" (Watanabe 1997). Unlike their male counterparts who are regarded as not as adventuresome and more susceptible to social pressures of conformity, young female consumers set the consumption trends for much of Japan. Consider this: according to the Japan Credit Rating Agency, about 68 percent of Japanese teens receive on average $220 a month, *plus* regular gifts of cash from parents and grandparents, "ranging from as much $1,700 for entering high school to $90 to celebrate birthdays and New Years'" (and this does not include money received from part-time work) (Watanabe 1997). According to one young woman, "We want to be cute. We want to have fun. We like the same things." Teens with such desires, from a business perspective, "represent the last, best bastion of potentially profitable group-think" (Watanabe 1997). However, many people do not look favorably upon young women presenting themselves in "untraditional" highly consumption-oriented ways. Some believe that female high school students "lack an inner core and suffer from the boredom of acquiring whatever they want without having to sweat for it" and possess a mentality of *genzai shikô* (living for the moment). A researcher at the Japan Youth Research Institute blames Japan's rigid society for not encouraging young women to be a more career-oriented society. "With teens like these, Japan is finished" (Watanabe 1997). According to another observer, "When I see those fake stars on the street, I cannot but wonder if they have their own individual personality" ("Readers' Forum: What do you think of the recent trend in which people dye their hair brown in chapatsu fashion?" 1996).

Contrasting Styles of Aesthetics-Ethics

How are productivist capitalism and consumptivist capitalism expressed as styles? This is too big a question to answer comprehensively, but in order to remain relevant to the topics of this book, I examine uniformity ("official ideology" of capitalist production) and non-uniformity ("antiofficial ideology" of popular consumption). A key difference between official and antiofficial ideologies is that the former possesses a clearly defined agenda along with strategies, while the latter is less concerned with pursuing specific goals determined by power centers. Here I want to reiterate that I employ "anti" not to mean direct, organized and purposeful resistance, but rather to mean indirect, unorganized and untargeted alienation vis-à-vis the dominant power structures. In this sense, the meaning of "anti" is closer to "contra" or "non". Though the official ideology is dominant, both it and the antiofficial ideology are both products of Japanese society's hegemonic (in the Gramscian sense) statist–capitalist nexus. Therefore, whether one is engaged in labor or leisure, these two forms of practice are linked since there is no production *sans* consumption and vice versa. The consumption of cuteness, whether by young children, teens, or adults, supports and drives productive forces, which in turn manufacture cute material culture for the purpose of capitalist accumulation. Consumerist desires and dreams are fundamentally inseparable from productivist demands and needs, and perhaps at a deeper level, the antiofficial ideology is part of "friendly authoritarianism", which "relies upon joyful, amusing, and pleasant entertainments such as songs, visual arts, and festivals to make sure that authority infiltrates without obvious pains" (Sugimoto 1997: 246).

Besides an ethical dimension, the official and antiofficial ideologies each possess their own aesthetic (see Table 6.1), though sometimes these two aesthetics–ethics come together: some private schools have "cute uniforms" (*kawaî seifuku*) (Aikawa 1994: 13) and in Mori's *Tôkyô joshi kô seifuku zukan* (Women's High Schools of Tokyo Picture Book of Uniforms (1985)) and *Misshon sukûru zukan* (Picture Book of Mission Schools (1993)) all the drawings of young women wearing uniforms are portrayed as cute in the sense of being infantilized (i.e. large, doe-like eyes, round faces, heads slightly large and out of proportion, etc.). They are also cheerfully (*akaruku*) smiling or have their mouths slightly open in what may be described as an expression of childlike, naive wonderment. Moreover, "University students are attracted to part-time jobs that have cute (*kawaî*) uniforms" (Watanabe 1994: 19) (also cf. examples of authority cuteness in the previous chapter). The most specific (if not the best) representation of the official uniformity aesthetic in terms of material culture are uniforms, with their (usually) straight lines, sharp angles, solid colors, symmetrical designs and smooth surfaces. Though the antiofficial aesthetic–ethic cannot be restricted to cuteness, *kawaisa* exemplifies expressions of non-uniformity. In terms of dress, non-uniformed clothing has rounded lines, curves, various colors, asymmetrical designs and perhaps an appliqué of small animals.

Here it may be noted that as something expressed visually, cuteness appears to gravitate toward the traditional Japanese aesthetic of *hade* (colorful, gaudy, flashy) and away from its opposite, *jimi* (plain, simple, subdued).[1] The *hade–jimi* dichotomy includes additional connotations of youth, spontaneity, fun-loving activities and quirkiness, versus maturity, control, sophistication and the staid. Cuteness is also closely associated with the notion of *akarui* (cheerful, sunny, lively), a linguistic staple of Japanese social life and advertisement. Perhaps a liking for "cheerful colors" explains a fad among young people to buy "flamboyantly colored" wristwatches, eyeglasses and electronic alarms (carried for personal protection) ("Brightly colored products to enjoy bright future", 1997). Needless to say, there is nothing cute about its opposite, *kurai* (gloomy) and while it is often considered chic for men to appear taciturn, women who do so are usually regarded as impertinent.

For the sake of argument and organization, we can speak of three types of acts or self-presentation styles linked to consumption that display sentiments of resistance. The first is appropriation: to adopt clothes, objects or a style of presentation that is foreign to what is usually expected by the community (e.g. *seken*). The second is subversion: to alter, damage or remove (nudity) one's ensemble or its components in some way. The third is conversion: rather than altering the garment itself, the wearer changes the *meaning* of the garment or ensemble. These three types are not exclusive, and any individual agent usually adopts tactics from each type. All types involve consumption to varying degrees. Below I offer some examples of each type.

Table 6.1. *The Aesthetics–Ethics of the Official Ideology and the Antiofficial Ideology*

Official Ideology: Capitalist Production	Antiofficial Ideology: Popular Consumption
Activity in Daily Life:	*Activity in Daily Life:*
Production	Consumption
Labor	Leisure
Work	Play
Reality	Fantasy
Style of Object/Clothes:	*Style of Object/Clothes:*
Uniformity	Non-Uniformity
Serious	Cuteness
Controlled	Uncontrolled
Order	Disorder
Covered	Exposed
Subdued (*jimi*)	Gaudy (*hade*)
Socioeconomic Relations:	*Socioeconomic Relations:*
Accumulation of Capital	Accumulation of Experiences
Social Role	Self-Expression
Groupism	Individuality
Official Policy (*tatemae*)	Personal Opinion (*honne*)
Planned	Spontaneous
Serious (*majime*)	Cheerful (*akarui, yôki*)
Formal	Informal
Scripted	Unprompted
Restrained	Unrestrained
Rehearsed	Unrehearsed
Arranged	Impromptu
Important	Trivial
Hierarchical	Egalitarian
Predictability	Unpredictability
Sociopsychological Dynamics Stressed	*Sociopsychological Dynamics Stressed*
"I" Observes "me"	"I" Merges with "me"
Performed Selves	Expressed Selves

Appropriation. White notes that there are two salient styles in Japan's teen culture: "cute and rebellious" (1994: 128–9) which can be placed on a continuum. Cute style has already been introduced in the previous chapter and will be further discussed below. At the rebellious or "nasty" end of the

> continuum are high punks, rappers and gangsters [who adopt *furio* style], though it should be noted that for the most part these are "baaad" styles (in the American approving sense) rather than evidence of bad *behavior*. Just as the Yoyogi Park Sunday dancers are in costume, so the neighborhood punk fashions are part of a performance as well. Punk ranges from an *haute* punk, expensive Italian leather and stylishly outlandish Madonna and hard metal outfits, to cheaper, home-riveted torn jeans and Korean leather jackets. Both affect unusual colors of hair, but the more conservative youth color with wash-out tints, removable in one rinse in a public bathroom. Punks of both sexes vie to create artistic to aggressively repellent facial makeup effects with cheek stripes and ghoulish green-grey eye sockets – not at school, of course (White 1994: 129, original emphasis).

Note should also be made of Japan's teenage bikers who use dress, language, motorcycles, cars and other accouterments to make it a point to be *medatsu* ("to be conspicuous") and who, despite their antiestablishment pretenses, are often (but not always) "well-groomed, and carefully dressed in elegant if bizarre costumes" (Sato 1991: 1). Furthermore, there are also other styles, such as *amekaji* (American casual style of dress), "preppy" (White 1994), the "outdoor" look, the British look and even "fascist fashion".[2] There is also the style of "conspicuous poverty". An example of this is the fad (most noticeable in Osaka) of carrying a flat, cloth shoulder bag that looks like a "pilgrim's scrip [cloth shoulder bag]". It is said that such bags give their carriers a "slender look". The "cheaper the bag looks", the more fashionable it is, and compared to expensive name-brand bags sold in department stores, their "'value is almost zero, as they are not creative-looking at all,' a scrip-toting girl scoffs". Some say they like it because it is as if they were carrying a "stuffed doll" (i.e. something cute) ("Teens have fashion in the bag", 1998).

Wearing make-up can also be a form of subversion for the simple fact that, though make-up becomes *de rigueur* once a young woman graduates from high school and enters the labor force or attends higher education, its use before graduation is usually forbidden. However, according to one survey, 56.2 percent of 1,000 students put on make-up after class (Nakanishi 1997a: 73). In any case, "Cute boys and girls both may use makeup, but keep to pale tints and natural tones. Schools almost invariably forbid makeup, so even these light cosmetics are relegated to weekend or evening use. Makeup kits for young teens resemble American children's play makeup kits and obvious makeup is rarely seen" (White 1994: 129).

Subversion.   Whether to make an antiestablishment statement or to simply express their fashion sense, many students violate school dress codes as pointed out in Chapter 3. As an editor of a fashion magazine for young people stated, "I think it's really interesting in Japan, the land of uniforms, how everyone – especially high school students – starts out with the same clothes but alters them to their own tastes" (Badtke-Berkow 1997). Many female students state that they attempt to present themselves as "cute" in their uniforms as a way to challenge school authorities (though admittedly it is often unclear what is "cute" about their presentation). Many male students seem to take delight in violating conventions of appearance by not buttoning their uniforms, letting their shirt tails hang out, carrying non-regulation accessories, wearing earrings, dyeing their hair, or even piercing their noses or lips. Some female students wear make-up in blatant violation of schools rules which forbid the use of cosmetics (or put make-up on after school while still in uniform), or alter their skirts by shortening or lengthening them. According to one male student, "I wear different shoes, change the jacket buttons, or wear tight-fitting or baggy pants. In this way I can show my personality." One female student explained that "even if I'm wearing a uniform, I can still enjoy some degree of fashion. For example, I can make my skirt just a little shorter than it should be, or wear short or long socks, allowing me to secretly show off my individuality." While off campus and not in uniform, students can adopt styles that twist conventional standards and call for attention. Some young men wear pants several centimeters below the waist, revealing their underwear in what is called the "slovenly style" (or hip-hop in the US). Or consider *degagutsu* (big shoes), *odekogutsu* (forehead shoes) or *bakagutsu* (foolish shoes), shoes for both males and females which are especially popular in Osaka and which may be thirty centimeters long with a sole more than ten centimeters thick. "Girls find it cute – the bottom-heavy silhouette is reminiscent of the footwear favored by Mickey Mouse or Charles Chaplin" ("Sizing up the big-shoes craze", 1997).

As an example of subversion, consider "lingerie-like dresses" that are now popular. "At present, boutiques are over-flowing with lingerie-like clothing, such as camisoles. Many magazines for young women feature articles on the latest fashion and camisoles are the new fashion trend" (see "Readers' Forum: What do you think about lingerie-like dresses now in fashion among young women?" 1998). Debate about this phenomenon was laden with moral judgments, ranging from strong support to condemnation. Another example of subversion concerns a phenomenon of the early 1990s: *otachidai gyaru* ("platform girls") were young women who would – in outfits hardly deserving to be called such – dance on stage in discos while others watched. *Otachidai gyaru* became a trend that included "sexiness contests" on TV. Men enjoyed gazing at and visually consuming dancers who were practically nude,[3] and for their part, the women enjoyed being gazed at. This phenomenon was "a happy symbiosis of exhibitionists and voyeurs: The women were there to dance, pose and provoke; the men, with their slick suits, salon tans and lots of hair gel, came to ogle and scheme [to pick up women]" (Fazio 1993). It should be noted that in Osaka such performances are not limited to women: "men are stripping to the waist and gyrating to the disco beat on stage, to the cheers of female onlookers" ("Men baring almost all at Osaka discos", 1993).

Conversion. Radically transforming the meaning of clothes, objects and other forms of material culture that have been imposed by a dominant power structure for one's own purpose is the most subtle of the three types of resistance.[4] But perhaps this form of resistance is the most effective, since the powers that be will be reluctant to have individuals stop wearing and using officially condoned items of material culture and yet fear their subversive uses. If a student dons a uniform yet does not alter it in any way but nevertheless *reinterprets* its meaning, there is very little a school can do. Traditionally, students have viewed their uniforms as a signal to others that they are not adults, but rather asexual individuals dependent on others. But Kataoka notes that in teen culture among some female students, the meaning of uniforms has changed, from "though I'm sexy in spite of my uniform" to precisely "because it's a uniform I'm sexy and cute" (1997: 123).[5] Cuteness itself has been appropriated by young people (especially young women) to mean "open-minded", "frank" and the "power of being liberated" (*kaihôteki na chikara*). In addition to being discussed in relation to what is fashionable, attractive, nice-looking, young people also use cuteness to mean "cool" (*kakkoi*) (nominal form, *kakkoyosa*). Being cute is also associated with being permitted a greater margin to be "chic" (*iki*) (Nakanishi 1997b: 115–21) and being "stylish" (*oshare*), which after all, affords the "feeling of being separated" from society (Washida 1996: 31). In short, cuteness allows a young person to express his or her *jibun-rashisa* ("self-likeness").

Another use of cute things, reported by Kinsella, turns its "male = superordinate, female = subordinate" message on its head: by adopting cute style, some women petulantly refuse to accept the traditionally subservient female role, so that cuteness becomes a way to defy socially sanctioned gender norms rather than support them (1995: 249). Kinsella also notes how, by idolizing childhood, young Japanese people implicitly reject their futures as responsibility-laden adults in society (1995: 241). By romanticizing their past, young people are able to scorn the "values central to the organization of Japanese society and the maintenance of the work ethic" (Kinsella 1995: 251). Thus, "Being cute meant behaving childlike – which involved an act of self-mutilation, posing with pigeon toes, pulling wide-eyed innocent expressions, dieting, acting stupid, and essentially denying the existence of the wealth of insights, feelings, and humour that maturity brings with it" (Kinsella 1995: 237).

Otachidai gyaru, students who violate school uniform regulations, local ruffians, young people dripping with gooey cuteness, and other individuals who breach dress conventions and rework dress codes prove that, contrary to the hopes and visions of hegemonic institutions, there are individuals who present themselves on the stage of society in an "un-uniformed" and "conspicuous" (*medatsu*) manner. Ironically, like fashion itself, presenting oneself as cute by purchasing material culture becomes a tyranny for the masses; following fashion is a type of uniformity. In the words of a male university student, "there's not much difference between school uniforms and regular clothes among young women who dress up. They are just wearing uniforms called 'fashion.'" The paradoxical nature of fashion explains its inherent instability: a goal everyone is charging at and to which one rushes in order to present oneself as distinct. Those who do not follow the trends are *utoi* ("be ignorant of", "unacquainted with", even "estranged from"), and it is debatable and depends on the individual, if those who do not follow trends are engaging in resistance.

Corporate Cuteness

"Who ever invented 'cuteness' was a genius," a male Japanese university student once commented to me. After all, unlike other certain forms of resistance consumption that are hard-edged, "cuteness is also safe and predictable; it doesn't test the margins of acceptability and provides a teen and industry stamp of approval" (White 1994: 127). What can be made cute and packaged for public purview is virtually limitless. One observer comments on how school pencils, erasers and notebooks are inevitably "cutely disguised with kittens with ribbons on their heads, little children with pink and blue hair who live among the stars, or perhaps a pink rabbit with one floppy ear" (Anton 1992b). The German company Steiff, which produces high-quality stuffed animals, has so far manufactured limited editions of nine types of Teddy bears only for Japan (Japan Teddy). These include Nagano Bear (for the Nagano Olympics) and Mifuyu (Beautiful Winter) ("The bear facts about Steiff teddies", 1998). Speaking of the 1998 Nagano Olympics, the official mascots were four owl-like "Snowlets" – from "snow" + "let's", which, organizers explained, "calls on everyone to join in the fun". These creatures, called Sukki, Nokki, Lekki and Tsukki (two boys and two girls), were put in stuffed-animal form (including life-size versions that greeted visitors) and found on an entire array of items, ranging from stationery, lunch boxes, ear muffs, to condoms ("Nagano suffers stuffed Snowlet shortage", 1998).

In addition to stuffed animals, assorted knick-knacks and advertisements, cuteness shows up in the most unexpected places and scenes: the fuselage of an All Nippon Airways airplane is covered with characters from the cartoon "Peanuts" ("ANA sorry for Snoopy's illegal flights", 1998). In one restaurant, hamburgers are shaped like hearts and stars. Other types of food are considered cute, and some carry gendered messages. For example, ice cream is considered "girl's food". No self-respecting Japanese man would be caught eating it. At least not the brightly colored, multilayered treats displayed in the windows of restaurants. Observing who eats what in a Japanese company cafeteria, Lo adds credence to this gendered division of food, when she writes that "There was an unconscious division of the sexes even in the cafeteria lines", and "Most women ate lightly and had ice cream or candies for dessert" (1990: 27).

As an example of how detailed, elaborate and intricate the aesthetic–ethic of cuteness can become, consider gloves for girls. Some have small animal heads or other detailed decorations on each finger tip. One pair in particular deserves description: the index finger was a father (hat, glasses, green tie); the middle finger a mother (hat with beads, lipstick, pearl necklace, earrings); the ring finger the daughter (winking, hat, red bow tie); and the pinkie a pet dog (lopsided ears, a bell) (the thumb of this black knitted glove was merely white-tipped). Such a glove allows a child to wear the family. To what degree such a glove socializes children about family life is debatable, but the iconic value of its embellishment and the designer's intent is clear. Or consider how cuteness can be stuck to the body: *neiru shîru* ("nail seals") – small stickers of Dumbo, Winnie the Pooh, 101 Dalmatians, Beauty and the Beast, Lion King, Sleeping Beauty – are not just for nails, but may also be stuck on one's ear lobes.

Anything, then, can be made to appear cute (though small animals, especially mice, hamsters and bear cubs, seem to be high on the list). Nothing is immune from this capital-driven aesthetic of the everyday. One commentator, tongue-in-cheek, suggests that the reason the indigenous Japanese *kamoshika* (an antelope-like animal) is being hunted to the point of extinction in parts of Japan is because it simply isn't cute. If only "it had the sense to market itself as a cuddly toy or the fluffy ball on the end of key-ring; then people would love it. After all, the "*kamoshika* has failed to grasp the first law of survival in Japan: In order to evolve, you have to be cute" (Hadfield 1991). The commodification of cuteness as perceived in an animal, or its lack, might make the difference between becoming extinct or remaining extant, since the "adoption" by a corporation can sustain mass interest in an animal. Animals, in fact, are a favorite theme of corporate cuteness. Female flight attendants who work aboard Japan Airlines jumbo jets were asked to wear Minnie Mouse ears with big red bows (and matching aprons decorated with Disney characters). Many attendants were not pleased with the plan and protested (Yamaguchi 1994). It should be added that the plane on which the attendants were to work was covered in Disney characters, such as Mickey Mouse (an attempt to upstage All Nippon Airways' Marine Jumbo, which is painted to look like a whale) ("JAL to offer 'Disney' jumbo service", 1994). Not to be outdone, All Nippon Airways announced it would decorate its planes with five characters from the popular cartoon Pokemon (from "Pocket Monsters"): Pikachu, Pippi, Myu, Myutsu and Kabigon. "Flight attendants' uniforms will feature similar Pokemon images as will the paper cups and seat covers" ("ANA elevates Pokemon to new heights", 1998). Such attempts seem to demonstrate the idea that women, as beings that for many men need to be "protected, cuddled, held and controlled", are often associated with animals.

Female children seem to receive extra doses of this saccharin-based commentary on social power, socializing her for her proper gender role. The child is allowed – indeed, encouraged – to inhabit a sugary world of make-believe. Shirts, shoes, socks, hats, underwear, school supplies and toys – all put cuteness into material form. When a mother takes her children out shopping, there are the playgrounds on the roofs of the stores where, at one I came across, life-sized mechanical pandas and other animals that can be saddled and ridden stood on all fours, waited to be mounted. There are also the restaurants that conveniently cater to tots (and no doubt mercifully to mothers, loaded down with shopping bags with screaming children in tow), serving special set meals for children prepared in trays shaped like cars, boats, or rocket ships. These are called *okosama ranchi*, "lunch for honorable children". As a very young girl matures, she graduates to the aesthetic of young cuteness, and then perhaps on to adult cuteness:

> The character items that fill the rooms and schoolbags of middle school children tend toward a pastel, sugary sweetness that seems to be outgrown in the United States by the age of eight. In fact, the Sanrio novelty company [see below] found in a market survey that their items sold to Japanese girls between the age of five

and the time of marriage would be bought in America only by girls from four to seven years old (White 1994: 126).

Some teens search out cute clothes and bric-a-brac in stores that specialize in such material culture. Larger stores have sections or entire floors devoted to cuteness, e.g. "Cute Cute" floor in Takashimaya Department store and a floor for young women called "Cute Zone" in Lumine Department Store in Tokyo.

There are other corporate uses of cuteness. For example, its softening function is often apparent in the manner that it anthropomorphizes commodities and objects, by making them more human and thus less threatening. If things can be talked to, and better yet, if they can respond, they become somehow more controllable. In advertising, besides providing things with limbs, heads and volition, even abstract ideas are anthropomorphized, fitted with arms and legs. Instruction manuals more often than not portray talking, walking, smiling household appliances that explain to the consumer how they should be cared for. Implicit in this way of dealing with manual readers is a great concern for how to address them. Technical, colorless, dry explanations are perhaps too impersonal, too direct. "When the imperative use of the imperative mood is unavoidable for effective appeal, it is made to be uttered by comedians, coquettish women, and children so that its offensiveness is reduced" (Lebra 1976: 72). And for the very young, perhaps even the notion that the inanimate world is really somehow alive in a friendly manner. With its bright colors, cheerful smiles and lovable figures, cuteness seems to shout out "The world is an amicable, safe and happy place! So let's be friends!"

An exemplary example of a recent fad in the realm of material culture that is often described as *kawaî* is "tamagotchi" (some romanize it as "tamagotch"). By pressing three buttons, a player gives food, medicine, exercise, etc., to a computerized, hand-held, egg-shaped electronic "virtual pet". With enough attention, it grows and matures, but if neglected, it weakens and dies (then the player resets the game). Its inventor, Aki Maita of toy-maker Bandai, explains how she conceived of the idea: "everyone wanted hamsters, mice – cute pets like that. At the same time there were a few pocket games which people were playing with . . . It seemed natural to combine the two: to cross a real pet with an electronic game" (Shah 1997). According to Maita, "We decided to make high school girls the target . . . We found they like characters that are [1] cute (*kawaii*) and round; which they can draw simply and quickly by themselves; which they can carry around with them and [2] show off to their friends. So we included all of these features in Tamagotchi" (note the two features Maita mentions indicated by brackets)

(McGill and Loney 1997). The name comes from *tamago* ("egg") and (*t*)*chi* ("cute", "lovable"); a tamagotchi is a "lovable egg" (Shah 1997).[6] "Seeing high school students as society's trendsetters, the toy company thoroughly researched what they want in a 'cute character' . . . It started with the high school girls, and then elementary school kids and office workers jumped on the fad" (Hani 1997). By the end of 1997 (its debut was in November 1996) 15 million units of this "portable pet" have been sold domestically and 20 million internationally (Arai 1997). When it first took Japan by storm, some would arrive at stores the night before in order to purchase one before they sold out. It is said that collectors will pay ¥20,000 for an electronic pet that originally sold for ¥2,000, and supposedly the original white ones are being resold for ¥120,000 (Kiritani 1997).

The original tamagotchi has generated imitations, spinoffs and new versions. For example, after raising a "boy" and "girl", players can have them "married" and make a baby by combining the two versions of the hardware, thereby creating a "family" ("Boy, girl versions of Tamagotchi set", 1997). Reasons for its popularity range from a desire to have a pet but, since this is difficult in urban Japan, "virtual pets" fulfill the need, making one feel part of a group ("everyone has one, so I should have one too") (though one student told me that the image of a single person standing somewhere playing with tamagotchi "looks lonely"), to giving women a chance to express their "maternal instinct" (though young men and elderly women also play with them). But whatever inherent enjoyment tamagotchi provide, their lightning-quick rise to popularity and subsequent fizzling out indicate their faddish nature. Indeed, after they became a hit, the impact of tamagotchi were being reported in the media: crime and counterfeits ("Men tempt kids with Tamagotchi virtual pets", 1997; "'Tamagotch' raids conducted in Osaka", 1997; "Tamagotch used in kidnapping attempts", 1997; and "Police copter joins manhunt for teen Tamagotchi thieves", 1997; "Tamagotchi passes 10 million mark", 1997); and international influences and incidents ("Thai princess sparks Tamagotch ban", 1997; "Tamagotch fans in Singapore fired from jobs", 1997; "Dead Hungarian Tamagotchis rest in peace", 1998).

Another development in consumer culture can be seen in the most basic micro-ritual of Japanese civility: the exchange of business cards (*meishi*), which "has long been the essential first step in seemingly every adult relationship . . . No salesperson, no banker, no journalist would be without a business card, unless he would also be without shoes, socks, and a shirt. And now this longtime ritual has been embraced by teenagers. Especially the girls". For many people, especially younger ones, *meishi* are used to indicate not what they are (company, department, rank, etc.), but who they wish to be, e.g. younger people, besides putting their school or pager number on a card, may write their favorite rock band or what they call a "live name", which "can be cute. It can be cool. It can be inspired by someone you admire . . . Most importantly . . . a live name is not the name your parents gave you" (Selby 1996). In other words, a "live name" signals a desire for self-expression (rather than the more role-oriented self-performance). Also, it was reported that an increasing number of people are keeping two different sets of *meishi*: one for their company or place of employment (for "professional role" and thus more oriented toward self-performance) and another for themselves (for "individuality" and thus oriented toward self-expression). Some *meishi* are quite high-tech. For example, a "bar code" version can be hooked up to computers for display of data and can dial if used in a special phone. The "talking" *meishi*, to be used with a small machine, can record and play back messages (Ma 1988; see also "Design school grads using creative cards in job search", 1998).

One recent fad that brings together high-tech, convenient acquisition, cuteness and self-presentation (as well as being "Small, cheap, quirky"; cf. Masuda 1998) is "Print Club" (or *purikura*). Print Club, manufactured by Atlus/Sega (though there are now many spinoffs), is a machine that takes one's picture and for about ¥300 produces a sheet of sixteen stamp-sized stickers. One can choose from a selection of twenty-seven frames – most of which are cute – that border one's face. These machines can be found at game arcades, train stations, hotels, banks, pachinko parlors, video shops, fast food outlets. The stickers they make are used for various purposes, but apparently the most popular is to exchange them with friends.[7] Indeed, individuals fill entire notebooks with stickers, thereby establishing, maintaining and strengthening interpersonal relations. According to sociologist Shinji Miyadai, a Print Club is a "memory-creating machine" (*omoide-seizô sôchi*) (Naito 1997). Exchanging such stickers is a form of "self-commodification" and self-presentation (which can be either self-expression or self-performance depending on its use and the individual) that says as much about the individual doing the exchanging as it does about the relationship. "The more stickers I have, the more comfortable I feel about my relations with others . . . This notebook is proof that I have lots of friends" (Naito 1996). The state, it may be added, has jumped on board the Print Club fad. In its "drive to improve letter-writing habits of young people", an informal panel of the Posts and Telecommunications Ministry has suggested that machines be installed that can make Print Club stamps (the Ministry already uses the cartoon character Doraemon – a robotic cat – on its stamps) (Kamiya 1998).

Another fad that is high-tech (at least in appearance) and illustrates how pop culture comically comments on hyper-rationalized society are "bar code" tattoos (which originated in American popular culture). Like so many other examples of Japanese popular culture, "It's so cute," according to one young woman. A graphic designer concurred: "The shape of bar codes is actually rather attractive. It is cute in an odd sort of way." The bar codes can be personalized, and "Many of the bar codes contain secret messages, such as 'I love you', or ' super cool', which can be read by a scanner. Other girls choose code numbers that correspond to the birthdays of their favorite celebrities." One observer notes that "the new craze may represent a modern resistance to an overly systematic life. People want to play a little joke with the symbol because bar codes are so ubiquitous that they almost seem to control our lives" ("Bar code 'tattoos' in vogue for Tokyo's material girls", 1997).

Cuteness and Entertainment

This cultural discourse on what constitutes cuteness, besides shaping gender images and relations, has profound economic ramifications on the entertainment industry. As a marketable sentiment, cuteness colors (some might say controls) entertainment. For example, consider the immense popularity of the movie (among all ages) *Koneko monogatari: The Adventures of Chatran* (*"koneko monogatari"* means "a kitten's story") in the mid-1980s. Watching the film "is rather like being mugged by marshmallows" ("It's a cat's life", 1986). What is notable about this movie is not so much its portrayal of a cat's adventures but the fact that no humans appeared in it.

Note also the popularity in the early 1990s of comic book and TV character Chibi Maruko-chan (who passes as an example of young cuteness), who "was plastered across the nation with all the restraint and subtlety of a North Korean publicity drive. Little sister was watching you." The public was "sprayed with Chibi Maruko-chan endorsement ads, drowned in a flood of Chibi Maruko-chan tie-in products before being battered into submission by the Chibi Maruko-chan song . . . She smiled from on your bank book. She beamed from your soft drink can. She admonished you in public awareness posters" (Levinson 1993). The fact that Chibi Maruko-chan is female speaks volumes: though small boys may be considered cute, somehow a small girl is thought to inspire sentiments of cuteness more readily, to the point of becoming a national heroine, evidence of the popularity of cuteness among adults.

Another example in the early 1990s of how cuteness follows entertainment trends was seen when dinosaur-mania hit both sides of the Pacific. But while American audiences enjoyed being scared by man-eating "terrible lizards" in *Jurassic Park* in the summer of 1993, Japanese audiences were given the chance to see a "cute dinosaur" named Rex. In the words of one movie critic, the star of *Rex kyôryû monogatari* (The Story of Tyrannosaurus Rex) "looks like a baby E.T. in dino drag and behaves like an infant chimpanzee" (Schilling 1993). What is pertinent for my present purposes is the gendered message: Rex's caretaker, teacher and loving companion is a Japanese girl regarded by many Japanese as irresistibly cute. Practicing for her future maternal role, she taught Rex to eat, do tricks and "even use a potty". Perhaps an idea of the movie's content can be gained from the critic's opinion that it was "the filmic equivalent of weak sugar water – cloying, insipid, uninspiring" and a movie made with "a big dollop of phony mysticism, drippy sentimentality, lame humor and blatant sexism" (Schilling 1993).

The aesthetic of cuteness is not limited to pop culture, and one critic discusses how cuteness has infiltrated Japan's art scene in an article called "Japan's incurable case of 'cuteitis.'" He describes one piece of an artist's photography exhibition, in which "everything is cute: kids in a pool swimming on rubber dolphins, a trailer home done up in lots of lace, a green and pink Jonathan's 'family restaurant.' There is not evidence of irony or critique here, only a lethargic choice to see the world through these very rose-tinted lenses" (Silva 1996). At another exhibit, the same critic describes sculpture as coming "close to being cute" and another work as "dangerously close again to being cute" (Silva 1997).[8]

Burikko, or "pretending children" (introduced in the previous chapter), is often used to refer to female young pop singers, models and movie stars, "usually making their debut at age fifteen in what promoters openly admit is an effort to appeal to Japanese men's 'Lolita complex'" (Cherry 1987: 39).[9]

Popular female stars (*tarento*) do not cultivate overt sexiness, which men find threatening and young women do not wish to emulate. According to Kinoshita (1991, 92): "Just barely past puberty, a *tarento* is a young girl who is plucked from the ranks of amateur beauty pageants and made into a star, with a recording contract, TV appearances, and ad campaigns. No need to be able to sing or act: these girls have the only thing that matters – *kawaii*" (cited in Cooper-Chen 1997: 20).

Note how a member of the all-female Shonen Knife band explains their success: "When we do want to add some irony or make a serious statement – say, if that statement was an almond – we'd try to coat it with chocolate – say a pop melody or cute lyrics. We intentionally try not to put in our opinions" (Fukami 1993). Not all Japanese female singers attempt to be cute, of course, but there is a huge industry for "chidols" (from "children idols"), girls who want (or are encouraged by their mothers) to become stars or at least appear in a TV commercial. Schools for singing and dancing, modeling agencies and special magazines cater to this interest (Nakajima 1997).

An example of what may be called "cutesy Lolita fashion" is Enomoto Kanako, the "ultimate cute and lovable high school girl". She plays the title character in the TV program *Osorubeshi, Otonashi Karen-san* (*Beware of Miss Karen Otonashi*). In the show Karen – described by one observer as "a girl who refuses to grow up" – wears outlandish but charming outfits that are "cute but funny", a combination of the fantastic, childish and camp ("Teen idol commits crimes of fashion", 1998). Karen resonates deeply with what a non-Japanese has to say about the "cult of cuteness" in North America: "Cute has to do with not wanting to grow up . . . A lot of young women today are anxious about making their way in the real world. If you're feeling threatened and you don't want to grow up and take responsibility, you want to look like a little girl and stay a little girl as long as possible" (Schomer and Chang, 1995). Such sentiments resonate with what one young student told me: "Why is there so much cuteness? I think it's because the way people think has become more infantile. They can sympathize with cute things. Perhaps it shows that they don't want to be an adult and want to be guarded forever like as if they were children."

Consider how shoes can be designed to fit into the "cutesy Lolita fashion". On display at a shoe fair was a "pink high-top vinyl sneaker with high heel and wedge sole. It looks virtually impossible to walk in." A company representative notes that such a style is "part of the Lolita trend":

> You'd wear these shoes with children's clothes, like a flair skirt covered with Disney characters . . . The fashion now is to have a childish look . . . Girls are saying that they are individuals. They are saying that they don't want to become mature adults . . . Our shoes are basically cute. *In Japan, cute is always in fashion* (Lazarus 1993; emphasis mine).

Tarento are another example of how the sentiment of cuteness is commercialized and commodified (and as an example that sometimes borders on child pornography cuteness), young singers are "packaged (discovered and given an image, attendant musical repertoire, and performing style) and promoted by production companies".[10] The ideal image is one of "youth and innocence" (Fujie 1989: 209). With this in the background, it might be worth noting that "busty Barbie dolls" did not sell well in Japan "until toy makers redesigned her into a cute pretender who appears less buxom, less glamorous, shorter, and younger" (Cherry 1987: 39). Called "Licca", she has bigger eyes and her overall look has the "decidedly innocent air of an elementary schoolgirl" (Watanabe 1992).

Part of the *tarento* (celebrity) industry is the endless stream of material culture associated with stars and celebrities:

> Idol shops cluster in popular teen districts and sell everything from pocket mirrors to sweatshirts to *noren*, the traditional door-way curtain, now in neon polyester with the image of a star on it. You can get also your idol on toothpaste or a packet of instant noodles. Addresses are listed in the magazines (White 1994: 122).

A recent fad illustrates how celebrities of the *tarento* variety exercise influence over popular culture. Many young women attempt to imitate the appearance of pop singer Amuro Namie who, it is said, is not considered "beautiful", but rather "homely" (or just "cute"). Thus, many young women regard Amuro as someone they "*can* emulate" (emphasis mine); "most of the girls who want to look like her don't have to go to too much trouble. They're probably already thin enough, which means all they have to do is lighten their hair, shave their eyebrows [using 'eyebrow design kits'], get a tan and buy the same shade of lip gloss" (Brasor 1997; see also Nakamura's "From Puffy to baggy socks: Japan's youth see green", 1998).

The Communicative Power of the Commercialization and Commodification of Cuteness

More than just a feeling or a way of describing something, cuteness is sentiment commercialized and commodified. The multivocal definitions of cuteness illustrate its remarkable power and plasticity as a concept; this is obvious in how cuteness permeates popular culture and the world of commodities and how it acts like a magnet, attracting vast sums of capital (especially the disposable income of young working women). The commercialized side to cuteness is by no means unrelated to its communicative function. This is because as a fetish that is admired, desired, bought and sold, the symbolism of cuteness is widely circulated, exposing individuals to the gendered messages it carries.

The materials, shapes, sizes and purposes of the objects that embed and encode sentiments of cuteness are virtually innumerable, indicating that in Japan, cuteness is not just a fad, but a standard style. "The marketing of cuteness has created a seemingly endless flow of products" (White 1994: 126). As for clothes, cuteness has become a basic style into which more transient fashions are mixed: preppy, punk, skater, folk, black and French (Kinsella 1995: 220).

Cute styles are bright for boys, lacy for girls, and boyishness is accentuated by wearing shirts and pants deliberately too large. Girls laciness is *not* in Japan Madonna-punk lace, but rather First Communion lace – but with a perky falseness, a look sometimes called *burikko*, or false innocent. A caricature of a burikko girl has a high-pitched voice, giggles helplessly when addressed, and squeals *"kawaiiiiii!"* (cute) or *"iyaa!"* (I hate it) when asked her opinion of a boy, a new soda drink, or a cartoon on TV (White 1994: 129).

In Osaka, a recent fashion is the British-flavored "romantic punk", though "it hardly resembles the violent look born in London in the 1970s. Instead, young Osaka women have given it a girlish tone, using white blouses and cute accessories. Some have taken to tying tartan scarves around their waists and wearing clothes made from kimono" ("British invasion in Osaka", 1997).

There is hardly a store that does not sell something cute, and some stores apparently sell nothing but articles of cuteness. The company Sanrio has specialized in designing 450 cute characters and 3,000 products since 1962 in 46 countries.[11] Popular characters include:

Keroppi, the goggle-eye frog; Pochacco, the soccer-playing, squeaky-clean pup; Pekkle, the aquatically challenged duck and wannabe lifeguard; Spottie Dottie, the stylish Dalmatian whose father was once chief fire dog with the New York City fire department; and Bad Badtz Maru, the hardcore penguin with his truculent frown and spiked feather-do. (Teenagers in particular like him) (Fox 1998).

The most well-known Sanrio character is "Hello Kitty", a white kitten with tiny eyes and large head that is seen everywhere in Japan (e.g. toys, handbags, stickers, coffee mugs, calculators, blankets, notebooks, Hello Kitty-shaped appliances such as telephones and televisions, phone cards, cameras, pocketbooks, watches, towels, pillows, toothbrushes, lunch boxes, pens, pencils, garbage pails, and at some banks, bankbooks and cash cards). Hello Kitty seems to be everywhere; on the cover of the catalogue for services at the Takano Yuri Beauty Clinic she wears a pink dress and says "Hello Kitty has become a softened Day Spa character". There is also the "Hello Kitty car", a small white passenger vehicle with "Hello Kitty wheel covers" and a choice of pink or blue "Hello Kitty seats". Some account for Hello Kitty's distinctive charm to the simplicity of her visage, referred to as "Zen cuteness" (Fox 1998). Hello Kitty is not just for young girls and teenagers (consumer fans of Hello Kitty are called "Kittilers"), but is also popular among young women and mothers; there are plans to target young men for the next line of Hello Kitty products. Sanrio profits are enormous, totaling ¥120 billion in 1998 (Saito 1998; Aoki 1997; "Kitty bankbook", 1998). A karaoke lounge (as other companies) has adopted the Hello Kitty theme to boost business:

Each of the lounge's 11 rooms boasts a different version of Sanrio Co.'s cat character. Pictures of Hello Kitty in Chinese dress, as an angel flying through the heavens, or clad in a kimono, have schoolgirls and young office ladies squealing with delight [and] devoted lovers of the icon are treated to more images on the video screen between songs, and the bathrooms feature Kitty toilet paper and towels ("Cat icon has merchandisers clawing in big revenues", 1998).

Exchanging Cuteness

One part of the commercializing and commodifying aspect of cuteness is its exchange value among many women. Giving and receiving cute objects may be viewed as an exercise in trafficking in sentiment. It says something about how the giver regards the receiver and vice versa. In Tokyo, young women who make a more or less conscious effort to be cute often gather in Harajuku, an area filled with boutiques and small eateries catering to those in their early teens. As a scene in which youth (as agents) can act out their self-presentations, Harajuku is one of the best places to observe cuteness publicly displayed and presumably admired.

A firsthand experience illustrates how significant the giving of cute items can be. As a faculty member at a college, I was invited to the tenth anniversary of the school's founding. This event was also held to celebrate the president's mother's birthday and I had the honor of sitting at the president's table with his mother. Held at a high-priced hotel in the *vierusaiyu no ma* (Versailles Room) whose glittering chandeliers, gold trimmings and giant mirrors provided the illusion that the hall was vastly bigger than it actually was, the event was a sparkling spectacle of beautifully attired young female students, extravagant dining and costly entertainment. But as if to "soften" all this glamour and add some warm-hearted sentiment to it, during the celebration the mother was presented on stage with life-sized Mickey and Minnie Mouse dolls. After the presentation, two waiters rushed over with chairs for the Mice couple, and seated them so they could join us at our table. A female professor sitting next to me, observing the irony of the situation, leaned over and said to me, "This indeed is a Mickey Mouse event." The mother petted and whispered a few words to them, and the president would lean over every now and then, smile, squeeze their noses and stroke their stomachs. But on a sadder note, Mickey and Minnie again made a public appearance some months later. When the president's mother passed away, they were seen again, sitting on the mammoth flower-festooned stage set up in the school for her funeral.

Mickey and Minnie Mouse, in fact, make as many appearances in Japan's popular culture as Hello Kitty. Sometimes they appear in person. According to one Japanese woman (who married at Disney World in Florida), "We tied the knot at a wedding hall near our hotel. Soon after we returned to the hotel, several Americans, each masquerading as Mickey Mouse, turned up at our room to give us blessings, and we danced together. It was like a dream" ("More couples break tradition, wed abroad", 1997).

Scenes and Spaces for the Performance of Cuteness

In Chapter 2, I discussed the notions of *seken, hitome, hitomae, soto, omote* and *tatemae*, which all strongly imply that a generalized gaze confronts people once they leave a group or their inner circle of family or friends. But if an awareness of a ubiquitous gaze keeps subjects positioned while being schooled, trained and primed for labor and while commuting, working and being managed, it also provides an audience for self-expression in certain places and spaces, or to remain faithful to the theoretical framework introduced in Chapter 2, certain scenes. Such self-presentations are deeply related to resistance consumption. For example, in Harajuku young people have their "I's" monitor their "me's", "perform" and "learn the joys of flaunting and being flaunted at" (Shoji 1998). It is also a respite from the gaze of the official ideology: "For the kids, Harajuku is a coffee break; it's a timeout from studying, worrying about exams, family pressures. As anyone who has ever been a Japanese teen will know, this little pocket of rest works wonders in what is a very difficult time in their lives" (Shoji 1998). Note that "The cultural brand here is undeniably 'street', but a street so sweetened and made gentle one seems to walk on marshmallows" (Shoji 1998), and note also the various permutations of cuteness found in Harajuku:

> Suitably, the kids display none of the anger, defiance and general punkiness of pubescence. Serene and smiling, they walk as if the air is laced with a marvelous tranquilizer (let's call it *"kawaii gas"*) that only they are exposed to. A stroll in the area is in fact a lesson in kawaii (cuteness): from the My Melody figurines displayed at Kiddyland (kawaii kawaii) to the Teddy Bear Museum (authentic kawaii) to the landmark prophylactics shop Condomania (naughty kawaii). As for the boys in their shorts and berets with pompoms and the girls in balloon skirts and floral print blouses complete with frills, lace and bows – well, it's kawaii gone galactic (Shoji 1998).

Condomania, it should be added, has a youthful, cheerful ambience and specializes in selling over 100 scented, textured, colored, toy-like and glow-in-the-dark condoms. There are other stores, whose patrons are mostly young women, that specialize in prophylactics (such as Peaches) that offer slightly risqué novelty goods alongside condoms . . . These include edible condom-shaped chocolates, lollipops in the shape of genitalia, condom-blossoming cacti called 'hybreed [*sic*] rubber plants' and pencils with skin-colored phallus-shaped rubbers . . . The condom pendant is particularly popular with young girls [who] wear it as a statement, wanting to shock your average conservative Japanese (Ferguson 1993).

Here it should be noted that condom manufacturers often sell their products in colorful, cheerful packaging, with names such as "My Sweet Home", ""Fruity", "Salad Party" and "Ice Candy Box" (cf. Watanabe 1994).

Areas similar to Harajuku (indeed, arguably the entire sociosemantic space of youth culture) offer individuals scenes (see Chapter 2), or places for posing, posturing and performing their selves. In such places "anonymous communication" (*tokumei no komyunikêshon*) occurs, especially via clothing which sends messages of cuteness (Kataoka 1997: 123). Cute objects (as forms of agencies) can be worn, informing others of one's own charming nature and how one would like to be considered by one's peers (especially those of the opposite sex).[12] Bright red ribbons, shirts with lovable creatures, carrying bags and furry key chains in the shape of animals, are tied, donned and carried along by girls (very young cuteness) and young women (young cuteness). Consider the small figures – cartoon personages or other Disney characters such as Mickey or Minnie Mouse – that so commonly dangle from book bags, knapsacks, backpacks, bags, purses, pocketbooks, even portable telephones. Though mostly girls and young women attach such items to their belongings, boys and young men also hang them on their belongings. Such colorful figurines are effigies, announcing to others one's devotion to the cult of cuteness. Besides public places, more restricted, intimate spaces can be made cute: in the book *Tokyo Style*, about the different dwellings of Tokyoites, there is a chapter called *"Kawasa to iu takaramono"* ("Treasures of Cuteness") which has photographs of rooms jam-packed with cute objects and colorfully illustrates how individuals surround themselves with cuteness (Tsuzuki 1997: 88–137).

Some students go to Harajuku and other gathering grounds of teen culture and transform their appearance:

They arrive at the station with a separate bag containing their Harajuku outfits and change in the restrooms which, over the years, have been enlarged and installed with full-length mirrors. They change again when it's time to go home and their parents are none the wiser [appropriation type of resistance]. These days girls just show up in their school uniforms, because as everyone knows, no street fashion comes close to the power and aura of a schoolgirl uniform [conversion type of resistance] (Shoji 1998).

Conclusion

Images of cuteness – bright colors, small children, lovable and friendly creatures, smiling, playful animals and personified objects that walk and talk – connect with normative principles, notions of power and gender definitions. No one is necessarily very aware of the normative associations being made. But that is just the point. As a child is socialized, she or he is bombarded through the senses with the sights and sounds of cuteness embedded in articles of everyday use and consumption. At the deep ideological, nonconscious level, sentiments relating to cuteness establish symbolic associations and connect with more abstract values. These associative processes are cognitive, and operate, to a large degree, without the conscious awareness of the individual. Bits and pieces of a normative framework are constructed. In this way, nonconscious mental operations work to form the bedrock of belief. The concrete (material culture) and abstract (ideology) reinforce each other. Communicated through commercialization and commodification, cute things become objectified sentiment, commenting on and supporting a normative discourse about power (male/female, parent/child, superior/inferior relations, etc.) definitions.

Notes

1. Over the last several decades, many knick-knacks inspired by folk art have lost their traditional appeal and become more "cute" (personal communication, Penny Herbert).

2. For other styles, see Miller (1998: 2–3). For a historical perspective of "street fashion", see *Sutorîto fuasshon 1945–1995: wakamono sutairu no 50 nen shi* (1995).

3. Nudity, especially when sexualized, is often a radical form of subversion and from the official point of view, problematic. In any case, the fact that it is intimately bound up with gendered self-presentation, commercialization and commodification proves its destabilizing power in modern Japan.

4. There are, of course, many examples of conversion, such as cross-dressing. A commercial with a woman wearing men's underpants attracted much attention, though it is reported that "Partners often swap garments as an expression of intimacy" (Nakamura 1998).

5. In another type of conversion, the female uniform is highly sexualized, as seen in pornographic magazines and comics (moreover, some female teens sell their underwear to shops who then put them on the market for men). "The going price on the black market for its (Shibuya Girls' High) uniforms starts at ¥100,000 and middlemen approach seniors for their ensembles months before graduation. These are sold to men with schoolgirl fetishes or, more recently, to college girls who wear them to attract male attention" (Shoji 1997).

6. Though others say the "tch" comes from "watch" since a tamagotchi is an "egg watch", – a watch on a chain that tells time.

7. Like all new technologies that become so popular (especially if among young people), the authorities have viewed, rightly or wrongly, Print Club with some suspicion; e.g. police have noticed how they are used for prostitution, and some arcades have message boards on which young women place a sticker of themselves and a phone number.

8. It should be noted that in Japanese, "cute" (*kawaî*) does not necessarily carry the ironic sense it usually has in English when used to critic works of art.

9. As widely reported, the "Lolita complex" is by no means limited to Japan. See Krier (1991).

10. Also referred to as *aidoru* or *tarento*, from "idol" and "talent", respectively.

11. Including the United States. Cf. Roberts' "U.S. teens say hello to Kitty and hang out on Cute Street" (1995).

12. However, to be regarded as cute, or to be *kawaigarareru* ("treated like a pet") or to be considered an *aiganbutsu* (prized article; pet), strongly suggests a lack of autonomy (*hishutai teki*) and a loss of individuality (cf. Nakanishi 1997b).

7

Final Thoughts: The Political Economics of Self-Presentation, Individuality and Individualization

In this book I have adopted a cultural psychological perspective to explore the linkages between socialization, subjectivity, self-presentation, body, state, economic production and material culture. I examined a politico-economic ideology (economic nation-statism) that has a vested interest in reproducing these linkages through uniforms, which are tangible symbols of the enormous power and extensiveness of politico-economic structures. These macro-structures form the matrix in which the use of objects, micro-practices and a concomitant form of subjectivity are structured. More specifically, my analysis has been informed by a dramaturgical approach whose aim was to tackle one of the dichotomies mentioned in Chapter 2 (self/society) by demonstrating how subjectivity articulates – via material culture – social forms (sociopolitical and economic institutions).

Perhaps one lesson everyday objects have to offer concerns how statefulness infiltrates – in an admittedly roundabout, oblique and circuitous manner – our most mundane thoughts and practices. "Certainly, the modern state involves itself chronically in the most intimate details of its citizens' day-to-day lives in a way which would be unrecognizable to the subjects of even the most despotic of premodern states" (Pierson 1996: 58). Recently some theorists have recognized "a blurring of the lines that divide state from society and an awareness of their complex interaction" (Pierson 1996: 92). The uses and meanings of material culture (e.g. cars, luxury items, banned substances, government ad campaigns, museums, exhibits, documentation, monuments, historical sites, public housing, public transportation, public space, military weaponry), provides us with a vast array of windows into the complexity of state/society interaction.

Uniforms are subjectivity rendered visible via material. The act of wearing a uniform is the product of massive politico-economic forces that bear down on the individual. But wearing a uniform also produces a form of subjectivity that these forces require for their reproduction. The important point to be made is that donning a uniform does not simply *reflect* the wearer's commitment to social norms; rather, the very act of donning a uniform *produces and reproduces* on a daily basis the subjective substructure of norms demanded by politico-economic structures. Such reproduction occurs over many years and social actors are not necessarily conscious of the normative pressure of society's gaze. However, at the unconscious level, they are cognizant of such pressures and consequently present selves (expressed and performed) that are tightly linked to capitalist production and reproduction.

Uniforms, of course, are certainly not unique to Japan, but their ubiquity in Japan points to some important linkages between politico-economic projects, bodily management, the construction of subjectivity and material culture in the form of dress. This penchant for uniformed dress is a product of modernity and is not due to some inherent culturalist or "traditional" tendency for conformity.

The more expectations the powers that be have for a certain group of people, the more concentrated its technologies of control over bodily covering and equipping. Thus, we are left with a simple if not surprising proposition: the more social control that is exercised, the more dress uniformity we can expect to find. Students, as the key socializing targets of the educatio-bureaucratic system, receive the most admonitions about dress (with the exception of military and security forces). More than white-collar employees, blue-collar workers must pay more attention to appropriate attire (their clothing and its outfitting are also, no doubt, motivated by safety concerns). More than men, women are expected to be more uniformed (e.g. "office ladies", "elevator girls", women's colleges with uniform rules, etc.). Moreover, as "natural" repositories of the national spirit and sentiment, women are expected to don the national costume (kimono) more than men on certain occasions.

The Role of Habit and the Complexity of Self-presentation

There are in general two theoretical lessons that I hope this book has illuminated. The first lesson concerns the habitual in social life. The notion of habit has a distinguished pedigree. Camic points out that in Durkheim's work, "This was the idea that, by its very nature, human action, whether individual or collective, oscillates between two poles, that of consciousness or reflection on the one side, and that of habit on the other side, with the latter pole being the stronger" (Camic 1986: 1052). Though some researchers have not ignored the role of habit and related notions (e.g. Mauss (1973) discussed *habitus*, which was developed by others, the most notable being Bourdieu (1977)), Camic writes that "contemporary sociology has virtually dispensed with the concept" (1986: 1040) since for some, there has been an emphasis on human action as "purposive, rational, voluntaristic, or decisional" (Camic 1986: 1040). "To many, the notion of habit immediately conjures up behavior that consists in a fixed, mechanical reaction to particular stimuli and is, as such, devoid of meaning from the actor's point of view" (Camic 1986: 1046). I suggest that the assumption that habitual action lacks intentionality requires serious rethinking. As I contended in Chapter 2, the acts of agents, whether "volitional" or "habitual", rest upon layers of nonconscious mentation built up over a lifetime of socializing and resocializing experiences. An act assumes prior knowledge, implicates hidden motives and is resonant with unspoken understandings. But if any single decision is a negotiation between contesting motives, an arbitration of conflicting demands or a compromise of competing desires, then so are dispositions, routines and "automatic" activities which are all part of *le quotidien*, i.e. mundane practices, microrituals and minor acts (such as bodily management and dress and how they are implicated in the nexus of state/capital/socialization/subjectivity/self-presentation).

The second lesson concerns the nature of self-presentation. Like the terms "self" and "agent", "self-presentation" saturates the social scientific literature. But often, in spite of much talk about the postmodern deconstruction of the "individual", the use of "self" and "agent" merely reproduces notions of a unified, individualistic, irreducible and self-contained "person". In this book I have attempted to tease apart the self, first by delineating the powerful politico-economic forces that construct it in Japan, and then by exploring its variegated presentations, performances, displays and exhibitions as articulated through material culture. As I have contended elsewhere, the Japanese ethnotheory of self (expressed versus performed selves), theories of acting (technical versus "method" acting), Goffman's view of "cynic" versus "sincere" personas, and what I have termed "identified 'I'–'me'" and "separated 'I'–'me'" (McVeigh 1997b: 216), basically correspond. These are all very different views of self, its artistic manipulation on stage, and its roles (both theatrical and social), and point to universal sociopsychological parameters. One theoretical lesson is that all exhibitions of self, whether consciously staged or spontaneously displayed, possess elements of subject/object distancing and subject/object identification.

Lessons from Japan: Capitalism, Consumerism and the Compartmentalization of Social Life

If anything, perhaps phenomena such as school rules, the rather rigid rules of bodily wrapping in standardized dress, highly routinized labor practices and the commodification of cuteness teaches us that we frantically produce, purchase and use objects not for an Orwellian Big Brother, but rather for countless friendly and neighborly "little sisters" (in Japan, perhaps best epitomized by Chibi Maruko-chan; see Chapter 6) and lovable, cheerful and cute creatures (in Japan, best epitomized by Hello Kitty; see Chapter 6). Though being watched by "little sisters" is annoying rather than ominous, pushy rather than threatening and meddlesome rather than oppressive, a hyper-consumerist capitalism legitimated by officious statism can be no less burdensome than other politico-economic arrangements. Indeed, businesses were disappointed when Masako Owada's marriage to the Crown Prince did not trigger a "Masako fashion-boom" in items and clothes she was seen wearing – deemed "Owada's favorites" – before and after the wedding (cf. Ashitani 1993 and "Stores hope to cash in on wedding", 1993).

Contrary to cultural clichés about the Japanese (their collectivism, group-centeredness and other-orientedness), it is pertinent here to point out that secrecy, the concealed and privacy are closely guarded in Japan. Because individuals often experience the pressures within units, retreating into one's own individuality becomes a refuge from the demands of a highly formalized social life. The result is a remarkably privatized self, concealed from the outside (*soto*) and behind fronts (*omote*). The distinction between expressed selves and performed selves/roles is relatively clear because intimate (*uchi–ura*) and ritualized (*soto–omote*) scenes are kept so distinct (at least ideally). If individuals are encouraged to ritualize their social landscape, a pre-disposition to theatricality should not be surprising, and this is, as I have argued elsewhere (McVeigh 1994, 1997b, 1998a), exactly what we find in Japan. The ubiquity of ritual and a polar view of self as intensely private (expressed) or highly dramatized (performed) resonate with this theatricality. Perhaps this, in part, explains the liking of cuteness (whether humorous, playful, erotic, corny, even trite or vulgar) which, it seems, often borders on camp – an artificiality of manner or style in which posing, posturing, commodification and commercialization all meet.

Whatever benefits of the dynamics of private/presented self, it in no small way bolsters sociopolitical atomization which encourages the formation of a mass society constituted by unitized or cellular structures. Such structures, isolated and unconnected, encourage the depoliticization of individuals. However, the argument can be made that atomization, for all its negative aspects, also provides people – comfortable and cozy in their units where they can consume – with a certain freedom from elite hegemony. And yet, "The contradiction of privatization lies in this, the more one thinks that a secure private sphere has been constructed – using the home, family and consumer goods as the basis – the more the bureaucratized, technocratic public sphere has succeeded in consolidating its control" (Ivy 1993: 250).

Japan offers a vision of the hyper-capitalist future – techno-bureaucratic, information-permeated and thoroughly rationalized – in which consumerism is deeply implicated in elite fantasies of nation-statist power and control, exercised through "guidance" (*shidô*) over the masses. Japan offers us examples of what happens when statist projects thoroughly penetrate society and how modernity can fragment psyche, generating a host of social roles. But such fragmentation is not necessarily unwelcome:

> Most Japanese are skilled at making the necessary transitions from one role to another in compartmentalizing their lives. In fact, Japanese often think of themselves as a chest of drawers and believe that the more drawers the chest has the more qualities he or she possesses – a sign of an interesting and well-developed personality by Japanese standards (Miyatake and Norton 1994).

This predilection for "compartmentalization" deserves attention because it offers an important clue about individuality (*kosei*) in Japan. An examination of dress uniformity *seems* to indicate a predilection for conformity, regulation and standardization. But such a conclusion is superficial, because ironically, what many Japanese actually do with the codes of dress uniformity – e.g. alter, supplement, subvert, convert, make cute – illustrate an adaptable, abounding and resolute – indeed, at times obstinate – individuality.

$$\mathscr{Appendix\ A:}$$
$$\mathscr{Surveys\ about\ Uniforms}$$

Table 1. *Male Uniforms in Saga Prefecture High Schools (multiple answers possible)*

			Type of Uniform	Number of Schools
Top	Form	Summer	Open Collar	30 (71.4%)
			Dress Shirt	7 (16.7%)
			Other	2 (4.8%)
		Winter	Stand-Up Collar	26 (61.9%)
			Blazer	15 (35.7%)
			(with Collar)	15 (35.7%)
			(with Necktie)	15 (35.7%)
		All Season	Dress Shirt	3 (7.1%)
			Necktie	2 (4.8%)
			Vest	1 (2.4%)
			Other	4 (9.6%)
	Color	Summer	White	39 (92.9%)
		Winter	Black	23 (54.8%)
			Navy Blue	14 (33.3%)
			Grey	3 (7.2%)
			Moss Green	2 (4.8%)
			Other (Dark Green, Grey + Green, Navy Blue Checked)	1 (2.4%)
		All Season	Green + Grey on White	1 (2.4%)
	Material	Summer	65% Polyester + 35% Cotton	20 (47.6%)
			50% Cotton + 50% Polyester	3 (7.1%)
			Other)100% Wool, 60% Polyester + 40% Cotton, 65% Polyester + 35% Linen)	

Table 1. *Male Uniforms in Saga Prefecture High Schools (multiple answers possible)* (continued)

			Type of Uniform	Number of Schools
		Winter	Polyester 65% + Cotton 35%	6 (14.3%)
			Wool 50% + Polyester 50%	5 (11.9%)
			Wool 100%	4 (9.5%)
			Polyester 100%	3 (7.1%)
			70% Wool + 30% Polyester	2 (4.8%)
			Other (50% Cotton + 50% Polyester, 70% Polyester + 30% Cotton, 80% Wool + 20% Polyester, 65% Wool + 35& Polyester, 80% Polyester + 20% Wool, 65% Polyester + 35% Wool, 80% Polyester + 20% Rayon)	
		All Season	65% Polyester + 35% Cotton Other (100% Cotton)	3 (7.1%)
Bottom	Form	Summer	Pants (Straight)	37 (88.1%)
		Winter	Pants (Straight)	36 (85.7%)
		All Season	Pants (Straight)	2 (4.8%)
	Color	Summer	Black	17 (40.5%)
			Navy Blue	8 (19.0%)
			Grey	7 (16.7%)
			White + Black Fretwork	2 (4.8%)
			Other (Black + Grey, Moss Green, Green + Navy Blue on Grey Checked)	
		Winter	Black	20 (47.6%)
			Navy Blue	8 (19.6%)
		All Season	Grey	8 (19.6%)
			Other (Black + Grey, Blue + Grey, Moss Green, Green Checked + Navy Blue on Grey, Black + Brown + Grey Fretwork, Grey + White + Black Fretwork	

Table 1. *Male Uniforms in Saga Prefecture High Schools (multiple answers possible)* (continued)

			Type of Uniform	Number of Schools
Material	Summer		50% Wool + 50% Polyester	10 (23.8%)
			65% Polyester + 35% Cotton	7 (16.7%)
			Other (50% Cotton + 50% Polyester, 100% Wool, 100% Polyester, 80% Polyester + 20% Wool, 70% Polyester + 30% Wool)	
	Winter		50% Wool + 50% Polyester	11 (26.2%)
			65% Polyester + 35% Cotton	6 (14.3%)
			100% Polyester	3 (7.1%)
			50% Cotton + 50% Polyester	2 (4.8%)
			Other (100% Wool, 65% Polyester + 35% Wool, 80% Polyester + 20% Wool, 70% Polyester + 30% Cotton, 80% Polyester + 20% Rayon)	
	All Season		50% Wool + 50% Polyester	2 (4.8%)
			Other (65% Polyester + 35% Cotton)	

Source: Isobe (1996: 102–3).

Table 2. *Female Uniforms in Saga Prefecture High Schools (multiple answers possible)*

			Type of Uniform	Number of Schools
Top	Form	Summer	Blouse	32 (76.2%)
			"Sailor"	7 (16.7%)
		Winter	Blazer	32 (76.2%)
			(with Lapel)	28 (66.7%)
			(with Necktie)	32 (76.2%)
			"Sailor"	3 (7.1%)
			(with Lined Lapel)	3 (7.1%)
			(with Lined Sleeves)	2 (4.8%)
			(Ribbon + Necktie)	2 (4.8%)
		All Season	Vest and Blouse	
			(with Opened Front)	30 (71.4%)
			(with Opened Sides)	2 (4.8%)

Table 2. *Female Uniforms in Saga Prefecture High Schools (multiple answers possible)* (continued)

		Type of Uniform	Number of Schools
		"Sailor" (Lapel, Lined Sleeves, Necktie)	1 (4.8%)
		Other	7 (16.7%)
Color	Summer	White	38 (90.5%)
		Other (Light Grey, Light Navy Blue, Light Blue, White + Grey Stripes)	
	Winter	Navy Blue	33 (78.6%)
		Black	4 (9.5%)
		Other (Grey, Caramel, Dark Brown, Moss Green, Dark Green, Navy Blue Checked on Green, Blue + Grey Checked on Navy Blue)	
	All Season	Navy Blue	23 (54.8%)
		White	4 (9.5%)
		Navy Blue Checked on Green	2 (4.8%)
		Other (Black, Grey, Beige, Moss Green, Checked + Navy Blue + Russet, Checked Blue + Grey on Green, Brown Checked on Navy Blue, Green Checked, Brown Checked)	
Material	Summer	65% Polyester + 35% Cotton	23 (54.8%)
		50% Polyester + 50% Cotton	4 (9.5%)
		75% Polyester + 25% Cotton	3 (7.1%)
		85% Polyester + 15% Cotton	2 (4.8%)
		Other (100% Wool, 60% Polyester + 40% Cotton, 55% Cotton + 45% Polyester, 65% Polyester + 35% Rayon)	
	Winter	100% Wool	18 (42.8%)
		70% Wool + 30% Polyester	5 (11.9%)
		65% Polyester + 35% Cotton	5 (11.9%)
		50% Wool + 50% Polyester	2 (4.8%)
		Other (80% Wool + 20% Polyester, 65% Polyester + 35% Wool, 70% Cotton + 30% Polyester, 50%	

Table 2. *Female Uniforms in Saga Prefecture High Schools (multiple answers possible)* (continued)

			Type of Uniform	*Number of Schools*
			Cotton + 50% Polyester, 100% Polyester)	
		All Season	100% Wool	13 (31.0%)
			50% Wool + 50% Polyester	6 (14.3%)
			70% Wool + 30% Nylon	2 (4.8%)
			Other (70% Wool + 30% Polyester, 65% Wool + 35% Polyester, 65% Polyester + 35% Wool, 70% Acrylic + 30% Wool, 50% Cotton + 50% Polyester, 65% Polyester + 35% Cotton)	
Bottom	Form	Summer	Pleated	28 (66.7%)
			Front Pleats	10 (23.8%)
		Winter	Pleated	26 (61.9%)
			Front Pleats	16 (16.7%)
			Other	2 (4.8%)
		All Season	Pleated	27 (64.3%)
			Front Pleats	4 (9.5%)
			Other	2 (4.8%)
	Color	Summer	Navy Blue	23 (54.8%)
			Grey	9 (21.4%)
			Navy Blue Checked on Green	2 (4.8%)
			Other (Blue Checked on Navy Blue, Checked Blue + Grey on Navy Blue, Checked Brown on Navy Blue, Navy Blue Checked + Black Gingham, Grey Checked, White + Brown Checked on Green + Navy Blue, White + Black Fretowrk)	
		Winter	Navy Blue	24 (57.1%)
			Grey	3 (7.1%)
			Green + Navy Blue Checked	3 (7.1%)
			Brown Checked	2 (4.8%)
			Other (Black, Navy Blue + Russet Checked, Blue + Grey Checked on	

Table 2. *Female Uniforms in Saga Prefecture High Schools (multiple answers possible)* (continued)

		Type of Uniform	Number of Schools
		Navy Blue, Brown Checked on Navy Blue, Blue + Caramel Checked, Brown + Black Checked, Brown + Green Checked, Green, Checked, Orange Tartan)	
	All Season	Navy Blue	21 (50.0%)
		Grey	3 (7.1%)
		Green + Navy Blue Checked	3 (7.1%)
		Brown Checked	2 (4.8%)
		Other (Black, Navy Blue + Russet Checked, Blue + Grey Checked on Navy Blue, Brown Checked on Navy Blue, Blue + Caramel Checked, Brown + Black Checked)	
Material	Summer	50% Wool + 50% Polyester	16 (38.1%)
		65% Polyester + 35% Cotton	7 (16.7%)
		Other (100% Wool, 50% Cotton + 50% Polyester, 70% Polyester + 30% Wool, 65% Polyester + 35% Rayon)	
	Winter	100% Wool	14 (33.3%)
		50% Wool + 50% Polyester	12 (28.6%)
		65% Polyester + 35% Cotton	4 (9.5%)
		70% Cotton + 30% Polyester	2 (4.8%)
		Other (50% Cotton + 50% Polyester, 70% Wool + 30% Polyester, 65% Polyester + 35% Wool)	
	All Season	50% Wool + 50% Polyester	10 (23.8%)
		100% Wool Polyester + 35% Cotton	8 (19.0%)
		Other (70% Wool + 30% Polyester)	3 (7.1%)

Source: Isobe (1996: 103–5).

Table 3. *Whose Opinion Was Sought When Changing Uniforms in Middle Schools, High Schools and Schools for the Handicapped in Saga Prefecture (multiple answers possible)*

Who	Number of Schools
Teachers	23 (76.7%)
Students	22 (73.3%)
Designers	12 (40.0%)
Guardians	10 (33.3%)

Source: Isobe (1996: 98).

Table 4. *Whose Opinion Was Sought When Changing Uniforms at 42 High Schools in Saga Prefecture*

Who	Number of High Schools
Teachers	18 (42.9%)
Students	14 (33.3%)
Guardians	4 (9.5%)
Other	6 (14.3%)

Source: Isobe (1996: 98).

Table 5. *How New Uniform Designs Were Decided at 292 Private Middle and High Schools*

	Women's Schools	Men's Schools	Coed Schools	Total
Designer	37	10	28	75
Agency	33	9	55	97
Within the School	34	25	52	111
Other	6	0	3	9

Source: Nomura (1993: 217).

Table 6. *Factors Considered When Changing Uniforms in Middle Schools, High Schools and Schools for the Handicapped in Saga Prefecture (multiple answers possible)*

Factor	Number of High Schools
Form	19 (63.3%)
Color	19 (63.3%)
Material	12 (40.0%)
Price	17 (56.7%)
School's Image	22 (73.3%)
Comfort	15 (50.0%)
Other*	4 (13.3%)

* "Other" includes "how easy to wash"; "if it suits everyone (e.g. physique)"; functionality"; "a form that is not out of date"; "suitable to the latest fashion"; "improves the school's image (*imêjiappu*)"; "easy to wear".
Source: Isobe (1996: 99).

Table 7. *Changes in Male Uniforms at 33 Middle Schools, High Schools and Schools for the Handicapped in Saga Prefecture*

Type of Uniform	Before Change	After Change	Number of Schools
Form:			
Summer Top	Sports Shirt	Polo Shirt	1 (3.3%)
Winter Top	Stand-Up Collar	Blazer	9 (30.0%)
		(or) Colored Stand-Up Collar	1 (3.3%)
Color:			
Summer	Black	Grey	2 (6.7%)
Bottom	Black	Gingham	1 (3.3%)
	Black	Navy Blue	6 (20.0%)
Winter Top	Black	Grey	1 (3.3%)
	Navy Blue	Dark Green	1 (3.3%)
	Navy Blue	Moss Green	1 (3.3%)
	Green	Navy Blue	1 (3.3%)
	Black	Navy Blue	2 (6.7%)
Winter	Black	Grey	2 (6.7%)
Bottom	Green	Brown Check	1 (3.3%)
Material:			
Winter Top	100% Polyester	100% Wool	1 (3.3%)
	100% Polyester	65% Polyester + 35% Cotton	1 (3.3%)
	50% Cotton + 50% Polyester	70% Cotton + 30% Polyester	1 (3.3%)
	50% Wool + 50% Polyester	70% Wool + 30% Polyester	1 (3.3%)

Source: Isobe (1996: 99).

Table 8. *Changes in Female Uniforms at 54 Middle Schools, High Schools and Schools for the Handicapped in Saga Prefecture*

Type of Uniform	Before Change	After Change	Number of Schools
Form:			
Summer Top	"Sailor"	Blouse	2 (6.7%)
	Overblouse (open sides)	Underblouse (open front)	2 (6.7%)
	Sports Shirt	Blouse with Necktie	1 (3.3%)
Summer Bottom	Box Skirt	Pleated Skirt	2 (6.7%)
Winter Top	"Sailor"	Blazer	6 (20.0%)
	Suit	Blazer	2 (6.7%)
	4-Button Blazer	3-Button Blazer	1 (3.3%)
	Navy Blue Necktie	Different Ribbons by Grade	1 (3.3%)
Winter Bottom	Box Skirt	Pleated Skirt	2 (6.7%)
	Long Skirt	Short Skirt	2 (6.7%)
	Pleated Skirt	Box Skirt	1 (3.3%)
	Pleated Skirt	Culottes	1 (3.3%)
Color:			
Summer Top	Blue	Grey	1 (3.3%)
	White	Stripes on White	1 (3.3%)
	Black Necktie	Grey	1 (3.3%)
Summer Bottom	Navy Blue	Grey	1 (3.3%)
	Navy Blue	Gingham	1 (3.3%)
	Navy Blue	Brown Checked on Navy Blue	1 (3.3%)
	Dark Navy Blue	Bright (*akarui*) Navy Blue	1 (3.3%)
	Grey	Navy Blue Checked	1 (3.3%)
Winter Top	Navy Blue	Navy Blue	4 (13.3%)
	Navy Blue	Dark Green	1 (3.3%)
	Navy Blue	Moss Green	1 (3.3%)
	Green Checked	Navy Blue	1 (3.3%)
Winter Bottom	Navy Blue	Brown Checked on Navy Blue	1 (3.3%)
	Navy Blue	Brown Check	1 (3.3%)
	Navy Blue	Navy Blue Checked and Green	1 (3.3%)
	Dark Navy Blue	Green and White Check	1 (3.3%)
	Green Checked	Brown and Blue Check	1 (3.3%)

Table 8. *Changes in Female Uniforms at 54 Middle Schools, High Schools and Schools for the Handicapped in Saga Prefecture* (continued)

Type of Uniform	Before Change	After Change	Number of Schools
Material:			
Summer Top	Unclear	75% Polyester + 25% Cotton	1 (3.3%)
	Unclear	50% Cotton + 50% Polyester	1 (3.3%)
Summer Bottom	Unclear	50% Wool + 50% Polyester	2 (6.7%)
Winter Top	100% Polyester	100% Wool	2 (6.7%)
	Unclear	100% Wool	1 (3.3%)
	50% Cotton +	70% Cotton + 30% Polyester	1 (3.3%)
	50% Polyester	70% Wool + 30% Polyester	1 (3.3%)
Winter Bottom	100% Wool	70% Cotton + 30% Polyester	1 (3.3%)
	50% Cotton +	70% Wool + 30% Polyester	1 (3.3%)
	50% Polyester	50% Wool + 50% Polyester	1 (3.3%)
	100% Wool		
	Unclear		

Source: Isobe (1996: 99–100).

Table 9. *Results of Changing Uniforms at 23 High Schools in Saga Prefecture (multiple answers possible)*

Results	Number of Schools
Decline in Clothing Violations by Students	13 (43.3%)
Students Became Cheerful (*akaruku*)	6 (20.0%)
Increase in School Applicants	4 (13.3%)
Other	(23.4%)

Source: Isobe (1996: 101).

Table 10. *What Has Been Noticed After Changing Uniforms at Private Middle and High Schools*

What Has Been Noticed	Number of Schools
Easy to Wear and Functional	61
Enriched Fashion Sense, a Stylish Image	43
Students Are Happy to Wear Them	37
Can Be Altered and Are Fun to Coordinate	33
They Suit the School's Tradition and Spirit (*kôfû*)	32
Economically Appropriate	31
High School-like (*kôkôsei-rashiku*) and They Have a Dignified Style	30
Made from Good Material; Durable	30
They Keep Clean (*seisetsusa*)	21
Without Following Fashion They are Simple and Basic	19
They Have a Cheerful (*akaruku*) and Lively (*hatsuratsu*) Sense	15
Other: Strange Clothes Are Not Worn, etc.	–

Source: Nomura (1993: 217; modified).

Table 11. *Uniform Ensembles at 38 Bus Companies*

Season	Ensemble	Number of Companies	%
	Blouse + Skirt	15	39.5
	Blouse + Skirt + Vest	10	26.3
	Blouse + Skirt + Jacket	8	21.1
Summer	Other	5	13.1
	Blouse + Skirts + Vest + Jacket + Coat	28	73.7
	Blouse + Skirt + Vest + Jacket	3	7.9
	Blouse + Skirt + Vest + Coat	2	5.3
Winter	Other (Two-Piece, etc.)	5	13.1

Source: Uno and Nogami (1994: 120).

Table 12. *Women's Uniform Ensembles at 108 Textile-Related Companies*

Season	Ensemble	Number of Companies	%
Summer	Blouse + Skirt (Note: a)	32	29.6
	Blouse + Skirt + Vest (Note: b)	18	16.7
	Blouse Only	10	9.3
	Blouse + (Slacks, Culottes, etc.)	10	9.3
	Vest + Skirt	10	9.3
	Two-Piece Dress	9	8.3
	One-Piece Dress	6	5.6
	Other	22	20.4
Winter	Blouse + Skirt + Vest (Note: c)	34	31.5
	Blouse + (Skirt + Slacks, etc.) (Note: d)	14	13
	Vest + Skirt (Note: e)	14	13
	Two-Piece Dress	14	13
	One-Piece Dress	5	4.6
	Blouse Only	4	3.7
	Other	23	21.3

Notes: (a) Ribbon, Jacket, etc.; (b) Polo Shirt; (c) Cardigan or Blouson; (d) Cardigan or Jacket; (e) Jacket, Blouson or Cardigan
Source: Uno and Nogami (1992: 140).

Table 13. *Uniform Ensembles at 31 Commercial Firms*

Season	Ensemble	Number of Commercial Firms
Summer	Blouse + Skirt + Vest (or Slacks)	17 (3)*
	Blouse + Skirt (or Slacks)	5 (1)
	Two-Piece Suit	3
	Blouse + Two-Piece Suit	1
	Blouse	1
	Skirt + Vest	1
	One-Piece Suit	1
Winter	Blouse + Skirt + Vest	8
	Blouse + Skirt + Vest + Cardigan	7
	Blouse + Skirt + Vest + Jacket	4
	Blouse + Skirt + Vest (or Slacks) + Coat + Jacket	3
	Two-Piece Suit	2
	Vest + Two-Piece Suit	1
	Blouse + Skirt + Cardigan	1
	Blouse + Skirt	1
All Season	Blouse + Skirt + Vest	2
	Blouse + Skirt + Vest + Jacket	1
	Skirt + Vest + Jacket	1

* Figures in parentheses indicate firms that have slacks
Source: Uno and Nogami (1993: 101).

Table 14. *Uniform Ensembles at 34 Banks*

Season	Ensemble	Number of Banks	%
Summer	Blouse + Skirt	33	97.1
	One-Piece	1	2.9
All Season	Blouse + Skirt	13	38.2
Winter	Blouse + Skirt	30	91.2
	Two-Piece Dress or Three-Piece	4	8.8

Source: Uno and Nogami (1990: 98).

Table 15. *Men's Uniform Ensembles at 23 Railroad Companies*

Season	Ensemble	Number of Companies	%
Summer	Jacket + Pants + Sports Shirt	8	34.8
	Jacket + Pants + Open-Collar Shirt	3	13.0
	Pants + Sports Shirt	8	34.8
	Pants + Open-Collar Shirt	1	4.3
	Jacket + Pants + Sports Shirt + Open-Collar	1	4.3
	Pants + Sports Shirt + Open-Collar	1	4.3
Winter	Jacket + Pants + Sports Shirt + Coat	10	43.5
	Jacket + Pants + Coat	8	34.8
	Jacket + Pants + Sports Shirt + Parka	1	4.3
	Jacket + Pants + Vest + Coat	1	4.3
	Jacket + Pants	2	8.7
All Season	Jacket + Pants + Sports Shirt + Coat	1	4.3

Source: Uno, Nogami and Sakurai (1991: 154).

Appendix B: Uchino Michiko's 1995 Questionnaires about Student Uniforms

First Questionnaire of 115 High School Students (47 Female and 68 Male Students)

(1) What do you think about high school uniforms?
  (a) They are necessary: 28
  (b) To some degree it is better to have them: 50
  (c) To some degree it is better not to have them: 18
  (d) They are not necessary: 17
  (e) Other: 2

(2) For those who answered (a) and (b) in question (1). Select a reason from those below (multiple answers are possible):
  – Because uniforms make for good discipline: 7
  – Because uniforms are economical: 16
  – There is no need to worry about clothes: 65
  – Because everyone is the same they feel at ease: 8
  – Ordinary clothes (*shifuku*) might be gaudy: 4
  – Other: I like them: 3; They look good: 4; They are convenient for ceremonial   occasions: 1

(3) For those who answered (c) and (d) in question (1). Select a reason from those below (multiple answers are possible):
  – Clothes are a matter of freedom: 32
  – Ordinary clothes (*shifuku*) are functional and easy to be active in: 19
  – Ordinary clothes are hygienic: 13
  – Ordinary clothes (*shifuku*) are able to cultivate fashion sense: 7
  – Other: It is better to have one's individuality come out: 1; I don't like uniforms: 1; Because of regulations I can't decorate my uniform: 1

(4) How do you think about how uniforms distinguish men and women?
(a) The distinction is natural: 82
(b) The distinction is strange: 17

Reasons for (a): Men and women are different: 8; if men and women are the same it is strange: 25; the distinction is natural and right: 5; I don't like it if men and women are the same: 7; Men and women can be easily distinguished: 3; It is better if men and women act the way they should (*rashiku suru*): 2; Somehow I don't like it: 5; Because the state had decided it there's nothing we can do: 1; I've never thought that they distinguish between men and women: 1

Reasons for (b): Women want to wear pants: 5; The distinction between men and women is not necessary – it is bad: 5; I want both men and women to show their legs: 1; There is no problem if we wear ordinary clothes (*shifuku*): 1; All people are brothers and sisters: 2

(5) Have you ever dislike wearing uniforms?
Yes: 56
No: 55

(6) For those who answered "yes" in question (5). What do you dislike about them?

Uniforms cannot be suitable to the climate and weather: 9; I worry about uniforms becoming dirty and wrinkled: 9; uniforms are hard to move in: 4; their design is bad: many answers; when I wear them on the way home: 1; When I am teased by students from other schools: 1; When I am solicited by cram and preparatory schools: 1; When others say something about my worn-out uniform: 1; When everyone is together: 1; When wearing uniform itself: 1; There's no freedom: 3; When I want to wear my own clothes (*shifuku*): 1; Uniforms are a vestige of militarism: 1; Students also have human rights: 1

Second Questionnaire of 155 High School Students (97 Female and 58 Male Students)

(1) Are there uniforms at your high school? What do you think about them?
(a) It would be better if we didn't wear them: 131
(b) We should wear them: 20
(2) For those who answered "no" in question (1). Select a reason from those below (multiple answers are possible):
    – Clothes are a matter of freedom: 106
    – Ordinary clothes (*shifuku*) are functional and easy to be active in: 82
    – Ordinary clothes are hygienic: 33
    – Ordinary clothes (*shifuku*) are able to cultivate fashion sense: 22

– Other: I'd like to pass time without wearing uniforms: 1; Students from "A" high school like ordinary clothes: 1; I can prepare something that is like a uniform myself: 1; The quality of uniforms is bad: 1; If everyone is dressed the same it gives me the creeps, it looks like the army: 3; Uniforms are a way to suppress the expression of individuality: 2; I have no money to buy uniforms: 1; I don't look good in uniforms: 1; Even though there is standardized clothing, it is better to have a situation in which it is left up to students to decide: 2

(3) For those who answered "yes" in question (1). Select a reason from those below (multiple answers are possible):
 – Because uniforms make for good discipline: 3
 – Because uniforms are economical: 11
 – There is no need to worry about clothes: 14
 – Because everyone is the same they feel at ease: 3
 – Ordinary clothes (*shifuku*) might be gaudy: 1
 – Other: Being student-like (*gakusei-rashî*) is good looking: 2; I should be aware of myself as a student: 1; There are people that wear ordinary clothes (*shifuku*) who do not think about what is appropriate to the place: 3; More than ordinary clothes (*shifuku*), uniforms help in self-control (*jiko yokusei*): 1; If we wear uniforms that look like ordinary clothes (*shifuku*) everyone will like them: 2; I can't stand the excitement. Young women who wear uniforms look good in them and are very pretty: 1

(4) Write down what you think would be the good points if uniforms were deregulated:
Comfortable and easy to move around in: 22; I can express my individuality: 19; Clothes would be suitable to the weather and climate: 52; There's no feeling of being constrained, I feel liberated: 23; My body feels good and it is easy to get what I want: 8; I can wear clothes that I like: 24; I can change my mood: 4; I can play without changing: 13; Others won't know what school I'm from: 1; I'm always clean: 2; There are no violations [i. e., of school regulations]: 2; Individual freedom: 6; I can look at each person as an individual: 4; The classroom would become more cheerful (*akaruku naru*): 1; The range of choices would become bigger: 12

(5) At schools that have uniforms, uniforms distinguish between males and females. What do you think about this?
Such a distinction is natural: 56; I don't think about it: 35; Men in skirts and women in pants is strange: 11; Such a distinction is functional – if viewed at a distance we can distinguish between men and women: 2; femininity (*onna-rashisa*) and masculinity (*otoko-rashisa*) is important: 1; To think about such a distinction is strange: 5; It is strange for only women to wear skirts: 10; such a distinction is unnecessary: 3; It is discriminatory: 1; It means to be

managed: 2; It is restrictive: 1; It is better to get rid of uniforms: 1; I don't understand the meaning of the question: 2; I don't know: 2; It has always been this way: 1; If we don't make such a distinction I want to see what kind of uniforms we would wear: 1

Bibliography

"Adults find kids' lotions softer on their skin" (1993), AEN 8 March, p. 9.

"AIDS awareness with art" (1992), JT 16 May, p. 2.

Aikawa R. (1994), "Ima naze seifuku ka: 'jiyû' to 'sekinin' no chiguhagu na kankei no naka de shimin-ken motsu 'seifuku'" ("Why Uniforms Now? 'Uniforms' Maintain Citizens' Rights among Uneven Relation between 'Freedom' and 'Responsibility'"), Kikan joshi kyôiku mondai (Women's Education Issues Quarterly) 59: 12–17 (April).

"Airlines kick in with special Cup flights" (1998), DY 31 May p. 5.

"Air Nippon attendants set to lose hats, gloves" (1998), DY 18 March, p. 3.

Allison, A. (1991), "Japanese Mothers and Obentôs: The Lunch Box as Ideological State Apparatus", Anthropological Quarterly 64(4): 195–208.

—— (1996), Permitted and Prohibited Desires: Mothers, Comics, and Censorship in Japan, Boulder: Westview Press.

Althusser, L. (1971), Ideology and Ideological State Apparatuses (Notes toward an Investigation on Lenin and Philosophy and Other Essays), New York: Monthly Review.

"ANA elevates Pokemon to new heights" (1998), DY 5 June, p. 3.

"ANA sorry for Snoopy's illegal flights" (1998), AEN 15 January, p. 4.

Anton, K. H. (1992a), "Traffic monitor draws doubletakes", JT 26 June, p. 16.

—— (1992b), "Children have no time to themselves", JT 28 May, p. 16.

—— (1993), "Compulsory fun in Shizuoka", JT 11 November, p. 16.

Aoki, N. (1997), "Hello Kitty has girls purring, Craze targets older women with TVs, toasters, cars", JT 27 December, p. 3.

"Apology issued over haircut comment" (1993), DY 21 November, p. 2.

Arai, N. (1997), "The little egg that hatched Bandai a flurry of success", DY 31 December, p. 3.

Ashitani, T. (1993), "No Masako fashion boom yet", JT 18 March, p. 3.

"As world watches Nagano, city endures culture conflict" (1998), JT 11 February, p. 23.

"Ax schools' hair rules, Rengo urges ministry" (1993), JT 6 October, p. 2.

Bachnik, J. M. (1992), "The Two 'Faces' of Self and Society in Japan", Ethos 20(1): 3–22.

Bachnik, J. M. and C. J. Quinn, Jr. (eds) (1994), Situated Meaning: Inside and Outside in Japanese Self, Society, and Language, Princeton: Princeton University Press.

Badtke-Berkow, L. (1997), "Brave new world of street fashion", JT 3 July, 13

"Bar code 'tattoos' in vogue for Tokyo's material girls" (1997), DY 13 September, p. 8.

Barry, J. G. (1970), *Dramatic Structure: The Shaping of Experience,* Berkeley: University of California Press.

Barshay, E. (1988), *State and Intellectual in Imperial Japan: The Public Man in Crisis,* Berkeley: University of California Press.

"Beautiful boys" (1998), JT 15 March, p. 14.

Becker, E. (1990), "The Self as a Locus of Linguistic Causality", in D. Brissett and C. Edgley (eds), *Life as Theater: A Dramaturgical Source Book* (2nd edition), New York: Aldine de Gruyter, pp. 117–28.

Becker, H. S. (1982), *Art Worlds,* Berkeley: University of California Press.

Bell, C. (1992), *Ritual Theory, Ritual Practice,* New York: Oxford University Press.

Benedict, R. (1946), *The Chrysanthemum and the Sword: Patterns of Japanese Culture,* Boston: Houghton Mifflin.

Berger, P. (1990), "Sociological Perspectives – Society as Drama", in *Life as Theater: A Dramaturgical Source Book* (2nd edition), D. Brissett and C. Edgley (eds), New York: Aldine de Gruyter, pp. 51–62.

Bestor, T. C. (1984), "Life in a Tokyo Neighborhood: An Anthropologist's Journal", *Japan Society Newsletter,* pp. 3–6 (December).

—— (1985), "Tradition and Japanese Social Organization: Institutional Development in a Tokyo Neighborhood", *Ethnology* 24(2): 121–35.

—— (1989), *Neighborhood Tokyo,* Stanford: Stanford University Press.

Blumer, H. (1931), "Science without Concepts", *American Journal of Sociology* 36: 515–33.

—— (1969), *Symbolic Interactionism,* Englewood Cliffs, New Jersey: Prentice-Hall.

Boles, J., P. Davis, and C. Tatro (1990), "False Pretense and Deviant Exploitation: Fortunetelling as a Con", in D. Brissett and C. Edgley (eds), *Life as Theater: A Dramaturgical Source Book* (2nd edition), New York: Aldine de Gruyter, pp. 299–316.

Bourdieu, P. (1977), *Outline of a Theory of Practice,* Cambridge: Cambridge University Press.

—— (1990), *The Logic of Practice,* Stanford: Stanford University Press.

"Boy, girl versions of Tamagotchi set" (1997), DY 22 March, p. 2.

Brasor, P. (1995), "Faster than a speeding Pop tart" JT 19 January, p. 14.

—— (1997), "Yes, you too can have the Naomi look!" JT 6 February, p. 14.

"Brightly colored products to enjoy bright future" (1997), JT 13 June, p. 13.

Brissett, D. and C. Edgley (eds) (1990a), *Life as Theater: A Dramaturgical Source Book* (2nd edition), New York: Aldine de Gruyter.

—— (eds) (1990b), "The Dramaturgical Perspective", in D. Brissett and C. Edgley (eds), *Life as Theater: A Dramaturgical Source Book* (2nd edition), New York: Aldine de Gruyter, pp. 1–46.

"British invasion in Osaka" (1997), DY 11 October, p. 8.

Burke, K. (1966), *Language as Symbolic Action: Essays on Life, Literature, and Method.* Berkeley: University of California Press.

—— (1969), *A Grammar of Motives,* Berkeley: University of California Press.

—— (1990), "Appendix I: The Five Key Terms of Dramatism", in D. Brissett and C. Edgley (eds), *Life as Theater: A Dramaturgical Source Book* (2nd edition), New York: Aldine de Gruyter, pp. 411–18.

Burns, E. (1972), *Theatricality: A Study of Convention in the Theatre and in Social Life,* New York: Harper and Row.

Buruma, I. (1983), *Behind the Mask,* New York: Pantheon Books.

"Bust the school uniform monopoly" (1997), JT 3 August, p. 18.

Camic, C. (1986), "The Matter of Habit", *American Journal of Sociology,* 19: 1039–87 (March).

"Cat icon has merchandisers clawing in big revenues" (1998), DY 14 May, p. 18.

Cherry, K. (1987), *Womansword,* New York: Kodansha International.

"Chiba schools OK short skirts in concession to fashion trend" (1992), DY 7 March, p. 2.

"Children's belongings to be checked" (1998), JT 7 February, p. 2.

"City to make teachers don uniforms" (1996), DY 2 March, p. 2.

"Color shirts are 'in,' but no-tie casual look is still 'out'" (1994), DY 1 January, p. 8.

"Cool as a cucumber" (1998), DY 3 June, p. 2.

Cooley, Charles Horton (1902), *Human Nature and the Social Order,* New York: Scribner's/Free Press.

Cooper-Chen, A. (1997), *Mass Communication in Japan* (with Miiko Kodama), Ames, Iowa: Iowa State University Press.

Coser, Rose (1962), *Life in the Ward,* East Lansing, Michigan: Michigan State University Press.

Cowherd, K. (1989), "'Cute' usage defies understanding by men", DY 15 August, p. 15.

"Curb exorbitant uniform costs" (1997), JT 10 August, p. 20.

"'Cute' grandma syndrome redefining societal norms" (1996), JT 5 October, p. 8.

Daijirin (Great Dictionary) (1988), Tokyo: Sanseidô.

Dalby, L. (1993), *Kimono: Fashioning Culture,* New Haven: Yale University Press.

Davis, F. (1992), *Fashion, Culture, and Identity,* Chicago: University of Chicago Press.

"Dead Hungarian Tamagotchis rest in peace" (1998), JT 22 January, p. 3.

Debord, G. (1977), *Society of the Spectacle,* Detroit: Black and Red.

Denzin, N. K. (1992), *Symbolic Interactionism and Cultural Studies: The Politics of Interpretation,* Cambridge, Massachusetts: Blackwell.

"Design school grads using creative cards in job search" (1998), DY May 4, p. 3.

"Designer uniform trend hits high schools" (1989), DY 22 January, p. 3.

Dewey, J. (1922), *Human Nature and Conduct,* New York: Holt, Rinehart & Winston.

Dittmar, H. (1992), *The Social Psychology of Material Possessions: To Have Is To Be,* New York: St Martin's Press.

Doi T. (1986), *The Anatomy of Dependence,* New York: Kodansha International.

"Doraemon ad in Russian welcomes Yeltsin's visit" (1992), DY 10 September, p. 3.

Dower, J. W. (1993), "Peace and Democracy in Two Systems: External Policy and Internal Conflict", in A. Gordon (ed.), *Postwar Japan as History,* Berkeley: University of California Press, pp. 3–33.

"Dress to impress" (1997), JT 28 September, p. 18.

"Driver wins right to color his hair" (1997), AEN 26 December, p. 4.

"Drive to be thin puts self-image at odds with standards" (1998), DY 10 June, p. 2.

Durignaud, Jean (1973), "The Theatre in Society: Society in the Theatre", in E. and T. Burns (eds), *The Sociology of the Theatre: Sociology of Literature and Drama,* New York: Penguin.

Edwards, W. (1989) *Modern Japan Through Its Weddings: Gender, Person, and Society in Ritual Portrayal,* Stanford: Stanford University Press.

Efron, S. (1998), "The Japanese kids are all right, so long as they are kept under full-time surveillance", JT June 21, p. 9.

El Guindi, Fadwa (1999), *Veil: Modesty, Privacy and Resistance,* Oxford: Berg.

"EU ready to yield on cuts", (1997), JT 8 December, p. 1.

Evreinoff, N. (1927), *The Theatre in Life,* New York: Benjamin Blom.

—— (1990), "Appendix II: The Never Ending Show", in D. Brissett and C. Edgley (eds), *Life as Theater: A Dramaturgical Source Book* (2nd edition), New York: Aldine de Gruyter, pp. 419–24.

"Execs snap up comic book on dealing with gangsters" (1993), JT 9 December, p. 3.

"Father arrested in school row over daughter" (1996), DY 2 May, p. 2.

Fazio, G. (1993), "Raving under pleasure dome", JT 13 August, p. 17.

"Females told to keep their loose socks out of dugouts" (1998), DY 24 June, p. 12.

Ferguson, J. (1993), "Condom novelties prove hit with kids: Trendy shops cash in on risque business", JT 18 June, p. 3.

"Firms welcome 1.1 million recruits" (1993), DY 2 April, p. 2.

Flannery, J. (1997), "Blond wants to blur Asian stereotypes", JT 17 July, p. 17.

For Beginners, eizu: sei, ai, byôki (AIDS: Sex, Love, and Illness) (1988), Tokyo: Gendai Shokan.

For Beginners, sei (Sex) (1987), Tokyo: Gendai Shokan.

Foucault, M. (1979), *Discipline and Punish: The Birth of the Prison,* New York: Vintage Books.

—— (1980), *The History of Sexuality,* New York: Vintage Books.

Fox, D. (1998), "Hello Kitty items a global rage in 'Zen cuteness'", JT 30 April, p. 15.

Friedmann, D. (1987), *Une Histoire du blue jean,* Paris: Ramsay.

"From the cradle to the toiletry market: young women go gaga for baby products" (1995), *The Nikkei Weekly,* 27 November, p. 20.

Frykman, J. and O. Löfgren (1987), *Culture Builders: A Historical Anthropology of Middle- class Life,* London: Rutgers University Press.

Fujie, L. (1989), "Popular Music", in R. G. Powers and H. Kato (eds), *Handbook of Japanese Popular Culture,* New York: Greenwood Press, pp. 197–220.

Fukami, A. (1993), "Shonen Knife's simple success story", JT 1 January, p. 15.

Funada S. (1992), *"Gakkô fuku ni taisuru chakuyôsha no ishiki ni tsuite"* ("On the Consciousness of Wearers towards Their School Uniforms"), *Nihon ifuku gakkai shi* (Japanese Journal of Clothes Research) 35(2): 13–59.

Geertz, C. (1980), *Negara: The Theatre State in Ninieteenth-Century Bali,* Princeton: Princeton University Press.

Gillis, J. (1981), *Youth and History,* New York: Academic Press.

"Girl's school ouster due to perm upheld" (1992), JT 31 October, p. 2.

Goffman, E. (1959), *The Presentation of Self in Everyday Life,* New York: Anchor Books.

—— (1961), *Asylums,* New York: Anchor Books.

—— (1974), *Frame Analysis: An Essay on the Organization of Experience.* New York: Harper and Row.

—— (1979), *Gender Advertisements,* New York: Harper and Row.

—— (1990), "Role Distance", in D. Brissett and C. Edgley (eds), *Life as Theater: A Dramaturgical Source Book* (2nd edition), New York: Aldine de Gruyter, pp. 101–12.

"Going ape" (1993), JT 2 February, p. 2.

Gramsci, A. (1971), *Selections from the Prison Notebooks* (ed. and trans. Q. Hoare and G. N. Smith), London: Lawrence and Wishart.

Hadfield, P. (1989), "Shakin' it – in the earthquake simulator", DY 31 October, p. 11.

—— (1991), "Darwin's second law: survival of the cutest", DY 26 February, p. 16.

"Hairstyle rights" (1996), JT 14 April, p. 14.

Hall, P.M. (1987), "Presidential Address: Interactionism and the Study of Social Organization", *Sociological Quarterly* 28: 1–22.

Hall, G. Stanley (1898), "Some Aspects of the Early Sense of Self", *American Journal of Psychology* 9: 351–95.

Hani, Y. (1994), "'Recruit suits' sales under way: Stores tailor selections to students' career choices", JT 29 March, p. 2.

—— (1997), "Virtual pet on a key ring: Tamagotchi craze sweeping the nation", JT 26 January, p. 2.

Hara T. (1996), "*'Seifuku jiyûka' no torikumi o kangaeru*" ("Thinking about a Bout with 'Uniform Liberalization'"), *Mirai o hiraku kyôiku (Education that Opens Up the Future)* 105: 64–9.

Harada T. and Hasegawa N. (1996), "The Present State of Uniforms in Nursery Schools and Kindergartens", *Nagoya joshi daigaku kiyô (Kasei shizen hen) (Nagoya Women's University Bulletin* [Domestic and Natural Sciences Edition]*)* 42: 21–32.

Hare, A. P. and H. H. Blumberg (1988), *Dramaturgical Analysis of Social Interaction,* New York: Praeger.

Hebdige, D. (1979), *Subculture: The Meaning of Style,* London: Routledge.

Hendry, J. (1986), *Becoming Japanese: The World of the Pre-School Child,* Honolulu: University of Hawaii Press.

—— (1993), *Wrapping Culture: Politeness, Presentation, and Power in Japan and Other Societies,* Oxford: Oxford University Press.

Hirosawa S. (1995), "*Ikitsuku hima mo naku: seifuku*" ("No Time to Rest: Uniforms"), *Sekai* (World) 10: 322–31 (September).

"Homeless employed in cleanup, but required to wear emblem", (1994), DY 15 July, p. 9.

Hoshino Y. (1994), *"Joshi kôsei seifuku konjaku monogatari: kanshô yô joseikan no minaoshi"* ("Past and Present Stories of Female High School Student Uniforms: Re- Examining Women's View of the Appreciation of Their Use"), *Kikan joshi kyôiku mondai (Women's Education Issues Quarterly)* 59: 4–11 (April).

Huber, T. M. (1994), *Strategic Economy in Japan,* Boulder: Westview Press.

Ida, K. (1997), "Coffee shop owner waxes hygienic: Store drums up customers with live video ear-cleaning service", JT 6 July, p. 3.

"Intl judo body OK's colored uniforms", (1997), DY 8 October, p. 1.

Ishi T. and Ôami M. (1995), *"Nabeshima ie no fukushoku ihin – dai yon hô: tokushi kangofujin-kai seifuku – kango fuku"* ("The Costume Heirlooms of the Nabeshima Family – Part 4: Voluntary Nursing Association Uniforms"), *Ôtsuma joshi daigaku kiyô – kaseikei (Ôtsuma Women's University Bulletin – Domestic Science)* 31: 1–18 (March).

Ishida Takeshi (1984), "Conflict and Its Accommodation: *Omote-Ura* and *Uchi-Soto* Relations", in E. Krauss, T. P. Rohlen, and P. G. Steinhoff (eds), *Conflict in Japan*, Honolulu: University of Hawaii Press, pp. 16–38.

Ishizuki M. (ed.) (1992), *Kindai nihon no gakkô bunka-shi (Writings on Modern Japan's School Culture)*, Tokyo: Shibunkaku Shuppan.

Isobe Y. (1993), *"Gakkô seifuku ni kansuru kenkyû – dai I hô: chûgakkô – kôtô gakkô no seifuku ni tsuite no daigakusei no iken"* ("Studies on School Uniforms – Part I: The Opinions of University Students on Middle School and High School Uniforms"), *Journal of the Faculty of Education Saga University* 40(3): 137–45.

—— (1996), *"Gakkô seifuku ni kansuru kenkyû – dai V hô: Saga-ken no kôtô gakkô no seifuku no jittai"* ("Studies on School Uniforms – Part V: The Real Conditions of High School Uniforms in Saga Prefecture"), *Journal of the Faculty of Education Saga University* 43(2): 95–112.

Isobe Y. and Eguchi C. (1996), *"Gakkô seifuku ni kansuru kenkyû – dai IV hô: seifuku yô nunoji oyobi fuzokuhin no shôhi seinô"* ("Studies on School Uniforms – Part IV: The End-Use Properties of Textiles Fabrics and Accessory in School Uniforms"), *Journal of the Faculty of Education Saga University* 43(2): 83–94.

It's a cat's life" (1986), *The Economist,* 11 October, p. 106.

"It's tight times for part-time workers" (1994), JT 15 January, p. 17.

Ivy, M. (1993), "Formations of Mass Culture", in Andrew Gordon (ed.), *Postwar Japan as History,* Berkeley: University of California Press, pp. 239–58.

JAL suchuwâdesu 9 nin no taiken sekkyakujutsu: Manâ–chotto î hanashi (The Experiences of 9 JAL Stewardesses in the Art of Handling Customers: Some Helpful Information on Manners) (1988), JAL Coordination Services Co., Tokyo: Seibun Dôshinkô.

JAL suchuwâdesu no iki iki manâ kôza (JAL Stewardess: Lectures on Cheerful Manners) (1989), JAL Coordination Services Co., Tokyo: Nihon Nôritsu Kyôkai.

"JAL to offer 'Disney' jumbo service" (1994), DY 1 August, p. 2.

James, W. (1890), *The Principles of Psychology* (2 vols.), New York: Holt.

"Japanese Business" (1994), DY 12 April, p. 6.

"Japan school uniforms under fire" (1997), AEN 15 October, p. 4.

"Japan's civilian army proud of its duds" (1992), JT 4 October, p. 15.

Jaynes, J. (1976), *The Origin of Consciousness in the Breakdown of the Bicameral Mind,* Boston: Houghton Mifflin Co.

—— (1990), "Afterward", in Jaynes, J., *The Origin of Consciousness in the Breakdown of the Bicameral Mind,* Boston: Houghton Mifflin Co.

"JOC critical of medalist's manners" (1998), JT 14 February, p. 23.

Johnson, C. (1980), "*Omote* (Explicit) and *Ura* (Implicit): Translating Japanese political Terms", *Journal of Japanese Studies* 6: 89–115.

—— (1982), *MITI and the Japanese Miracle,* Stanford: Stanford University Press.

Joseph, N. (1986), *Uniforms and Nonuniforms,* New York: Greenwood Press.

Kageyama, Y. (1997), "U.S. finally learns how to export to Japan: Just take those old pants and beat-up shoes and label them 'vintage,'" JT 2 August, p. 3.

Kamiya, S. (1998), "Posts may adopt 'purikura': Ministry panel suggests letter-writing boost for young", JY 8 August, p. 3.

Kataoka Y. (1997), *"Joshi kôtôsei ga fuyû nichijô to machi"* ("The Mundane and Town in which Female High School Students Float"), in Nakanishi S. (ed.), *Kodomotachi no sabukaruchyâ daikenkyû (Great Research on Children's Sub-culture),* Tokyo: Rôdô Junpô, pp. 122–41.

Kawachi, Kyotaro (1996), "School dress code has teachers howling", DY 13 March, p. 7.

"Kawaî tte nanda tsuke" (1990), *Asahi,* 14 March, p. 2.

Kelly, W. W. (1997), "An Anthropologist in the Bleachers", *Japan Quarterly* 44(3): 66–79 (December).

"Kiddy cosmetics" (1998), DY 7 March, p. 13.

Kinsella, S. (1995), 'Cuties in Japan', in L. Skov and B. Moeran (eds), *Women, Media, and Consumption in Japan,* Honolulu: University of Hawaii Press, pp. 220–54.

Kiritani, E. (1994), "Uniforms give clues to rank, status", DY 29 September, p. 7.

—— (1996), "Hand in glove", DY 9 November, p. 8.

—— (1997), "Bringing up baby", DY 22 February, p. 8.

Kitamura T. (1996), "'Kyôshokuin no seifuku' de kyôiku wa yoku naru no ka" ("Does Education Improve with 'Teacher Uniforms'"?), *Kyôiku: kyôiku kagaku kenkyûkai II hen* (Education: Education Science Society II Edition) 4b(8): 112–14 (August).

"Kitty bankbook" (1998), DY 2 April, p. 18.

Krier, B. A. (1991), "Kids in provocative dress a growing trend", DY 21 January, p. 7.

Landers, P. (1996), "In Japan, flight attendants idolized as feminine ideal", AEN 10 April, p. 5.

Lapenta, J. (1983), "Seifuku", in *Discover Japan* (vol. 2), Tokyo: Kodansha, pp. 114–15.

Lazarus, D. (1992), "Toilet togetherness for you and your cat", JT 17 May, p. 11.

—— (1993), "Quick now, how is a shoe like a toilet?" JT 20 November, p. 14.

—— (1994a), "Are we having a good hair day, guys?" JT 24 April, p. 15.

—— (1994b), "Seeing Japan through a magnifying glass", JT 27 November, p. 14.

"LDP courts voters with 'ryu' doll" (1996), JT 30 July, p. 3.

Lebra, T. S. (1976), *Japanese Patterns of Behavior*, Honolulu: University of Hawaii Press.

—— (1984), *Japanese Women*, Honolulu: University of Hawaii Press.

—— (1992), "Self in Japanese Culture", in N. Rosenberger (ed.), *The Japanse Sense of Self*, Cambridge: Cambridge University Press, pp. 105–20.

LeCallier, L. (1988), "'Tax terror' hits Hungary", DY 2 November, p. 3.

LeTendre, G. (1994), "Guiding Them on: Teaching, Hierarchy, and Social Organization in Japanese Middle Schools", *Journal of Japanese Studies* 20(1): 37–59.

Levinson, H. (1993), "Shin-chan latest manga menace", JT 24 June p. 14.

Lewicki, P. (1986), *Nonconscious Social Information Processing*, New York: Academic Press.

Lo, J. (1990), *Office Ladies, Factory Women: Life and Work at a Japanese Company*, New York: Sharpe.

Lock, M. (1993), "Cultivating the Body: Anthropology and Epistemologies of Bodily Practice and Knowledge", *Annual Review of Anthropology* 22: 133–55.

Lyman, S. M. (1975), *The Drama of Social Reality*, New York: Oxford University Press.

Ma, K. (1988), "Ready for a 'talking' business card? *Meishi*", DY 5 December, p. 3.

"Mad for uniforms" (1998), DY 25 January, p. 14.

Mangham, I. L. and M. A. Overington (1990), "Dramatism and the Theatrical Metaphor", in D. Brissett and C. Edgley (eds), *Life as Theater: A Dramaturgical Source Book* (2nd edition), New York: Aldine de Gruyter, pp. 333–46.

Masuda, Y. (1998), "Small, cheap, quirky – formula for fast sellers in slow times", AEN 26 May, p. 5.

Matsuzaki, T. (1997), "Exercise show mirrors changing times", DY 16 October, p. 18.

Mauss, M. (1973 [1936]), "Techniques of the Body" (trans. B. Brewester), *Economy and Society* 2(1): 70–88.

"Maverick assemblyman fights dress code, graft" (1997), JT 7 October, p. 3.

McGill, P. and M. Loney (1997), "How I made billions for Bandai", AEN 18 May, p. 5.

McVeigh, B. (1994), "Ritualized Practices of Everyday Life: Constructing Self, Status, and Social Structure in Japan", *Journal of Ritual Studies* 8(1): 53–71.

—— (1995a), "Society in the Self: The Anthropology of Agency", *Tôyô Gakuen Daigaku Kiyô* (Tôyô Gakuen University Research Bulletin) 3: 33–48.

—— (1995b), "The Feminization of Body, Behavior, and Belief: Learning to Be an 'Office Lady' at a Japanese Women's College", *The American Asian Review* 13(2): 29–67.

—— (1996a), "Commodifying Affection, Authority and Gender in the Everyday Objects of Japan", *Journal of Material Culture* 1(3): 291–312.

—— (1996b), "'Cultivating 'Femininity' and 'Internationalism': Rituals and Routine at a Japanese Women's Junior College", *Ethos* 24(2): 314–49.

—— (1997a), "Wearing Ideology: How Uniforms Discipline Bodies and Minds in Japan", *Fashion Theory: The Journal of Dress, Body & Culture* 1(2): 1–26.

—— (1997b), *Life in a Japanese Women's College: Learning to Be Ladylike*. London: Routledge.

—— (1997c), "*Seken:* The Sociopsychology of Being Observed in Japan's Political Economy", paper presented at the 42nd International Conference of Eastern Studies, Tokyo (May 31).

—— (1997d), "States of Gendered Subjectivity: How the Japanese State Produces Femininity", in Uchiyamada Y. (ed.), *Jiendâ to "daisan sekia no joseitachi"* (Gender and "Third-World Women"), Kokusai Kaihatsu kôtô kyôiku kikô, Kokusai kaihatsu kenkyû sentâ (Research Center for International Developmnent, Foundation for Advanced Studies on International Development), pp. 53–75.

—— (1998a), *The Nature of the Japanese State: Rationality and Rituality,* London: Routledge.

—— (1998b)", Students Who Pretend Not to Know: The Official Gaze and University Education in Japan", paper presented at the Second Asian Studies Conference, Sophia University, Tokyo (June 20).

—— (1998c), "Linking State and Self: How the Japanese State Bureaucratizes Subjectivity through 'Moral Education'", *Anthropological Quarterly* 71(3): 125–37.

—— (forthcoming), "'Micro-Rituals' that Ritualize Bodies: Learning to Be Ladylike at Japanese Women's College", *Journal of Ritual Studies,*

—— (n.d.), *The Japanese Ministry of Education: Strategic Schooling and the Construction of Japanese Identity* (book manuscript under review).

Mead, G. H. (1910), "What Social Objects Must Psychology Presuppose?" *Journal of Philosophy, Psychology, and Scientific Methods* 7: 174–80.

—— (1934), *Mind, Self and Society,* Chicago: University of Chicago Press.

—— (1938), *The Philosophy of the Act,* Chicago: University of Chicago Press.

"Men baring almost all at Osaka discos" (1993), DY 21 October, p. 3.

"Men tempt kids with Tamagotchi virtual pets" (1997), JT 5 June, p. 3.

Messinger, S. E., H. Sampson, and R. D. Towne (1962), "Life as Theater: Some Notes on the Dramaturgic Approaches to Social Reality", *Sociometry* XXV: 98–110.

Messinger, S. E., H. Sampson, and R. D. Towne (1990), "Life as Theater: Some Notes on the Dramaturgic Approach to Social Reality", in D. Brissett and C. Edgley (eds), *Life as Theater: A Dramaturgical Source Book* (2nd edition), New York: Aldine de Gruyter, pp. 73–84.

"*Metoro Q & A*" (1998), *Metoro natsu matsuri gaido* (Metro Summer Festival Guide) 17: 25 (1 July).

Miller, L. (1998), "New Body Aesthetics for Men", paper presented at the 1998 Association for Asian Studies, Washington, DC.

Mills, C. W. (1990), "Situated Actions and Vocabularies of Motive", in D. Brissett and C. Edgley (eds), *Life as Theater: A Dramaturgical Source Book* (2nd edition), New York: Aldine de Gruyter, pp. 207–18.

Mitchell, T. (1990), "Everyday Metaphors of Power", *Theory and Society* 19: 545–77.

Mitchell, T. (1991), "The Limits of the State: Beyond Statist Approaches and their Critics", *American Political Science Review* 85(1): 77–96.

Miyatake, F. and J. Norton (1994), "In Japan, many parts to play", JT 6 January, p. 14.

Mizui, Y. (1998a), "Something old, something new", DY 16 May, p. 18.

—— (1998b), "Yukata gains popularity as outdoor wear", DY 20 June, p. 7.

Mizutani, O. and N. Mizutani (1987), *How to Be Polite In Japanese,* Tokyo: Japan Times.

"More couples break tradition, wed abroad" (1997), JT 22 May, p. 8.

Morikawa, K. (1998), "Ridiculous rules protect teens from 100% cotton", AEN 20 June, p. 4.

Mori N. (1985), *Tôkyô joshi kô seifuku zukan (Women's High Schools of Tokyo Picture Book of Uniforms),* Tokyo: Yudachi-sha.

—— (1993), *Misshon sukûru zukan (Picture Book of Mission Schools),* Tokyo: Fusô-sha.

Morimura, S. F. (1993), "Japan's marriage industry is booming", *Japan Scope* (spring), pp. 39–43.

"Most companies see black hair as beautiful" (1996), DY 2 July, p. 3.

Musgrove, F. (1965), *Youth and the Social Order,* Bloomington, Indiana: Indiana University Press.

"Nagano suffers stuffed Snowlet shortage" (1998), DY 20 February, p. 27.

Naito, Y. (1998), "Are men just big tweezes?" JT 30 April, p. 15.

Naito, Y. (1996), "'Print club' craze: Latest fad has teenagers stuck on stickers", JT 27 June, p. 3.

—— (1997), "Print club forever", JT 17 August, pp. 12–13.

Nakagawa A. (1994), *"Seifuku to kodomo no jinken: kôsoku no oyobu ihan o kaku suru mitsu no shiten"* ("Uniforms and Children's Rights: Three Viewpoints that Demarcate the Limits to Which School Rules Go"), *Kikan joshi kyôiku mondai (Women's Education Issues Quarterly)* 59: 30–6 (April).

Nakajima, M. (1997), "Children's show business becoming big business", DY 8 December, p. 5.

Nakamura, A. (1996), "Teachers up in arms over city plan for them to don uniforms in school", JT 17 March, p. 3.

Nakamura, K. (1998), "Underwear ad drives kids wild", DY 9 April, p. 13.

Nakamura, Y. (1998), "From Puffy to baggy socks: Japan's youth see green", JT 1 January, p. 6.

Nakane C. (1970), *Japanese Society,* Berkeley: University of California Press.

Nakanishi S. (1997a), *Kodomotachi no sabukaruchyâ daikenkyû (Great Research on Children's Subculture),* Tokyo: Rôdô Junpô.

—— (1997b), *"Yasashî – omoshiroi – kawaî"* ("Kind, Interesting and Cute"), in Nakanishi Shintarô (ed.), *Kodomotachi no sabukaruchyâ daikenkyû (Great Research on Children's Subculture),* Tokyo: Rôdô Junpô, pp. 82–121.

"New face mask takes blinkers off kendo" (1998), DY 26 January, p. 3.

"New police uniforms show designer touch" (1992), DY 8 October, p. 2.

Noguchi, P. (1990), *Delayed Departues, Overdue Arrivals,* Honolulu: University of Hawaii Press.

"No jacket (or tie) required, as metropolitan government goes summery" (1998), DY 31 May, p. 2.

Nomura M. (1993), *"Shiritsu joshi chûgaku – kôtô gakkô no seifuku ni tsuite: sonoseiritsu to gaiteiki o mukaeta genjô"* ("Concerning Private Women's Middle and High School Uniforms: Their Formation and The Present Conditions that Welcome a Period of Reform"), *Nihon shigaku kyôiku kenkyûjo kiyô (Japan Private School Education Research Institute Bulletin)* 28(1): 199–223.

—— (1994), *"Seifuku ni kansuru seito no ishiki ni tsuite: ankêto chôsa yori"* ("On the Consciousnes of Students Towards Their Uniforms: From a Questionnaire Investigation"), *Nihon shigaku kyôiku kenkyûjo kiyô (Japan Private School Education Research Institute Bulletin)* 29(1): 229–57.

"N.Y. education board urges uniforms for schoolchildren" (1998), DY 26 March, p. 20.

Onozuka, J. (1996), "Beauty in the eyes of Japanese shortsighted", DY 21 July, p. 14.

Ortner, S. B. (1979), "On Key Symbols", in W. A. Lessa and E. Z. Vogt (eds), *Reader in Comparative Religion,* New York: Harper and Row, pp. 92–8.

"Osaka teachers begin anti-uniform fight" (1996), DY 6 March, p. 2.

Otake, T. (1998a), "Teens take shine to 'fashionable' knives", JT 7 February, p. 2.

—— (1998b), "High-fashion bikes hit Harajuku streets", JT 1 June, p. 3.

Ôya K. (1995), *"Seifuku no sampi o meguru 'kodomo-kan'"* ("'Children's View' Concerning the Debate about Uniforms"), *Gendai kyôiku kagaku (Modern Education Science)* 38(2): 52–5 (February).

Park, R. E. and E. W. Burgess (eds) (1921), *Introduction to the Science of Sociology,* Chicago: University of Chicago Press.

Peirce, C. S. (1934), *Collected papers of Charles Sanders Peirce,* Vols. 5 and 6 (ed. C. Hartshone, trans. P. Weiss), Cambridge, Massachusetts: Harvard University Press (Belknap).

Perinbanayagam, R. S. (1982), "Dramas, Metaphors, and Structures", *Symbolic Interaction* 5(2): 259–76.

—— (1985), *Signifying Acts,* Carbondale, Illinois: Southern Illinois University Press.

"Personal image business is starting to take off" (1990), JT 18 October, p. 3.

"Pet pampering proves popular productive pastime" (1993), JT 9 July, p. 13.

Pierson, C. (1996). *The Modern State,* London: Routledge.

Pin, E. J. and J. Turndorf (1990), "Staging One's Ideal Self", in D. Brissett and C. Edgley (eds), *Life as Theater: A Dramaturgical Source Book* (2nd edition), New York: Aldine de Gruyter, pp. 163–82.

"Police copter joins manhunt for teen Tamagotchi thieves" (1997), JT 1 March, p. 2.

Prendergast, C. and J. D. Knotternus (1990), "The Astructural Bias and Pre-suppositional Reform in Symbolic Interactionism: A Noninteractionist Evaluation of the New Studies in Social Organization", in L. T. Reynolds, *Interactionism: Exposition and Critique* (2nd edition), Dix Hills, New York: General Hall, pp. 158–80.

Prown, J. D. (1988), "Mind in Matter: An Introduction to Material Culture Theory and Method", in R. B. St. George (ed.), *Material Life in America, 1600–1800*, Boston: Northeastern University Press.

"Pupil sues middle school over strict haircut regulations" (1993), DY 1 November, p. 2.

"Pussycat attack" (1998), JT 7 August, p. 14.

Quinn, C. J. Jr. (1994), "The Terms *Uchi* and *Soto* as Windows on a World", in J. M. Bachnik and C. J. Quinn, Jr. (eds), *Situated Meanings: Inside and Outside in Japanese Self, Society, and Language*, Princeton: Princeton University Press, pp. 38–72.

Raz, J. (1992), "Self-presentation and Performance in the *yakuza* Way of Life: Fieldwork with a Japanese Underworld Group", in R. Goodman and K. Refsing (eds), *Ideology and Practice in Modern Japan*, London: Routledge, pp. 210–34.

"Readers' Forum: Can school uniforms effectively curb juvenile violence?" (1998), DY 25 April, p. 6.

"Readers' Forum: What do you think about lingerie-like dresses now in fashion among young women?" (1998), DY 27 June, p. 6.

"Readers' Forum: What do you think of the recent trend in which people dye their hair brown in chapatsu fashion?" (1996), DY 30 November, p. 7.

Refsing, K. (1992), "Japanese Educational Expansion: Quality or Equality", in R. Goodman and K. Refsing (eds), *Ideology and Practice in Modern Japan*, London: Routledge, pp. 116–29.

Reynolds, L. T. (1990), *Interactionism: Exposition and Critique* (2nd edition), Dix Hills, New York: General Hall.

Roberts, V. (1995), "U.S. teens say hello to Kitty and hang out on Cute Street", JT 20 December, p. 3.

Rohlen, T. (1983), *Japan's High Schools*, Berkeley: University of California Press.

Rosenberger, N. R. (1989), "Dialectic Balance in the Polar Model of Self: The Japan Case", *Ethos* 17: 88–117.

Saito, S. (1998), "Kitty comes to the rescue", DY 25 March, p. 13.

Sakamoto H. (1986), *Kôsoku no kenkyû* (Research on School Regulations), Tokyo: Sanichi Shobô.

—— (1989), *Kyôshi no kenkyû* (Research on Teachers), Tokyo: Sanichi Shobô.

Samuels, R. (1994), *Rich Nation, Strong Army: National Security and the Technological Transformation of Japan*, Ithaca, New York: Cornell University Press.

Satô A. (1988), *Kashkoi onna wa kawaiku ikiru (A Clever Woman Lives In a Cute Manner)*, Tokyo: PHP Kenkyû.

Sato, I. (1991), *Kamikaze Biker: Parody and Anomy in Affluent Japan*, Chicago: University of Chicago Press.

Sawaguchi, T. (1997), "Salon caters to young clients," JT 17 June, p. 3.

Sayle, M. (1998), "How Rich Japan Misled Poor Asia", *JPRI* Working Paper No. 43. Japan Policy Research Institute (March).

Schechner, R. (1977), *Essays on Performance Theory 1970–1976*, New York: Drama Books Specialist.

—— (1982), *From Ritual to Theatre: The Human Seriousness of Play*, New York: Performing Arts Journal Publications.

—— (1985), *Between Theatre and Anthropology*, Philadelphia: University of Pennsylvania Press.

—— (1988), *Performance Theory*, New York: Routledge.

—— (1992), *The Future of Ritual*, New York: Routledge Chapman & Hall.

Schechner, R. and W. Appel (eds) (1989), *By Means of Performance: Intercultural Studies of Theatre and Ritual*, Cambridge: University of Cambridge Press.

Schechner, R. and M. Schumar (eds) (1976), *Ritual, Play, and Performance*, New York: Seabury Press.

Scheper-Hughes, N. and M. Lock (1987), "The Mind-ful Body: A Prolegomenon to Future Work in Medical Anthropology", *Medical Anthropology* 1: 6–41.

Schilling, M. (1993), "A star isn't born in 'Jurassic' lite", JT 20 July, p. 17.

Schomer, K. and Y. Chang (1995), "The Cult of Cuteness", *Newsweek*, 28 August, pp. 54–8.

"Schools bring uniforms back to improve image" (1997), DY 10 April, p. 3.

Scott, M. B. and S. Lyman (1990), "Accounts", in D. Brissett and C. Edgley (eds), *Life as Theater: A Dramaturgical Source Book* (2nd edition), New York: Aldine de Gruyter, pp. 219–42.

Selby, H. (1996), "Teen creed: have 'meishi' will travel", DY 6 December, p. 3.

Shah, T. (1997), "The housewife who donated an egg to the world", *You* (November) (9): 48–50.

Shilling, C. (1993), *The Body and Social Theory*, London: Sage Publications.

"Shiseido, Kao offer virtual makeup", (1998), DY 30 June, p. 9.

Shoji, K. (1997), "We wish we all could be Shibuya teens" JT 22 October, p. 14.

—— (1998), "Harajuku, sweeter than marshmallows", JT 11 March, p.14.

Shweder, R. A. (1990), "Cultural Psychology: What Is It?" in James W. Stigler, Richard A. Shweder, and Gilbert Herdt (eds), *Cultural Psychology: Essays on Comparative Human Development*, Cambridge: Cambridge University Press.

Silva, A. (1996), "Japan's incurable case of 'cuteitis,'" JT 8 September, p. 13.

—— (1997), "Koyanagi hops on bandwagon with show of new *otaku* crafts", JT 6 July, p. 12.

Simmel, G. (1909), "The Problem of Sociology", *American Journal of Sociology* 15: 289–320.

"Sizing up the big-shoes craze" (1997), DY 1 November, p. 9.

"Sky-high pride" (1998), AEN 12 June, p. 4.

"Small is big" (1997), JT 26 January, p. 18.

Stone, G. P. (1990), "Appearance and the Self: A Slightly Revised Version", in D. Brissett and C. Edgley (eds), *Life as Theater: A Dramaturgical Source Book* (2nd edition), New York: Aldine de Gruyter, pp. 141–62.

"Stores finding big bucks in little pets" (1998), AEN 26 May, p. 5.

"Stores hope to cash in on wedding" (1993), JT 13 January, p. 3.

Strawn, Perri Johanna (1999), *Teaching Nationalism in the Crucible: Changing Identities in Taiwan High Schools after Martial Law*, Unpublished PhD dissertation, Yale University.

"Student's hair cut to appease gangster" (1994), DY 12 January, p. 3.

"Students judge schools by their uniform" (1992), JT 21 June, p. 18.

Sugimoto, Y. (1997), *An Introduction to Japanese Society*, Cambridge: Cambridge University Press.

Sugiyama Y. (1994), *"Shiritsu gakkô bûmu to seifuku: ojôsan burando no seifuku wa tôshi ni miau?"* (The Private School Boom and Uniforms: Do Young Ladies' Brand Name Uniforms Mean an Investment?), *Kikan joshi kyôiku mondai* (Women's Education Issues Quarterly) 59: 24–9 (April).

Sutorîto fuasshon 1945–1995: wakamono sutairu no 50 nen shi (Street Fashion 1945–1995: A 50-Year History of Young People's Fashion) (1995), Akurosu Editing Office (ed.) Tokyo: Parco.

Takasu K. (1988), *Kawaî onna ni narukokoro no jikigaku: mesumeru ga toguiionna e no 5 hôsaku (The Magnetism of the Heart – Becoming a Cute Woman: Mesmer Explains the 5 Rules for Becoming a Good Woman)*, Tokyo: Shôdensha.

"Tamagotch fans in Singapore fired from jobs" (1997), DY 6 June, p. 3.

"Tamagotchi passes 10 million mark" (1997), JT 19 July, p. 12.

"'Tamagotch' raids conducted in Osaka" (1997), DY 30 May, p. 2.

"Tamagotch used in kidnapping attempts" (1997), DY 13 April, p. 2.

Tambiah, Stanley J. (1979), "A Performative Approach to Ritual", *Proceedings of the British Academy* 65: 113–69.

Taniguchi T. (1995), *"Shinsen datta seifuku haishi no torikumi: kaki joshi kyôiku mondai kenkyûkai ni shusseki shite"* ("The New Bout of Abolishing Uniforms: Attending a Summer Research Session of Women's Education Issues"), *Kikan joshi kyôiku mondai (Women's Education Issues Quarterly)* 65: 107–9 (October).

Tatsuta, K. (1997), "New generation suggests kimono has had its day", JT 4 January, p. 3.

"Teachers nix brown hair, blue nail polish on poster" (1996), DY 4 October, p. 2.

"Teachers put pins in students' shoes to stop them rebelling" (1998), JT 22 February, p. 2.

"Teen idol commits crimes of fashion" (1998), DY 22 January, p. 12.

"Teens have fashion in the bag" (1998), AEN February 14, p. 9.

"Thai princess sparks Tamagotchi ban" (1997), DY 14 June, p. 3.

"The bear facts about Steiff teddies" (1998), DY 11 April, p. 9.

"The Twain Meet: In Japan, many parts to play" (1994), JT 6 January, p. 14.

"To hell with school uniforms!" (1997), JT 6 June, p. 18.

"Tops for tots" (1992), JT 29 September, p. 10.

Toyama, H. (1997), "Kimono or Skirt? The Female Fashion Controversy in Meiji Japan", paper presented at the New England Conference of the Association for Asian Studies, Wesleyan University (October 17–18).

"Toymakers give fresh face to cosmetics mart" (1995), DY 15 July, p. 3.

Trueheart, C. (1998), "Eager minds or pack mules? French schoolkids bear burden of weighty education", JT 18 May, p. 10.

Tsuzuki K. (1997), *Tokyo Style*, Tokyo: Arts Collection.

Turner, B. S. (1984), *The Body and Society: Explorations in Social Theory*, Oxford: Blackwell.

—— (1991), "Recent Developments in the Theory of the Body", in M. Featherstone, M. Hepworth, and B. S. Turner (eds), *The Body, Social Process and Cultural Theory,* London: Sage, pp. 1–35.

Turner, R. H. (1990), "Role Taking: Process versus Conformity", in D. Brissett and C. Edgley (eds), *Life as Theater: A Dramaturgical Source Book* (2nd edition), New York: Aldine de Gruyter, pp. 85–100.

Turner, T. (1974), "Cosmetics: The Language of Bodily Adornment", in J. P. Spradley and D. McCurdy (eds), *Conformity and Confict: Readings in Cultural Anthropology,* Boston: Little, Brown, pp. 96–105.

Turner, V. (1967), *The Forest of Symbols: Aspects of Ndembu Ritual,* Ithaca, New York: Cornell University Press.

—— (1969), *The Ritual Process,* Chicago: Aldine Publishing.

—— (1974), *Drama, Fields and Metaphors: Symbolic Action in Human Society.* Ithaca: Cornell University Press.

Uchino M. (1995), *"Fusorio koso ga utsukushî: seifuku no danjobetsu kyôsei wa seisabetsu"* ("Lack of Uniformity is Beautiful: Compulsory Male-Female Distinctions are Sexual Discrimination"), *Kikan joshi kyôiku mondai (Women's Education Issues Quarterly)* 63: 54–60 (April).

"Uniformity rules" (1997), JT 7 May, p. 16.

"Uniforms are symbol of professionals" (1994), DY 2 February, p. 8.

Uno K. and Nogami A. (1990), *"Ginkô no joshi jûgyô-in no seifuku"* ("Women Employers' Uniforms in a Bank"), *Ôsaka shôin joshi daigaku ronshû (Ôsaka Shôin Women's University Essay Collection)* 27(17): 93–101.

—— (1992), *"Sen-i kanren kaisha no joshi jûgyô-in no seifuku"* ("Women's Employers' Uniforms in Textile-Related Companies"), *Ôsaka shôin joshi daigaku ronshû (Ôsaka Shôin Women's University Essay Collection)* 29(10): 133–45.

—— (1993), *"Shôjikai no joshi jûgyô-in no seifuku"* ("Women Employers' Uniforms in Commercial Firms"), *Ôsaka shôin joshi daigaku ronshû (Ôsaka Shôin Women's University Essay Collection)* 30(5): 95–105.

—— (1994), *"Basugaido no seifuku"* ("Bus Conductress' Uniforms"), *Ôsaka shôin joshi daigaku ronshû (Ôsaka Shôin Women's University Essay Collection)* 31(3): 115–23.

Uno K., Nogami A. and Sakurai M. (1991), *"Tetsudôgyô no danshi jûgyô-in no seifuku"* ("Male Employers' Uniforms in the Railroad Industry"), *Ôsaka shôin joshi daigaku ronshû (Ôsaka Shôin Women's University Essay Collection)* 28(13): 149–56.

Washida S. (1996), *"Jinsei o 'seifuku' ni shite imasen ka"* ("Don't We 'Uniform' Life?"), *Haha no tomo (Mother's Friend)* 523: 26–31 (December).

Wataguchi Y. (1996), *"'Sensei no seifuku' sôdô kara mieru gakkô no ima"* ("Looking at Schools Now from the Perspective of 'Teacher Uniforms' Disturbance"), *Shinbun kenkyû (Newspaper Research)* 541: 24–6 (August).

Watanabe S. (1994), *"Soshiki ni ubawareru 'jiko kettei-ken': 'josei nomi' seifuku no shûhen"* ("The 'Right of Self-Determination' Deprived by the Organization: The Circumference of 'Only Women Wear Uniforms'"), *Kikan joshi kyôiku mondai (Women's Education Issues Quarterly)* 59: 18–23 (April).

Watanabe, T. (1992), "'Doll wars' challenge female ideal: Japan likes 'cute.' American likes 'sexy.' So, Barbie and Licca duke it out in toydom", DY 31 October, p. 8.

—— (1994), "Condoms elevated to chic, art: But fewer youths, pill's arrival may crimp market leader", JT 8 September, p. 4.

—— (1997), "The boom brigade: Japanese teen queens rule the trend market", JT 8 June, pp. 9, 11.

Watson, C. M. (1990), "The Presentation of Self and the New Institutional Inmate: An Analysis of Prisoners' Responses to Assessment for Release", in D. Brissett and C. Edgley (eds), *Life as Theater: A Dramaturgical Source Book* (2nd edition), New York: Aldine de Gruyter, pp. 183–200.

Weiss, L. and J. M. Hobson (1995). *States and Economic Development,* Cambridge: Polity Press.

White, M. (1987), *The Japanese Educational Challenge,* Tokyo: Kôdansha.

—— (1994), *The Material Child: Coming of Age in Japan and America,* Berkeley: University of California Press.

Whyte, L.L. (1978), *The Unconscious Before Freud,* New York: St Martin's Press.

Yamada H. (1993), *"Seifuku ga kirarenai nara hadaka de aruke"* ("If You Don't Wear a Uniform Walk in the Nude"), *Rôdô undô (Labor Movement)* 333: 224–30 (April).

Yamaguchi, M. (1994), "JAL stewardesses feel goofy in Minnie ears", JT 7 September, p. 3.

Yato, T. (1997), "World of Japanese judo gets thrown for a loop", DY 18 December, p. 67.

Yoshida K., Egawa F. and Yokoyama K. (1989), *"Seifuku ni kansuru hifuku kikôgakuteki kenkyû"* ("Climatological Research on Clothing of Uniforms"), *Mukogawa joshi daigaku kiyô (Mukogawa Women's University Bulletin)* 37: 47–53.

Young, M. and P. Willmott. (1962), *Family and Kinship in East London,* Baltimore, Pelican.

Zelinsky, W. (1988), *Nation into State: The Shifting Symbolic Foundations of American Nationalism,* Chapel Hill: University of North Carolina Press.

Zenkoku kakushu dantai meikan (National Directory of Organizations) (1993), Shiba (ed.), *jô-chû-gekan* (Volumes 1, 2, 3), Tokyo: Shiba.

Index

accessories, 5, 9, 106, 128
act, 8, 9, 19, 35
Adult Day, 109
aestheticization
  of clothes
  uniforms, 115, 116
agency, 8, 9, 19, 37–8, 39, 48, 51, 98, 110
agent, 8, 9, 19, 28, 30, 31, 39, 42, 48, 51,
  52, 97, 185
  see also agentiveness
agentiveness, 97
  see also agent
anomic situations, 24, 36
anonymous communication, 76, 179
appearance, 86
  see also looks
asociality, 23
atmosphere, 27
atomization
  sociopolitical, 186
  see also mass society

Bachnik, J. 21, 46n5
backstage, 22
Barbie doll, 150
Benedict, R., 26
blue-collar workers, 28, 39, 130
bodily adornment, 109
bodily gestures, 22
bodily management, 5, 8, 35, 73, 184
bodily movement, 23
bodily practices, 3
body piercing, 99
body, 2, 7, 10, 14, 18n9, 30, 32, 39, 53, 80,
  108, 113, 118, 183
  defined, 13
  female, 105
  'Westernization' of, 15
Bourdieu, P., 78, 185

bullying, 70, 71
bureaucratic ethos, 120
Burke, E, 8, 18n7, 19

capital/ism, 2, 9, 40, 80, 110, 121, 160, 185
  consumerist 8, 35, 186, 187
  dress uniformity and, 12
  hegemony and, 10
  production and, 15, 157, 158, 162, 184
capitalist developmental state, 40, 46n6
capitalist elite, 51
capitalist projects, 4, 11, 43
cheerfulness, 53, 99n1, 116, 125, 126, 129,
  162, 199, 200
  cuteness and, 142, 144, 148, 149, 150,
  161
civility, 24, 170
  see also etiquette, manners
class differences
  uniforms and, 84–5, 88, 89
cleanliness, 54, 86, 87, 88, 89, 92, 108,
  116, 125, 126, 200
clothes
  ordinary, 53, 67, 81, 83, 84, 87, 113,
  122, 205, 206, 207
  privatization of, 66
  see also uniforms
cognition, 4, 29
  see also mind, psyche, subjectivity
colleges (women's), 10, 177
  see also universities
companies, 25, 79, 107, 170
consciousness, 13, 29, 184
  construction of, 30, 34
  features of, 19, 31
  self and, 31
conspicuousness, 88, 89, 113, 158, 163, 166
consumerism, 2, 8, 35, 186, 187
  see also consumption

225